SISTERS IN DEATH

SISTERS IN DEATH

The Black Dahlia, the Prairie Heiress, and Their Hunter

ELI FRANKEL

Citadel Press
Kensington Publishing Corp.
kensingtonbooks.com

CITADEL PRESS BOOKS are published by

Kensington Publishing Corp.
900 Third Avenue
New York, NY 10022

All Kensington titles, imprints, and distributed lines are available at special quantity discounts for bulk purchases for sales promotions, premiums, fund-raising, educational, or institutional use. Special book excerpts or customized printings can also be created to fit specific needs. For details, write or phone the office of the Kensington sales manager: Kensington Publishing Corp., 900 Third Avenue, New York, NY 10022, attn Sales Department; phone 1-800-221-2647.

10 9 8 7 6 5 4 3 2 1

First Citadel hardcover printing: November 2025

Printed in the United States of America

ISBN: 978-0-8065-4376-5

ISBN: 978-0-8065-4378-9 (e-book)

Library of Congress Control Number: 2025937911

The authorized representative in the EU for product safety and compliance
is eucomply OU, Parnu mnt 139b-14, Apt 123,
Tallinn, Berlin 11317; hello@eucompliancepartner.com

For May Wiesenfeld (1912–1996)

CONTENTS

PART III   CARL BALSIGER

AUTHOR'S NOTE

Los Angeles has no history. It's a statement of undisputed fact, repeated over and over. And it always makes my skin crawl. The layers of sediment beneath LA's asphalt and stucco may reveal a more nuanced saga than the excavations of ancient sites in Europe or even East Coast cities, but it is a thrilling one, nevertheless. From nineteenth-century adobe structures to long-shuttered sixties tiki bars, to silent-era movie sets literally buried beneath sand dunes, Southern California is a region abundant with the ruins of our modern age.

As an avid student of the city's rich past, I've been particularly drawn to its dark side, a history of murder and crime rivaling that of any world metropolis many times its age. Outrageous and flamboyant on the surface, the city has an equally colorful and appalling history beneath it. And no case has gripped the fevered imagination of multiple generations more than the Black Dahlia. The reverse image of Hollywood glamour, the story of Elizabeth Short's sojourn through Southern California has remained a specter, a haunting reminder that behind the beautifully lit façade of Los Angeles is darkness.

The Black Dahlia is inescapable in Hollywood, where the case is still casually mentioned at dinners and business meetings. Like so many others, I was drawn in at an early age by the mystery of Elizabeth Short, the film noir world she inhabited, and the cast of characters with whom she interacted, among them the rogue's gallery of potential suspects. I devoured every book, every online article, every social media post I could find on the subject but remained a passive hobbyist. After all, everything that could be written about the case had been written.

But something gnawed at me. Nearly every account begins with the discovery of the horrifying bisected body at 10:50 A.M. on January 15, 1947, in full public view just inches from the sidewalk. What about all the other passersby who used that heavily trafficked street in the hours after sunup? How could someone not have seen such a prominent corpse until midmorning? Only one person could have possibly known the answer to that question, and I wasn't even sure if she was alive.

Within days, I was in contact with Betty Bersinger, the woman who had found the body nearly seventy-five years earlier. Her responses to my questions were familiar, the same she had given since 1947. Making contact with complete strangers and asking them to speak about their past is walking a tightrope. Probe too little, you get too little. Push too far and the conversation can end abruptly. But upon my pressing the issue, she revealed an astounding fact that turned the case on its head.

My question set in motion a hundred more questions. A hobby turned into a mission as I lobbed hundreds of phone calls to sons, granddaughters, nieces, great-nephews of deceased participants in the story, most of them yielding nothing while a special few provided a treasure trove. The research project would net inordinate amounts of seemingly unrelated facts and narratives. It was like trying to put together a ten-thousand-piece puzzle with fifteen thousand puzzle pieces.

Finally, I discovered a tiny announcement in a 1936 Kansas City newspaper that placed one of the Black Dahlia's long overlooked lead suspects in the same room as another murder victim who had been killed in eerily similar circumstances. If it were mere coincidence, it at least begged further investigation. Little did I know at that time how much investigation it would require.

The hunt to track down the details of the suspect's life was a long and painstaking road, requiring travel to Missouri and Kansas, thousands of primary sources, and scores of interviews. For every door that closed, another would open, leading to more doors that opened. History can be rigid and unyielding, but it can also unleash its secrets when pushed in just the right place.

While the life story of the perpetrator was a central focus, it was the stories of the victims—both those who survived and those who didn't—that truly captured my attention and heart. Upon the discovery of her body in 1947, Elizabeth Short was quickly transformed into the Black Dahlia, a role she was never suited to play but into which she would nonetheless be cast by a press and public eager to create a character befitting her dark and tragic end. Through it all and into the modern day, the real Beth Short became a useless distraction from the tawdry noir figure that would define the narrative.

Through the testimony of those who knew her best, her own words in letters, and a closer look at patterns of her behavior, the real twenty-two-year-old woman emerges. That was the Beth Short I wanted to write about. There is always a temptation in true crime to lavish attention on the killer, but the victims' life stories bloomed through the research phase and refused to be an afterthought. Ultimately, this book is about them.

—Eli Frankel

INTRODUCTION

THE KEY QUESTION

I t is one of the most infamous moments in the annals of true crime, an encounter of such stark and shocking contrasts that it has become the de facto introduction to nearly every narration of the greatest cold case in United States history. Some of the details may subtly shift between each retelling, but the story always remains the same and never ceases to grab attention.

On the morning of January 15, 1947, in the quaint, working-class neighborhood of Leimert Park in South Central Los Angeles, twenty-seven-year-old Betty Bersinger set out to walk the few short blocks between her home and a nearby commercial district where she intended to get a pair of shoes fixed. Accompanying her was her three-year-old daughter, Anne. On her regularly traveled route down Norton Avenue, Betty would pass a weed-strewn lot, two blocks in length.

Housing construction had suffered during World War II, but now this stretch of empty real estate stood at the ready to join the suburban sprawl surrounding it on all sides. Parcels on the block had been subdivided, depressions in the curb laid for future driveways. For years, the expanse of dirt and weeds had served as a convenient location for locals to dump trash. On the morning of January 15, it became a convenient location to dispose of a corpse that would redefine the city of Los Angeles.

Some versions have Anne playing in the weeds, then suddenly crying out for her mother's attention. Other versions have Betty pushing Anne in a stroller, stopping abruptly when she sees it. She then runs screaming in terror to the nearest house. Yet other versions claim Betty calmly walked on, having glanced to her side only for a moment and mistaking what she saw for a mannequin. Farther down the block, she realizes something is not right and calls the police to investigate.

Remaining consistent across all versions of the story is what Betty encountered at 10:50 A.M. on January 15, 1947: the body of twenty-two-year-old Elizabeth Short, cut neatly in half, the two parts facing up and separated by a gap of several inches. Horrific wounds across the body detailed a map of torture. Large pieces of skin and flesh were carved out and missing. Various knife and razor cuts had been made across the body, some in graphic crisscross fashion, others a flurry of tiny slices, yet others prominent and deep. Dark, circular depressions around her neck, wrists, and legs evidenced long periods of restraint by leather or wire before her death. Even more shocking was what had been done to her face. Three-inch gashes had been ripped from both corners of her mouth nearly to the ears, forming a contorted, twisted smile. The body had been drained of blood and scrubbed clean with a coconut-fiber brush, appearing stark white in the sun, in contrast to the victim's jet-black hair.

Photographs of the horrendous scene were cleaned up for newspapers, a pretty face in repose painted over the ghastly carved cheeks and a blanket artistically added to cover the bisection. Though the mutilations would not be publicly viewed, the description in print alone was enough to grip the imagination of Angelenos and propel the story to the front pages of newspapers across the country.

One fact of the crime scene grabbed the most attention and remains to this day the most puzzling, tantalizing, and frightening aspect of the discovery of the body. No description of the case ever fails to mention it. In fact, it has become the defining feature. The body wasn't discarded in a back alley, or left in a car, or hidden in a home. It had been laid out in the grass mere inches from a heavily trafficked public sidewalk. A streetcar line emptied out hundreds of passengers daily just a block away. The two halves of the body had been carefully placed, lined up, and posed for public view on Norton Avenue, with its considerable foot traffic from dawn to dusk.

No doubt the location had been chosen for a reason. The empty block in the early morning hours would have allowed the killer a modicum of privacy when the body was laid out, but by sunup, the display of a bisected, heavily tortured corpse inches from the sidewalk guaranteed an audience and maximum shock value. Whoever did this wanted the world to see their work.

Betty Bersinger would be the person fate chose to discover that work. The press could not have found a more ideal first witness to the horrifying display. Here was the postwar American housewife—neatly dressed, pretty, poised, active—stepping unwittingly into a scene of utter depravity and sadism that reflected back at this wholesome young mother the darkest recesses of the human mind. In a world still grappling with the horrors of war and the evil men visit upon each other, Betty Bersinger became a stand-in for every American trying to normalize their lives after years of trauma.

Bersinger was hounded by the press, to whom she told and retold her story. Different reporters injected their own flare for the dramatic, which became the source of discrepancies in her story. Though she closely guarded her privacy, Bersinger would allow a handful of interviews in later decades, and her account remained remarkably consistent. Her memory of that day never flagged, every detail remaining crystal clear, her story never deviating.

As Betty explained, "It was about the time kids were going off to school, riding their bikes or whatever, and I had to go by this lot that was undeveloped . . . And as I was walking along, I happened to glance over at my side and I saw this strange sight. It looked like a mannequin that had been cut in half and was separated and was lying there. And I didn't glance at it too long because I had my little girl with me. And I thought, 'gosh,' as I walked on further. I thought that just didn't seem right to me. And I could see these kids with their bicycles, and I said maybe it'll scare those kids if they ride to school and see this, so I better call somebody to come and at least have a look and see what it is. But the thought of a dead person did not enter my mind. I thought it was a mannequin because it was so white."

In another interview, she offered even more detail regarding the body. "I glanced to my right and saw this very dead, white body. My goodness . . . it was so white. It didn't . . . look like anything more than perhaps an artificial model. It was so white and separated in the middle. I noticed the dark hair and this white, white form."

Bersinger's accounts prove she did not just casually glance for a moment to her side and walk on, unsure of what she saw. The sight was so striking that it burned an image into her memory she would never forget. Likewise, for anyone who has seen the photographs of the bisected body of Elizabeth Short, the image is unforgettable.

But there is a problem with Bersinger's story. In every interview, she consistently states she saw a truncated white form with black hair. The figure was so white she believed it was a mannequin. But the photographs of the body on Norton Avenue display a horrifically tortured form, gaping areas of open muscle and flesh, visible organs, a ten-inch open laceration across the face, overwhelming trauma to the head—all within inches of where Bersinger was standing. Nobody could mistake the form visible in those photographs for a white mannequin.

When investigators and reporters arrived minutes after Bersinger called the police, they would experience utter shock and horror, even after years of exposure to the worst crime scenes in Los

Angeles. Their memories of that day would fill books and articles for decades to come, and none of them would describe anything resembling a mannequin. Betty Bersinger could not have glanced to her right and formed the image she described, based on the undeniable photographic evidence showing the two halves of the heavily mutilated body laid out, facing up, inches from the sidewalk.

In addition, Bersinger mentions seeing children riding their bicycles on the street. It is inconceivable that they would not have noticed such a prominently posed bisected corpse, which the police established had been placed on Norton Avenue around 6:30 A.M. Witnesses in the neighborhood claimed they walked by the location as late as 8:30 A.M. and didn't see anything. With all of the foot traffic common to Norton Avenue, how could someone fail to have noticed the startling figure displayed along the sidewalk until nearly 11:00 A.M.?

Because the body wasn't there.

At 11:05 A.M., Bersinger's phone call came into the complaint line of the LAPD. At 11:07 A.M., a "390 down"—police scanner code for "intoxicated individual passed out"—was dispatched to radio unit 34, Officers Frank Perkins and Wayne Fitzgerald. At 11:09 A.M., Perkins and Fitzgerald arrived at Norton Avenue. Five minutes later, at approximately 11:14 A.M., car 34 radioed LAPD's University Division, requesting backup. Homicide Bureau chief Captain Jack Donohoe was immediately notified. At 11:18 A.M., Officers S. J. Lambert and J. W. Haskins of University Division arrived at the scene, followed quickly by Sergeant Marty J. Wynn of Homicide Division and a succession of sergeants, lieutenants, police photographers, Scientific Investigative Unit investigators, and crime lab technicians.

At 11:30 A.M., Harry Hansen and Finis Brown, the two homicide detectives who would lead the investigation, arrived at the packed crime scene. Newspaper reporters and photographers had already assembled en masse, stepping around the body while taking notes and photos, preparing to breathlessly report in print and on the radio every detail of the scene as well as Hansen and Brown's first observations.

But as close as reporters got to the body, as much information as they pried out of the police, investigators were able to hold back three crucial details. The police would use these pieces of information in questioning potential suspects, as only the killer would know the answer. Two of those questions and their answers were eventually revealed, but one remained a secret, and does so to this day. The police referred to it as "the Key Question."

A 1971 *Los Angeles Times* article about Harry Hansen states, "Within this group of questions was one that was relevant yet so bizarre and remote that its answer was beyond even a wild guess, but obvious to the killer. Police called it 'the Key Question,' and will admit only that it deals with some fact about the condition, appearance, or attitude of Elizabeth Short's body at the time it was discovered." Hansen goes on to deny that a rumored marking on her body or any rearrangement of her organs was the basis of the Key Question. "Hansen asked the question of approximately 500 people. Not one ever responded correctly. Not one even came close."

Though he never revealed any more details, Hansen left a very important clue in his description of the Key Question. His choice of words, "at the time it was discovered," is the giveaway. Reporters and photographers stood inches from the body. They witnessed and catalogued every aspect of its condition, appearance, or attitude. If there was something about the condition, appearance, or attitude of the victim's body that only the killer would have known, then some aspect of the positioning of the body shifted between "the discovery" and the moment reporters first arrived.

Betty Bersinger discovered the body, but she did not touch it. At 11:09 A.M., Officers Fitzgerald and Perkins arrived and were alone at the crime scene. At 11:18 A.M., the second set of officers, S. J. Lambert and J. W. Haskins, arrived. What happened in the crucial nine-minute gap between the arrival of the first and second set of officers that would alter the condition, appearance, or attitude of the body?

The answer lies with Betty Bersinger. At 103 years old, the woman who first stepped into the story of the Black Dahlia murder would be the last to leave it, having outlived every other participant. Until her death in October 2023, she lived in a retirement home and retained all her faculties. In one last interview, conducted with the author, she provided details of what she experienced that morning that she had never divulged before. When asked why she had never shared this information, her response was simple: "Nobody ever asked."

On the morning of January 15, Betty Bersinger's attention was caught by a white form, but it wasn't inches from the sidewalk. It was approximately twelve feet away—hidden in the weeds. Betty took several steps into the grass to get a better look and saw only the upper torso, cleanly bisected. She did not see the legs, pelvis, buttocks, or face. She assumed it was a mannequin because it was so white and didn't have a lower torso. She then returned to the stroller and continued down the block, knocking on the first door she came across to call the police.

But if Betty Bersinger saw the torso lying twelve feet away in the weeds, how and when did it move to the sidewalk?

Officers Fitzgerald and Perkins arrived at the crime scene at 11:09 A.M. In a 1997 interview, Wayne Fitzgerald recalled, "The first thing we thought was that it was a mannequin. That someone was playing a trick because there was no blood. Then we realized what the hell we had." They, too, at first believed the form in the weeds was a mannequin. But when they pulled the upper torso out, they then realized "what the hell they had." Underneath the upper torso, they found the lower half of the bisected body. It had been placed in the weeds by the killer first, with the upper portion then laid over it, face down.

That is why Betty Bersinger only saw the top half and not the legs or the face. She was staring at Elizabeth Short's back, which was virtually the only part of her body that wasn't mutilated. Washed and scrubbed, it appeared like a white form.

Perkins and Fitzgerald moved the bisected halves over to the sidewalk, where the grass was much shorter and where they could see the entire form. They laid the two segments down, face up, separated by only a few inches. Without realizing it, they had just created a tableau that would define this murder and capture attention for generations to come.

Though they were first on the scene, Perkins and Fitzgerald's account was quickly wiped from any official record. The LAPD Dead Body Report, the first to be written and submitted for the investigation to follow, was tasked to S. J. Lambert, one of the second set of officers to arrive after the nine-minute gap. In the official district attorney timeline of arrivals to the crime scene, Lambert is the first to arrive at 11:18 A.M., following Betty Bersinger's discovery of the body, Perkins and Fitzgerald's arrival at 11:09 A.M. is completely missing.

Sergeants Harry Hansen and Finis Brown's internal LAPD/follow-up report directly contradicted Bersinger's own account, in which she believed she had seen a mannequin: "She said that she [was] walking to the store with her three year [sic] daughter when she noticed the body lying in the grass, and without taking a second look, and not wanting her baby to see a body in that condition she hurried on to 39th Street and stopped at the nearest house to find a telephone." Hansen then dismisses any follow-up questioning of Bersinger. "Mrs. Bersinger's testimony is not considered pertinent."

How could the testimony of the first person to see the body in its untouched state a full twenty minutes before the police arrived not be considered pertinent? Because Hansen did not want anyone asking her what she actually saw.

Contrary to every account of the Black Dahlia, the severed body of Elizabeth Short was not "posed" by the killer. It was not set out for maximum shock value, the two halves not lined up carefully along the sidewalk. Instead, the body had been discarded, thrown away like the trash that had been tossed for years in the weeds of Norton Avenue's 3900 block. This was the final insult to a young woman who endured unthinkable pain and degradation at the hands of a killer who had no use for her once his work was done. He never sought to sensationalize her or the slaying, never meant to send a message. His only thought was to get rid of the corpse. Dropping it in tall weeds would at least hide the evidence a bit longer from discovery. He did not anticipate, nor could he foresee, the infamy that would soon arrive once the body was pulled from the weeds.

The myth of the "posed" Black Dahlia has been central to the analysis of the many theoretical perpetrators proposed over the decades as the killer of Elizabeth Short. Each suspect has been examined through the lens of this bizarre act of morbid exhibition. Even famed FBI profiler John Douglas assessed that the killer wanted the world to see the vengeance he had wreaked upon Elizabeth Short for having "wronged" him.

Indeed, the posing of the body has actually helped inspire the suspect list itself. The act of presenting a severed and mutilated corpse in a public place is so brazen it suggests an outsized ego and bravura akin to a comic book supervillain. In turn, the list of suspects who have been "discovered" in recent years reads like a litany of exotic super geniuses, brilliantly outmaneuvering the police, always a step ahead. All of these narratives were mistaken in their presumption that the killer posed the body for public view. The correct narrative forces a reexamination of the killer's profile. The disposal of the body wasn't the work of an evil genius. It was the work of an awkward but fiendish amateur.

After a firestorm of fear, publicity, and the largest manhunt in Los Angeles history, the Black Dahlia was largely forgotten until the case came roaring back to life decades later, with thousands of TikToks, YouTube videos, websites, books, films, and shelves of merchandise devoted to the gripping mystery. As recognized and monetized as Jack the Ripper, the Manson Family, Ted Bundy, and the Zodiac Killer, the Black Dahlia is arguably the most famous cold case in American history. Fueling its infamy is the enigma of Elizabeth Short herself—her mysterious associations, her random travel destinations, her last desperate movements. But the greatest enigma remains her murderer. The gaping black hole at the center of the story is the absence of a name, a face, a backstory of someone capable of such a unique atrocity. Her killer was never found. No suspect was even charged with the murder.

What challenged investigators in the years following the murder continues to challenge modern-day inquiries: Elizabeth Short's last months were a whirlwind of chance encounters, short-lived friendships, come-and-go acquaintances, first and second dates, and roommates at motels, apartment buildings, and houses. Hundreds of possible suspects emerged among the copious encounters, each name leading to five more names, leading to yet more. Overwhelmed by the innumerable paths, detectives committed enormous resources to identify a viable suspect and make an arrest, and yet came up empty. It is the definition of a riddle wrapped in a mystery inside an enigma.

But one name would stubbornly remain in the LAPD's crosshairs even as the investigation stalled and eventually turned cold. Having played a central role in Elizabeth Short's baffling escape from Los Angeles a month before her murder, the suspect ignited detectives' suspicions when they looked into his past. What they discovered was the key to unlocking the mystery of the Black Dahlia.

That key would not be found in Los Angeles in 1947. It was hidden in an eerily similar murder committed six years earlier in Kansas City, Missouri. The victim was a wealthy heiress raised on the prairie who had ties to this same suspect. Her gruesome 1941 slaying would prove to be the dry run for the Black Dahlia murder six years later. Having escaped the LAPD's efforts to pin him with both murders, the suspect has evaded all modern investigation. Now, the curtain will be pulled back, and the missing pieces to the Black Dahlia murder will finally fall into place.

PART I
LEILA WELSH

CHAPTER 1

HEIRESS OF
THE PRAIRIE

P rairie Township, with its tall, flowing Indian and bluestem
grasses, is dotted with gently rolling hills, low woodlands,
and small glades where wild turkeys flourish. Just shy of
Missouri's border with Kansas, it marks the gateway to the dramatic grasslands of the Midwest.

The violent struggle between Free Staters and pro-slavery South-
erners in the years leading up to the Civil War shed much blood in
this seemingly peaceful terrain, with enmity and vengeance con-
tinuing to rip communities apart to the end of the nineteenth century. The arrival of the Missouri Pacific Railroad into the township
in 1865 turned the remote village of Lee's Summit into an important
grain-shipping destination and brought with it Easterners who had
no use for antebellum feuds.

In 1916, Leila Adele Welsh was born in Prairie Township just as
it was letting go of the last vestiges of its violent past. Cole Younger,
who had ridden with Jesse James, robbing banks and trains across
the Midwest, was living out his final days down the road from the
hundred-acre Welsh family farm on Outer Belt Road. Leila's mother,
Marie Fleming, had grown up in rural Kentucky and met her husband, George Welsh, while attending the University of Missouri.

In 1905, the young couple married and moved to a series of small, dusty towns across Oklahoma, where George found work as a lawyer. Marie yearned for a home suitable to raising children, so George returned to his native Kansas City, eventually settling thirty miles and a world away on the prairie farm. Their first child, James, died when he was only eleven months old. Soon Mary Frances was born, followed by George Jr. in 1912, and then Leila four years later.

From the moment Leila was born, the quiet and shy George Jr. was drawn to her, acting as older brother, caretaker, and best friend. Leila's social graces and warmth helped cover his many social anxieties. The farmhouse was spacious and the possibilities outdoors endless for the two children as they explored a world not far removed from the Missouri of Mark Twain. Each morning, Marie packed their lunch and George walked his sister a quarter mile down a country lane to a one-room prairie schoolhouse where grades one through eight were taught by a single teacher. Marie anxiously awaited their return home to dote on their every need. As unshakeable was the bond between sister and brother, so, too, was their bond with Marie, who made them the center of her world.

The Welsh family home was modestly furnished, their clothes simple, their needs even more simple. But the Welshes were not like everybody else in this humble farm community. Thirty miles away, in Kansas City, their family name loomed large. George Sr.'s father, James Welsh, had arrived in Kansas City in the 1880s, toiled in the dry goods business, and then lot-by-lot built a real estate empire through his James B. Welsh Realty and Loan Company, helping transform Kansas City from a backwater cow town into a metropolitan jewel that was central in the vast network of American industry. George Sr.'s three children were in line to inherit the family's vast real estate fortune, which is exactly why he and Marie escaped to a modest farm well outside the reach of his enormously powerful father. But in time, Kansas City would pull in the Welsh children like a magnet.

When real estate titan James B. Welsh's wife, Mary, died in 1904, he married her sister Leila McKee, who would need no introduction in the society pages of Kansas City newspapers. J. B. Welsh may have been widely admired, but Dr. Leila Welsh was revered and universally praised as a pioneer in women's education. The press extolled, "[She] has done more for the education of her sex than any woman in the middle states."

Having attended Western College for Women in Oxford, Ohio, where she earned a doctor of laws degree, she fought for admission to the all-male Centre College in Kentucky, where she became one of the first women in the nation to earn a PhD. She served as president of two colleges, led the American Association of University Women, and traveled extensively, lecturing and championing women's admittance into higher education. Dr. McKee had remained unattached until late in life. Once married, she maintained her career and many influential board positions.

Her greatest joy was her namesake and grandniece, Leila Adele Welsh. A special relationship had developed early and grew stronger with every trip Leila made up to Kansas City to visit her treasured aunt. The stately family home at 233 W. 56th Street was one of Kansas City's most enviable mansions. There, Aunt Leila introduced her grandniece to the magical city that was fast becoming a center of culture, music, art, and, most importantly, women's education. Leila found a model of independence, ambition, and self-reliance in her aunt, values rarely instilled in girls of the era.

While George Sr. and Marie attended a small country church near the farm, Leila was treated as a VIP at the grand Second Presbyterian Church in Kansas City's fashionable Country Club District. Her great-uncle, James McKee, had served as an officer and pastor of the church for many years, and Aunt Leila had contributed handsomely, making the Welshes the church's most prominent family. Leila regularly attended Second Presbyterian with pride, sitting beside her aunt in the front pew, the admiration and envy of the large congregation.

Each time Leila returned from the whirlwind trips to the city, her life on the farm felt uninspired, limited, and remote. Nonetheless, Marie tried to act as a counterbalance to Aunt Leila's ambitions, teaching her daughter Leila humility, simplicity, modesty, and a deep appreciation for the importance of family. As Leila matured into her teenaged years, she grew to embody the best of both women. Dressing simply and unattracted to material goods and status, she centered her life around her family. She also swore off the distraction of romantic attachments and poured herself into schoolwork at Lee's Summit High School.

When Leila turned eighteen, there was no question she would leave the farm behind and follow in her aunt's inspiring footsteps to Western College in Oxford, Ohio. After a year away, though, she yearned for home. But which home? Her mother's embrace on the austere farm she was raised on, or her aunt's world of explosive possibilities in Kansas City? At first, she would attempt to straddle both worlds, moving back to the farm and enrolling at the newly opened University of Kansas City in the fall of 1935. But soon, the thirty-mile commute would prove too much.

Her brother George, too, had left home for college but had dropped out and returned to the farm. He had recently found work at a law firm in Kansas City and shared Leila's fatigue over the exhausting travel to and from the farm. With both her children back, Marie would not allow herself to be separated from them again and agreed to find a home in the city where all three could live together. Her husband, George Sr., had become ill and would not be able to travel with them. But frequent visits to the farm would keep

Leila and George grounded even while the many temptations of the city would undoubtedly challenge the simple rural values she had worked so hard to instill in them.

Kansas City in the 1930s was a contradiction, a town with two diametrically different faces. One face looked south into the suburbs, where a network of lavish country clubs served the growing wealth of the Midwest metropolis. The city had suffered the deprivations of the Depression like any other American city, but refused to fold, occupying itself with every social distraction it could muster. White, Protestant, middle-class, and upper-class families enjoyed rich social schedules of dinner banquets, themed galas, luncheons, garden parties, charity events, and black-tie affairs. While leafy, expansive country clubs served as anchors for the southern half of Kansas City, downtown served as the anchor for the other face of the city.

Kansas City was run not by a mayor or council. It was ruled by the Pendergast political machine, which had kept a forty-year stranglehold over city government with its unbreakable majority bloc of Democrat voters. In return for their steadfast loyalty, Boss Tom Pendergast handed his voters coveted city government jobs, housing, and access to his influence through a citywide network of precinct and block captains.

The Pendergast machine had long benefited from a skim off the profits of saloons and dance halls and would not allow Prohibition to meddle with its coffers. Alcohol flooded the "wide open town" of 1920s Kansas City, birthing hundreds of nightclubs and bars, which in turn attracted a synthesis of jazz, blues, and ragtime musicians. With the onset of the Depression, Pendergast pulled in huge Works Progress Administration (WPA) construction projects that dramatically altered the skyline of the city and created thousands of jobs. As the dustbowl ravaged the Midwest, Kansas City remained the one place that had money to spend, and it pulled in the best jazz musicians from cities as far away as New Orleans and Chicago. It also pulled in prostitutes, bookies, gambling parlor operators, criminals, and the Mafia, who would all have a free hand as long as tribute was paid to the Pendergast machine.

In 1933, the sprawling and stately University of Kansas City opened in the Rockhill neighborhood, a testament to the growing professional class of the city. Students flooded in from suburban Kansas City to "KCU," attracted by the outstanding faculty and wide selection of academic programs. Just as attractive was the extensive social life that blossomed on campus, the Depression be damned. By the time Leila arrived in the fall of 1935, the classes that had preceded her had established social dominance in the strict hierarchy of the school.

At the top of the social ladder were the fraternities and sororities that dominated the campus. Composed of Kansas City natives who had grown up within thirty blocks of each other in the Country Club District, the KCU Greeks had all attended the same high schools, churches, and country clubs. Members of a tight-knit community, their names read like characters out of The Great Gatsby: Punky Vanderhoof, Farel Swanson, Red Calloway, Patsy Porterfield, May Messenger, Buck Belwood, Marjory Lovejoy.

The Greek system at KCU maintained control over the student body through a two-tiered system of governance sanctioned by the school's administration. Non-Greeks were excluded from student government and were denied invitations to splashy dances, banquets, and formals, which formed the highlight of the school's social calendar. So exclusive was the KCU Greek community that fraternities and sororities did not seek recognition from national Greek organizations, a practice unheard of at other schools. Sheltered from the Depression and insulated from the rest of the student body, KCU Greeks were in an elite and highly restricted class of their own.

With her simple prairie background, Leila did not appear to be a candidate for a sorority. Yet everyone knew of her lineage and impending inheritance, and so Leila was quickly recruited into Cho Chin, one of the top sororities. Marie had hoped Leila would not fall prey to the fast crowd of Greeks at the school, as had Aunt Leila McKee, who wanted her to remain focused on her education. But Leila had spent her whole life isolated on a farm, always dutiful and responsible. For the first time, she had an opportunity to break free of the role she had always played.

If there were any doubts whether Leila would be accepted into the chic, well-connected set among the Greeks, they were quickly dispelled. She instantly became one of the most popular new students on campus. Her rural naïvety, kindness, sunny disposition, glowing smile, and smoldering beauty made her an instant attraction among the jaded city-bred students who had "seen it all." Introduced to a social calendar unlike anything she had ever experienced, Leila was swept up in extravagant banquets and posh dances at the Kansas City Country Club, the Mission Hills Country Club, the Muehlebach Hotel, the Baltimore Hotel, the Garrett, and even out at ritzy Lake Quivera.

All members of fraternities and sororities owned tuxedos and colorful formal gowns, many drove convertibles, nearly everyone smoked cigarettes, and even men wore fur coats, which were all the rage. The first Pan Hellenic dance was thrown in the fall of 1935 at Meadow Lake Country Club, where Leila was introduced to the superstars of the KCU Greek system. *UNews*, the school newspaper, gushed about the lavish affair. "Everyone seemed present. Webb, Swanson & Swanson, Balsiger, Macintosh, Collins, Sage's Johnny, Campbell, et al ad infinitum."

The most anticipated event of the spring season was Hobo Day, when the student body dressed up in their parents' turn-of-the-century hoop skirts and frock coats to enjoy a stream of dances, picnics, and parties. The highlight of the day was a mile-long caravan of cars with a police escort that deposited hundreds of students in downtown, where they ran wild through buildings, throwing firecrackers into hallways and shooting off blanks with pistols, terrifying office workers. After shutting down classes at a local junior college, the KCU students were outraged to find their tires slashed in revenge.

Romantic attachments came and went with wild abandon, and "juicy libel" was printed for all to read in the school's ubiquitous *UNews*, which spared no student's modesty nor privacy: "Tops Miller, that gorgeous Cho Chin, calmly breaks a date with one APO to go with another. The unlucky boy was none other than 'boy am I good' Wilhite, and the affair was the APO private spring formal dance." "Fred Somers tells us that he does not like to have his name mentioned in this column. So, we won't tell anybody that he thinks he's doing right well with Sue Holland." "Speaking of Rome and Nero—'Rome' Burkhead burns while 'Nero' Wilson fiddles. That cute violin is Jane Baldwin."

Fraternity men who traded girlfriends like baseball cards vied for Leila Welsh's affection, but she had sworn off dating and rejected all advances, making her the object of jealousy and even greater desire. Scurrilous rumors were printed about her in the school newspaper: "We'll start right off with a bang this week, and let you all wonder who the out of town man is that is calling Lea Welsh 'honey' these days. We know, you guess. . . ." The persistent rumors were a scandal for Leila, who thought of her aunt Dr. Leila McKee Welsh and her warnings to stay true to her academic ambitions.

Of all the fraternities at KCU, none was as notorious as Kegon, which had been the first formed on campus and whose members were infamous for their womanizing and partying. The KCU yearbook had not spared its judgment of the raucous crew's sexual conquests: "These boys are sometimes referred to as 'sots' [heavy drinkers] in the worst of society. After spending their time vainly chasing the prettiest girls in school, these guys sit back and tell about their successes. They're strong and they're tough, woolly and rough, they say. Sole reason for existence—to let the world know that Kegon is the best fraternity this side of everywhere." The emblem the yearbook chose for Kegon was "a nice, overripe, rotten, and very swollen tomato."

The *UNews* reported, "The Kegons were out in full color and just like last year were attempting to take a monopoly on the prettiest girls present." The school paper even seemed to offer a coded warning to female students, "Kegon—you will probably be dead (literally) when you get home—if and when. They are a fast goin', hard drinking (yes, we mean cokes) lot, but if you ever end up standing up straight you can really take it."

Kegon grabbed center stage not only in the Greek system but also for the entire school. In student government, Kegon member John Chaney headed the Student Fraternity and Sorority Co-Operative Party, or Co-Op Party, which represented the Greek system. Chaney had sailed through election for president of the student council with his right-hand man and enforcer by his side—a gangly, odd student named Carl Balsiger, who served as Chaney's campaign manager and spokesman. During the election, Chaney had been pressed by *UNews* for more specifics on his platform. His breezy two-word response was "See Balsiger."

In the platform was a decree that all first-year students wear a cap and ribbons in KCU's blue and gold at all times on campus, with the establishment of an Enforcement Committee to roam the school and mete out corporal punishment to any freshman found not wearing the school's colors. Carl Balsiger headed the Enforcement Committee and took special pleasure in hunting down both men and women who failed to display the cap and ribbons. Once caught, the offending student was forced to bend over as Balsiger administered a series of painful paddlings to their posterior.

All students dutifully complied, except for one. Leila Welsh refused to wear the ribbons, and when caught rebuffed the inevitable paddling and walked away in disgust. *UNews* caught wind of her shocking defiance and asked her why she would not wear the required school colors. Her simple response was printed in the newspaper: "Because it doesn't match my dress."

The student council oversaw all campus-wide affairs and was the most important and powerful student committee at the school. Though it purported to represent the entire student body, only members of Greek houses were allowed to select candidates for office, handing John Chaney and the powerful Co-Op Party effective control over every student election. An editorial in the *UNews* sharply criticized the rigged system: "This damnable Co-Op party keeps all opponents in the dark by creating its own rules and regulations through its mouthpiece, the so-called Student Council. Have you ever even seen a copy of the all student constitution, supposedly the Magna Carta of school politics? No? Neither have I. But they tell me I couldn't understand it if I did see it." "'This is a joint,' said one upperclassman, 'and the damn Co-Op party controls all the elections. They always have.'"

The opposition Vo-Camp Party, which represented the "unaffiliated" non-Greek students, soon staged a revolt. A petition to allow all students to vote for candidates of their choice was circulated across campus and successfully adopted by the school. Swept up in the campaign, Leila Welsh turned her back on the Greek system and ran for office on the Vo-Camp ticket, which dominated the elections. Leila was elected secretary of the student council, third in line of power. The results shattered the stranglehold John Chaney, Kegon, and the Co-Op Party had on student government and ended Carl Balsiger's Enforcement Committee.

Leila's new leadership role took center stage in her life, but she still found time for the glittering social events that dotted the KCU social calendar. At the end of her freshman year, she attended the lavish Spring Formal at the Meadow Lake Country Club at 75th and State Line. Though the event was restricted to KCU fraternity and sorority members, her sorority sister Marjorie Bybee had invited a neighborhood friend from Independence, a city on the outskirts of Kansas City. As glamorous as her social life had been throughout the last year, Leila had avoided the many requests for dates from men on campus and stayed true to her self-imposed abstinence from romantic attachments. But the moment she was introduced to Richard Funk, her resistance melted away. She instantly knew this man would be her destiny.

CHAPTER 2

LOVE TRIANGLE

I f ever there was a time Richard Funk felt out of place, it was the night he attended the University of Kansas City Spring Formal at Meadow Lake Country Club. Surrounded by the elite of the Greek system, his well-worn, cheap suit made him an obvious outsider among the well-heeled, insular crowd. Funk had been raised in a blue-collar family and was neither expected nor had the funds to attend college, much less the distinguished University of Kansas City. Funk's father was an electrotyper at the *Kansas City Star* newspaper. He raised his son to work hard, volunteer, and stay away from the distractions of the city, like the gala he was now attending as a guest of KCU sorority girl Marjorie Bybee.

Richard followed his father's example to the letter of the law, becoming a leader in Boy Scout Troop 128, where he headed up the Christmas toy drive. At sixteen, he went to work as a Western Union messenger boy and never missed a day. He spent his off hours designing and building small model airplanes out of wood and glue. So, when the Jimmy Allen Air Races were announced in July of 1934, Funk went to work designing his greatest airplane yet, spending weeks crafting each small part to perfection.

On the day of the races, two thousand Kansas Citians showed up to watch the sixty entrants compete with their model airplanes made of wood, paper, and rubber bands. As expected, the planes each sailed less than two hundred yards. But when Richard released his masterwork, it rose up toward the sky and kept going. The crowd gasped as the plane miraculously climbed higher and higher. Official timer Milton Mullins ran after the plane with stopwatch in hand, but after eight minutes and twenty-one seconds, the airplane disappeared into the clouds. Nobody could believe what they just witnessed.

Though he had just set the record in fifty states, Funk was nowhere to be found by the roaring crowd. He had already left to continue his bike messenger duties. Only later in the day did he find out he had won the contest and the grand prize of a gold watch and round-trip ticket to St. Louis on Trans World Airlines.

Richard wasn't entirely surprised at the disinterest shown him by the privileged fraternity and sorority members at the KCU Spring Formal. They seemed to have a shorthand with each other that was like a different language and had no interest in anyone outside their tight circle. Richard knew one of the upperclassmen, former Enforcement Committee leader Carl Balsiger, with whom he had attended Southwest High School. He and Balsiger had also served together as officials in the Order of DeMolay, a national Masonic service group for teenaged boys that had been founded in Kansas City and counted Walt Disney among its distinguished alums.

Richard's family owned a summer cottage at Lake of the Forest, a small middle-class lake community thirty miles outside the city, where Balsiger's family also owned a summer home. Despite their having so much in common, Balsiger, too, showed little interest in socializing with Funk. Richard contemplated his exit just before Marjorie Bybee brought him over to meet her closest sorority sister, Leila Welsh.

Richard couldn't believe that of all the attendees at the party, the most beautiful girl was also the friendliest. In her evening gown with her hair in Marcel waves, Leila was a breathtaking vision. Her smile lit Richard up as the two found instant chemistry. They talked and danced through the evening, drawing judgmental glances from the other attendees. There was no doubt Funk would ask for a formal date, and to her own surprise, Leila heartily accepted.

Richard may have been serious and contemplative, but in Leila's presence he felt confident and joyful, her glow bringing out an exuberance in him. Their dates steadily increased over the months, a slow, traditional courtship rather than the slapdash affairs that were so common among the youth in fast-paced Kansas City. Richard brought her to every dance thrown by the Order of DeMolay, and in turn he was her date at the many KCU social events. Leila may have been an heiress and Richard an entry-level clerk at Skelly Oil Company, but their differences never invaded the intimate, luminous space they had created for each other.

As close as the relationship grew, Leila still held back a piece of her heart. By senior year, many of her friends in various sororities were beginning to consider marriage to their KCU boyfriends. But like her aunt Dr. Leila McKee, Leila had never warmed to the idea of marriage, and she was certain it would be a long time before she would ever contemplate it. Richard was never quite sure whether she was seeing other men and never asked. Leila never asked if he was seeing other women but knew in her heart he had devoted himself completely to her. She struggled to understand why she hadn't made the same commitment.

In 1938, Leila graduated from KCU and, following in the footsteps of her aunt, entered a career in education. She spent the next year teaching first grade at Ruhl–Hartman School, where she became a much-beloved teacher. But in 1939, she left Kansas City, her mother Marie, brother George, and boyfriend Richard Funk for a teaching position seven hundred miles away in tiny Knoxville, Illinois. Soon after arriving, she met handsome, strapping Elery "Gabby"

Boynton, who coached basketball at Princeville High School in nearby Peoria, Illinois, and who lived just four blocks from her in Knoxville.

While Richard Funk was dependable, dutiful, and level-headed, Elery had been a star athlete in high school and college and was exciting and unpredictable, a live wire in a quiet town. He had declared his love for her three weeks after they first met, while Richard had still not told her he loved her in four years of dating. Against her better judgment, Leila fell head over heels in love with Boynton, labeling him "the very sweetest and most perfect boy I ever met." She even brought Gabby with her on multiple trips back to Kansas City, where he met her friends. And yet, through the love affair, she still wrote a steady flow of letters back home to Richard, who waited and wondered if Leila would ever return to him, unaware she had fallen in love with another man.

In spring of 1940, Marie Welsh wrote her daughter, pleading for her return home. Leila was close with her mother and had shared every detail of her life with her. Neither of them could continue living apart, and soon Leila returned to Kansas City, leaving Gabby Boynton heartbroken at her departure. She wrote him letters and promised a reunion, but details were scant.

Over the summer, Leila's relationship with Richard Funk heated up again. Weekends were spent at his family's summer home at Lake of the Forest, where dinners and dances at the rustic clubhouse and long walks along the water's edge brought them closer than ever. Richard yearned to express his love to her, but something always held him back. He sensed her resistance, her inner struggle. Leila thought of Gabby and tried to bury her feelings, but still sent him letters. One ended with the directive to "Please destroy this."

In February of 1941, Leila, her brother George, and Marie made a seven-hour drive to the Army Air Corps' Scott Field in Illinois, where Leila's sister Mary Frances and her husband, Quartermaster

Captain Jack Turner, were stationed. While Marie doted on her only grandchild, Leila and George took a two-hundred-mile side trip to Knoxville, where Leila was reunited with Gabby. Their romantic interludes were constrained by George's presence, but Boynton found his moment for a last-ditch plea for Leila's love.

Richard Funk had been kept in the dark about the trip, so when he stopped by Leila's house at 6109 Rockhill Road, he was surprised to learn from the maid that the Welsh family had left for Illinois and Leila had gone to see a boy she had been dating. Though Leila had never fully committed to their relationship, Richard was still stunned. Their summer at Lake of the Forest had been magical, and they were seeing each other several times a week now. He had to know if she was seeing someone else and if she loved him.

Upon her return to Kansas City, Leila fell ill with the flu and was holed up for days in her bedroom. She kept her window open for fresh air and to cool down her temperature. Marie brought her soup on a tray and nursed her back to health. By Wednesday, March 5, 1941, Leila felt well enough to see Richard. They spent the evening at friend Dick Lowden's house, playing cards and games. Leila was still recovering from her illness, and the mood was light. Richard just couldn't bring himself to confront her yet.

Two days later, they attended the Philharmonic and then walked to the Town Royale cocktail bar for drinks, where Richard finally gathered the courage to ask her about the trip to Illinois and the mystery man she had gone to see.

Leila told him everything. She had carried on a relationship with Elery Boynton while she lived in Knoxville, and she had made the recent trip to Illinois as a test to see how she felt about him. But there was more. Just after she had returned to Kansas City, she had received a letter from Boynton in which he proposed marriage. Leila had struggled with her feelings but came to realize she could not marry him and had let him know. Just two days ago, she had received the official "break-up" letter from Elery: he had moved on and was dating someone else.

Richard was blindsided. He had suspected Leila was seeing other men but not seriously, at least not enough to merit a marriage proposal. It was a bitter pill. He had planned to propose to her, himself, but everything was thrown off now. Five years of dating and he still hadn't told her "I love you," though he felt it deeply. He could not remain in the dark any longer. He would wait until their date on Saturday night to tell her how he felt and to press for a decision about their future.

At 6:45 P.M. on Saturday, March 8, 1941, Richard arrived at 6109 Rockhill Road. He had ascended the concrete steps to the Welsh home a hundred times, usually bounding for the front door. But this evening, his steps were slowed by the weight of his uncertain future with Leila. As always, Marie Welsh greeted Richard warmly at the door, though he wondered what she knew of Leila's relationship with Elery Boynton. Had the recent trip convinced her Leila's heart belonged with another man?

The warm air inside the compact bungalow home provided Richard quick relief from the winter chill. Leila's brother George stepped into the living room to gather Richard's coat. Though the two weren't close, George had grown to admire Richard's quiet confidence and the social skills that had made him a leader in the community at such a young age. If only he, too, could possess such fine qualities.

Following in the giant footsteps of his grandfather, George had pivoted into real estate in the last year, but the few sales he had made of modest family homes paled next to the real estate empire his legendary family had built. Like Leila, George would come into his inheritance soon, though he secretly feared he would never live up to the expectations that came with such an entitlement, which represented more than just money. The name, Welsh, cast a long shadow over his measly accomplishments. George frequently cast off the family shadow at the Golden Arrow Inn, where he had amassed a $1,500 bar tab, or at Dierks Smoke Shop, where dice games had landed him $1,100 in debt.

Richard knew better than to ask where Leila was. This was always the ritual: small talk with Marie and George while Leila remained hidden in her room applying the last touches of light makeup. Sitting at her vanity, Leila was still struggling with the sudden end of the relationship with Elery Boynton. But she had finally made her mind up on the matter. She would not marry anyone—not now, not forever. No matter the disapproval that would be heaped upon her, she was finally at peace with the independence she treasured.

She loved Richard and the two had grown closer than ever since the summer, but he had never declared his feelings or intentions. Which might have been for the best. Leila felt pangs of menstrual discomfort—it was that time of the month. She thought about taking a sedative for the pain, but it would only make her sleepy, and this was a night of energy and gaiety. No, she would wait until later to take the pill.

Leila entered the living room bursting with anticipation of the night's event at the Municipal Auditorium. The Police Circus had been running all week. Tonight was the final and command performance. Friends had told her tidbits about the death-defying stunts she and Richard would see—the Flying Wallendas shakily riding bicycles on a suspended wire, the Antaleks performing a high-perch contortionist act. Leila's excitement boosted Richard. After all, he had secured the precious tickets.

Downtown always came alive after dark, but this Saturday night bloomed brighter than ever. The circus crowd was fourteen thousand strong, all swarming at once to the entrances of the massive

Municipal Auditorium, an art deco monument to the triumph of Kansas City. Hundreds who were hopeful for tickets were turned away at the door while Richard confidently escorted Leila to their seats. The crowd's energy was electrifying. Despite the ominous news out of London and the Selective Service draft that was slowly peeling their boys away, at least here Kansas City could feel safe. And the man responsible was also the man of the hour.

Tall, lean, and sharp featured, Lear Reed was only eighteen months into his new job as chief of the Kansas City Police Department, but he could retire tonight and still be regarded as the most consequential chief in the department's history. It was he who had broken the back of the Pendergast machine, the crime syndicate that had ruled Kansas City from the highest political suites through rivers of payoffs made possible by its army of burglars, prowlers, bookmakers, and slot machine operators, all immune from arrest.

Only a year before, gambling parlors had outnumbered grocery stores. A former FBI G-man, Reed had been personally selected by Missouri Governor Lloyd Stark in 1939 to clean up what had become nationally known as the worst police department in the country. Reed sliced through the KCPD's ranks, firing hundreds of corrupt cops, then shut down the gambling rings, conducted extensive arrests of criminal networks, and placed an iron thumb over the city.

The machine had fought back. Reed had been visited by shadowy figures flashing thousands of dollars in bribes, had bags of poison candy sent to him through the mail, and had been lured to hotel rooms where half-naked women attempted to coax him into compromising situations. Even the city's ways and means committee was rumored to have held secret meetings in apartments to plot his destruction. None of it worked. Reed had survived every frame-up, every hunt for compromising dirt, every death threat. Tonight's Police Circus was a benefit for the ascendant KCPD. But for Lear Reed, it was more than that. It was his triumphal statement of conquest. His legacy now secure, he was untouchable.

The Ringling Bros. and Barnum & Bailey Circus may have been king of the big top, but the Hamid-Morton Circus claimed the mantle of largest indoor circus in the world, a three-ring behemoth that crisscrossed the country attracting colossal audiences. Yes, there were clowns and exotic animals, but it was the danger acts that brought the crowds in, and Hamid-Morton always delivered. Leila tensed as Captain Roman Proske, "the most daring of all animal trainers," placed his head into the mouth of his Bengal tiger, his neck certain to be sliced. Peejay Ringen, "the man who laughs at death," prepared to ride his bicycle from the ceiling of the auditorium down a steep incline, only to leap from the bicycle into an impossibly small tank of water. Circus owner Robert Morton bluntly warned the crowd, "If he misses, he bashes his brains out."

Leila grabbed Richard's arm and held on tightly as the Great Peters appeared and climbed his rigging eighty feet high. His neck was placed into a tight noose, he tensed, and then dove into the air, somehow surviving certain decapitation. Death was at hand in nearly all of the thirty acts that performed that night, each one pulling Leila tighter into Richard's embrace.

As was his custom, George Welsh had dozed off on the living room couch, still in his day clothes. Though he had a bedroom in the tight attic space above, he often passed out for long stretches of sleep in the living room. Marie thought better of waking him and read her book in a nearby chair with only a small reading lamp illuminating the room. The book helped distract her from worrying about Leila. She was in Richard's good hands, but the city was still filled with peril.

Every day brought new stories of stickups and prowlers in the surrounding neighborhoods. It sometimes felt as if every hoodlum in the country ended up in Kansas City, despite the boasts of the new chief of police. At 10:30 P.M., she rose from her chair to retire for the night. Though she would remain half-awake in bed until Leila returned, she would never see nor hear the figure watching her through the window.

As the crowds poured out of Municipal Auditorium, Chief Reed stood by and watched every face, savoring the joy and excited chatter of the circusgoers. They had him to thank for this night and all the other peaceful nights to come. Among the throngs whizzing by him were Leila and Richard. When they stepped out into the chilly air, they were met with clogged traffic and a cacophony of car horns. The parking garage would be at a standstill. Richard recognized a good excuse to extend their date and proposed they go for a drink while the congested motorists worked their way out. Leila wanted to attend church the next morning, but a 9:00 A.M wake up would allow her a few more hours with Richard.

The pair window-shopped up crowded Wyandotte Street, when Leila bumped into Phyllis Wetherill, her sorority sister and best friend. The pair had been inseparable since Leila's return to Kansas City, and fate seemed to pull them together like magnets. Accompanying her was Isabelle Bash, another Cho Chin sorority sister, and her husband, Charles Rouse, a former member of the Kegon fraternity and now a coworker with Richard at the Skelly Oil Company. While the group chatted, Phyllis wondered if Leila had broken the news to Richard yet.

Shortly before 11:00 p.m, Leila and Richard stepped into the Hotel Phillips, then walked across the palatial lobby and into the Tropics Room, a tiki bar fitted with sounds of thunder, flickering lights, and a rainstorm behind the bar. While Richard sipped on his usual rum collins and Leila on her usual Coca-Cola, Marie Welsh awoke from her half slumber. She checked the clock. Leila should have been home by now. The moon was dim, and the darkness outside looked impenetrable to her.

Outside, the temperature was settling into the low thirties, with a sharp wind from the northwest blowing at twenty miles per hour. The ground was still covered in a light dusting of snow, but the melt had begun and conditions outside were soggy. A trail of fresh footprints snaked across the backyard, leading to the north window of Leila's bedroom. A knife was thrust below the bottom frame of the window screen, allowing for it to be swung out from its upper hooks. Fingers gripped at the window, but it was locked tight from the inside.

Two houses away, Marguerite Garner felt something was not right. She was home alone with her six-year-old son, her husband and mother yet to return from the theater. It wasn't just the unusual sound of neighborhood dogs barking at midnight, but something else she could sense. She couldn't put her finger on it. Marguerite drew down every curtain in her home and nervously sipped coffee in the kitchen. Minutes later, she heard glass breaking.

While Richard and Leila chatted beneath paper-mache palm trees, Chief Reed pressed the flesh at the swanky Beaux Arts Ball, which in true Kansas City fashion really got swinging past midnight. He allowed himself one drink as politicians, business leaders, and dubious important figures of the city congratulated him on a highly successful benefit circus. Reed found himself distracted by the event's risqué modern dancing, which offended his old-fashioned sensibilities. Things had changed too quickly. Too much too fast. He dismissed his own prudishness but began edging for the exits.

A gloved hand reached through a smashed pane of glass, fumbled for a doorknob, and turned it. Inside was a garage. Eyes scanned the dark room, and boxes filled with old clothes were quietly turned over. The detached garage belonged to John Blackman, whose dog was barking wildly from the basement of the adjoining house.

It wasn't unusual for the dog to be alarmed by a foreign sound, but this was different. The intensity of his howls roused Blackman from bed. He peered out of his second-floor window into the small backyard below. Steps beyond it, the Welsh home. Had he lingered a moment longer, he would have seen a prowler stepping out of his garage, tossing a pile of clothes to the ground, rummaging through them, and pulling out Blackman's own white undershirt.

The dark figure added the shirt to a collection of tools and instruments, none of which came from the garage. They had been carefully assembled, brought to this place at this time for their specific intended use. Cradling the package, the intruder waited on a mound of dirt under a large cedar tree, eyes boring into the east window of Leila Welsh's bedroom.

At 1 A.M., the intruder heard a car pull up to the front curb of the Welsh home. The wait was over.

CHAPTER 3

PROWLER

By the time Richard's car pulled up to the curb at 6109 Rockhill Road, the banter about the circus had run its course. He shut off the engine and sat quietly with Leila, trying to gather the courage to tell her for the first time that he loved her. But the moment never arrived. Instead, Richard leaned in, they embraced, then kissed passionately. Several more minutes of small talk followed by yet more kissing came and went with no mention of love or marriage. He would tell her he loved her next time.

At 1:30 A.M., Leila exited Richard's car, and he escorted her to the front door. She kissed him good-bye on the porch and entered the home. As he turned to leave, Richard glanced through the glass panel in the door and noticed George asleep on the living room couch.

Before retiring, Leila attended to familial duty, waking her mother to let her know she was home, safe and sound. Marie asked about the circus as Leila opened the window for fresh air, the gas furnace having turned the room stuffy. Leila sat on the bed and told her about the wonderous performances, but soon grew tired. She asked to be woken at 9:00 A.M. for church, then kissed her mother on the forehead. Marie squeezed her hand one last time.

Leila's bedroom was mere steps from her mother's, only a narrow bathroom dividing them. She closed the door behind her and immediately went to open the north window, as she regularly did. Having grown up in the country, she was used to open windows and unlocked doors. She wasn't about to change her way of life now, despite her mother's concerns about prowlers.

The window jammed. She pulled again, but it was caught on the screen, which was oddly hanging off its bottom hinges. There was another window on the east side of the room, but its screen had gone missing the year before. Still, she wanted the cold air. Leila unlatched the east window and lifted it.

She stepped into her tiny closet, changed into baby blue pajamas, and meticulously folded her clothes, placing them on a chair in the corner of the room. She brushed her teeth, washed her face of makeup, and swallowed a pill for her menstrual cramps. It would tranquilize her just enough to sleep through the pain.

Two houses northeast of the Welsh home, Lois Malsness and her husband arrived home from a rare late night out. Usually, they were the first ones to bed in the neighborhood, but tonight, she commented to her husband, they would be the last ones to bed. She drove the babysitter home, then listened to her favorite radio program from Hollywood on the drive back. At 2:20 A.M., she parked in her driveway but remained in the car for twenty minutes to finish listening to the broadcast.

Twenty feet away from her on the other side of her garage crouched the intruder, staring through the east window at Leila Welsh, who was deep asleep under a blue chenille bedspread. At 2:40 A.M., Lois entered her home. She drank a glass of water in the kitchen and looked out across her backyard directly toward the Welsh home. She saw nothing.

Marie Welsh woke with a start. She had heard a thud. No, two thuds. Seconds later, the Welshes' next-door neighbor Ruth

Kennedy awoke as well. Her three-year-old son, Johnny, was crying for her. Ruth was alarmed. A sound sleeper, Johnny never woke this early. Something must have startled him. His window faced the Welsh home next door, but there was no sound, no movement outside.

Marie paused to consider the sound that had awoken her. It was unusual—deep and close. She wondered if the furnace had broken or if George had fallen off the couch. She rose and stepped into the living room, where she found George still asleep on the couch. She turned the reading light off in the living room and returned to bed. Just before falling asleep, she glanced at her clock. It was 3:00 A.M.

Marie slept soundly until 7:30 A.M., when George's stirrings in the kitchen woke her. Though it was Sunday, he faced a packed schedule of real estate showings, and she knew he would step out without eating. George had prepared coffee and an early exit, but Marie's protestations forced him to sit through a hearty breakfast. He was soon gone, leaving the house eerily quiet. Marie considered waking Leila and stepped to her door but heard no sound on the other side. Honoring the request for a late wake up, Marie passed the hour tidying up the home until 9:15 A.M. It was time.

Leila's bedroom door didn't open freely; it was caught on something, an obstruction. Marie pushed harder until the door relented, dragging something with it across the wood floor. She peered inside. Inexplicably, Leila's vanity chair had been propped up against the door. The room was cold. Marie went to close the east window, but a strange smell caught her attention, then the sound of something dripping. She turned to her daughter—the blue bedspread had been pulled up over Leila's head, shielding her from view.

Marie's gaze lowered to an expansive pool of blood on the floor. Confused, Marie called out, "What's the matter, honey, have you had the nosebleed?" Silence. A primal terror struck her. She stepped onto a small bedside rug adorned with the image of a puppy, an island in the red pool of blood. Marie fumbled her hand beneath the bed covering and touched Leila's ice-cold forehead. When she pulled her hand out, it was covered in blood.

Marie's screams jolted Ruth Kennedy, who ran out of her home to meet her hysterical neighbor in the backyard. Marie could barely speak, sputtering that something had happened to Leila. Ruth tried to calm her. She could hear neighbors stirring at the sound of Marie's wails. Ruth grabbed her around the waist and guided her back inside. She instructed Marie to wait in the living room while she went to see about Leila.

Kennedy steeled herself for what was to come. She walked toward the lake of blood beneath the bed, stepped onto the island formed by the rug, and ripped back the bed cover. Leila's body was splayed on its left side, a gaping hole in her skull still dripping blood into the red-soaked mattress. She was nearly decapitated; her head was lolling down, the neck sliced, slashed, and stabbed completely through, with only the exposed vertebrae keeping it attached to the body. As Kennedy stood frozen, a blood-soaked man's undershirt dropped out of the open neck wound where it had been stuffed and fell to her feet. Kennedy's screams rivaled Marie's.

Two houses down, at 6105 Rockhill Road, Marguerite Garner stepped into her backyard for fresh air after a fitful night of sleep. The invigorating moment was interrupted when a young voice called out to her. Three-year-old neighbor Johnny Kennedy shouted that Leila Welsh had died. Marguerite dismissed the impossible news and stepped back inside her home.

A short while later, her six-year-old son ran to alert her that soldiers were marching outside. Marguerite peered out the window and was shocked to see police officers walking about the neighbor's yard. She ran to the Welsh home to find Ruth Kennedy consoling a distraught Marie Welsh. Hysterical with grief, Marie cried out,

"Why does this have to happen to me?" Frantic relatives of the Welsh family arrived, and the terrible screaming began again.

Marguerite felt herself in the way and quietly left to return home. As she stepped to the back door of her house, she noticed something she had missed earlier that morning. Though her back porch had just been cleaned the day before, it was now covered in muddy footprints. No neighbor, no police officer had been to her home yet. Whoever made the prints had visited her porch in the dark.

Just after 10:00 A.M. Lear Reed's phone began to ring. He had been hoping for a few more hours of sleep, having returned home at 5:00 A.M. after making the rounds visiting patrolmen on duty across the city. It wasn't the words, but the tone of Homicide Detective Lester Haupt's voice that got to him. "Hello, Chief—we've got a dead girl over here on Rockhill Road. Yep—murder—all chopped up— pretty messy job." Haupt sounded shaken. Reed had seen him cool as a cucumber at crime scenes that had rattled veteran homicide detectives. The unspoken message was received—this wouldn't be like the others.

Chief Reed arrived at the Welsh home soon after, the scene at Rockhill a study in contradictions. The quaint homes lining the middle-class neighborhood were indistinguishable from hundreds like them in all directions, built to raise families and provide a foundation of security not only for Kansas City but also for America. And yet here they were, crowds of gawkers held back by police officers surveying the crime scene and awaiting a glimpse of the horrors within. As Reed walked past, he wondered what had drawn decent people to witness the mutilation of their own neighbor.

He passed through the front door and first scrutinized not the home but the many faces of those inside, as his FBI training had taught him to do. Staring back at him was a quiet and deep unease.

"Come in, Chief," an officer invited. "Right back here." A detective motioned in the direction of the bedroom. To his officers' surprise, Reed stepped away from them and wandered every room but Leila's, scanning furniture and decor, memorizing the layout of the house. He would read every detail of the Welsh way of life before he would allow himself to see the victim.

All eyes were on Chief Reed as he finally walked the hallway to the bedroom. Jackson County Coroner Cecil Leitch awaited him inside. Reed had witnessed the bloodiest slayings across the Midwest at the height of the 1930s gangland crime wave, had survived Kansas City's Union Station Massacre of 1933, had tracked down Pretty Boy Floyd and Alvin Karpis, had discovered the bodies of countless victims of kidnappings, drownings, beheadings, and hangings. Nothing could prepare him for the moment he would first see the murdered body of Leila Welsh.

Reed explained, "Never have I viewed a scene of this type that impressed me as indelibly as that looked upon in the bedroom of Leila Welsh. Her throat had been gashed to the vertebrae. It gaped wide open as though a V had been cut out. The killer had drawn his long knife across that throat not once but a number of times. He had sawed, hacked and stabbed, replaced his blade and hacked more. The bed clothing was soaked with blood. The mattress was saturated. Blood had flowed downward, towards the middle of the girl's body. Over the edge of the bed her blood had run, not yet completely coagulated."

The drawstring of the blue pajama bottoms had been slashed and the pants pulled down, revealing Leila's buttock. There, at the junction with her upper thigh was a horseshoe-shaped cavity in her flesh, five inches across and an inch deep. Bloodless, the walls of the gap were smooth and fully exposed, a near perfect puzzle piece of skin, flesh, and fat—sliced, torn out of the body, and missing. A final desecration lay on the calf of her left leg, peeking out the bottom of the bed covering. A symbol had been written on her skin in blood, resembling the letter *S* or *G*.

Reed struggled not only with the horror of the death scene but also the gnawing question why. His training had prepared him to contain his revulsion and focus on the motivation of the crime. But nothing in his long years of experience could explain this butchery. Peering closer at Leila's exposed neck, he noticed unusual notches on the bones of the vertebrae. In the pillow beneath were visible stab marks where the blade had penetrated through the neck. Coroner Leitch saw an opportunity to break the silence and offered a blunt observation: the body had been purposely bled out. That was the only way to explain the lack of blood in the cavity of flesh cut from the thigh.

But it wasn't the severing of the neck that had caused most of the blood loss. It was the hole in the skull out of which blood had poured, soaking the mattress. "That's why he brought the hammer," Leitch stated matter-of-factly. Reed finally saw it: a heavy railroad "track chisel" hammer lying on the throw rug by the side of the bed—the tool that had punctured the skull of Leila Welsh and had likely killed her.

Reed had little time to absorb the shocking appearance of the murder weapon as Leitch continued his relentless unraveling of the killer's modus operandi. He explained that it would have taken up to half an hour for the body to bleed out enough before the killer could have cut the flesh from the thigh without any trace of blood in the cavity. Half an hour the killer had waited, Reed thought. An eternity in a room just steps from other sleeping residents. An eternity in a room with a large open window exposed to the prying eyes of nearby houses crowded all around.

Reed noticed the crowd of onlookers standing outside the window at this very moment, watching his every move in what should have been a very private setting. He had no time to sort out the unfortunate public spectacle, however, as yet another surprise left by the killer awaited him. The pink curtains and hanging rod of the east window had been violently pulled off the wall and laid over the windowsill, the end of the rod balancing precariously over the sill and onto a sitting chair. No doubt the killer had entered and left through the east window, but why would he tear off the heavy curtains and drape them over the windowsill?

John Wagaman from the police lab stepped into the room with his photography equipment to document the as-yet undisturbed crime scene. Close behind him, Detective Haupt called to Reed, "Chief, you need to see something." Reed followed Haupt out the back door of the house and into the backyard, where Officers Charles Aust and Joe Trabon, who had been first on the scene, were scrutinizing the ground. Several feet from the east window, the weathered handle of a long-bladed butcher's knife was jutting out of the lawn at a forty-five-degree angle. It was the blade used to cut Leila's neck, thrust to the hilt into the soil.

If Reed felt the discomfort of prying eyes on him in the bedroom, his every utterance could now be easily heard by the hovering crowd that was held back only by a rope hastily taken down from the Welsh clotheslines and repurposed as a police perimeter. First the hammer and now the butcher's knife. The killer's instruments of death had been left behind in plain view. Were they discarded . . . or displayed?

With the discovery of the knife, the backyard became center stage for the expanding crime scene. Detectives competed with the crowd as they roamed for evidence. They would soon find more than they could have bargained. A pile of discarded clothing was found scattered along neighbor John Blackman's garage, forcing the police perimeter wider. Promising evidence of footprints throughout the yard had been compromised by spectators walking about, though several prints close to the knife were left relatively intact.

Despite all the activity around him, Chief Reed's attention drifted away from the Welsh property. He stared down the long corridor of backyards sandwiched between the homes facing Rockhill Road and those facing Harrison Road, the next street over. No fences or gates separated the yards, making for easy passage through the open alley between the row of homes. Reed suddenly saw it. He turned to his second-in-command, Captain Harold Anderson, and declared, "That was his escape route."

George Welsh was on his third hour of showing homes to client Ralph Robertson when he became aware something wasn't right. As the pair arrived at the next showing, George found a note affixed to the front door. It was from his uncle Edgar Fleming, instructing him to come home immediately. Abandoning Robertson meant another potential sale wasted. Still, this was highly unusual. George jumped into his car.

He was stunned by the scene awaiting him outside his home, the presence of his uncle Edgar an alarming sign. But before he could walk inside, his aunt Helen called him over to her car. George was surprised to find the family doctor, Graham Asher, in the driver's seat. In the back seat sat his mother, staring silently at some hazy point in the far distance.

Helen dropped into the front passenger seat, and Dr. Asher drove the car out onto the road. George sat quietly, intuiting a demand of silence. The car drove four blocks to Helen and Edgar's home. George watched incredulously as Dr. Asher helped a frail Marie out of the car and into the house. Helen held George back on the front steps. "George, it's Leila." His breath caught as she struggled to say the words. "Leila's dead."

George felt the life drain out of him, a flood of warm memories on the farm with Leila suddenly a torrent of pain. His legs buckled and his body sank to the pavement as if his bones had vanished.

Helen struggled to keep him upright. In an instant, George had gone into the trancelike state he now shared with his mother. Inside the Fleming home together, Marie and George would become so anguished that Helen would tell the police, "They were in a state bordering on collapse."

Even in Kansas City, where the nation's most daring crooks and gangsters came to succeed or die trying, a lowly patrolman like Officer Lawrence Ober faced nothing but the most mundane of radio calls—drunk drivers, domestic disputes, disturbances of the peace. The most exciting assignment of the year had been department-issued canoe training at a community pool. But the order he received from Captain Harry Anderson the morning of March 9 would finally set his heart and career racing.

He and five other officers had been unexpectedly called up and ordered to the corner of 61st and Rockhill Road. There, Anderson ordered them to search the neighborhood's backyards for a very unusual item. A twenty-four-year-old woman had been murdered just four houses away. A part of her body had been removed by the murderer, who detectives believed fled by foot. They were to search lawns, hedges, porches, and trash bins for a piece of human flesh. Not skin. Flesh. An inch thick, five to six inches in diameter, nearly circular but slightly horseshoe shaped. It would have skin on one side and on the other tissue, fat, a layer of muscle.

Dumbstruck, the other officers moved slowly, each man unsure whether he wanted to be the one to find the flesh . . . or not. But Officer Ober felt no such misgivings. He could see the streets crowding with onlookers as word spread. This was big. His mind so set on the mission, any thought of the girl behind the flesh evaded him.

While the other officers moved as a group south on Rockhill Road toward the Welsh home, Ober slipped away north onto the next block. He scoured every inch of ground one property at a time, walking through thick shrubbery, examining basement windows, crawling under porches. His house-by-house search eventually took him to the backyard of 6032 Harrison Street, where he spotted something unusual in the yellowed grass: a white cotton glove.

His instructions were to find a piece of flesh, but something about the glove gave him pause. It was bunched up, though the fingers were splayed out. That was a telltale sign of a glove torn off in haste. He examined it—no trace of blood. If the glove had been worn by a killer who tore out a piece of human flesh, doubtless there would have been bloodstains. Ober scoured the yard and found the matching second glove twenty feet away from the first. The forefinger of the glove was stained with blood.

Two doors south, at 6042 Harrison Street, Mabel Murphy was barricaded in her home, waiting for the Welsh commotion outside to die down. Earlier in the day, she had been visited by police officer Alvin Hymer. After a cursory glance across her backyard, he left. A neighbor called at 12:00 P.M. to inform her officers were walking through her backyard. Just after lunch, her husband, Walter, suggested she look outside to see if the police had trampled the yard they had worked so hard to maintain.

Mabel stepped from her porch onto the manicured, yellowed grass. As she looked with pride at the flawlessly smooth lawn, a strange object attracted her attention. She picked it up. Her fingers touched a sticky, gelatinous surface. Turning it in her hand, she suddenly recognized the familiar bloom of human skin. Mabel nearly collapsed, calling out for Walter to come quickly. He stood guard over the flesh while Mabel ran to find a police officer. Officer Ober had just delivered the gloves to his superiors when she found him and summoned him to her home.

Chief Reed and an entourage of detectives hurried the half block up Rockhill Road to the Murphy's yard. There it lay: the missing flesh, a human puzzle piece in the unfolding Welsh jigsaw. Reed would find one last piece just steps away in a small snowbank by a neighbor's garage. Melting ice from the eaves was dripping down, forming a pool of water in the snow. It was stained blood red. After losing the flesh and gloves, the killer had washed Leila's blood away in the dripping trail of water as he continued north through the backyard alley.

Reporters from the *Kansas City Star* were now on hand, fully documenting every explosive discovery of evidence, but Reed would manage to keep hidden from the press one tool the killer had used. He quietly directed Captain Anderson to search for a two-tined carving fork, the type usually paired with a carving knife and used specifically for slicing meat. Reed would ensure that this weapon and the reason for its search would never be divulged to the public.

From the discarded clothes found outside the Blackman garage to the footprints, the bloody undershirt, the hammer, the collapsed curtains, the plunged knife, the flesh, the gloves, and finally the pool of blood, the killer had left a terrible but abundant trail of evidence. Surely, Reed thought, the laboratory men would discover some telltale clue that would lead to the killer. He was wise to trust in his department's crime lab, now one of the best in the nation, in no small part owing to his familiarity with the FBI's crime lab.

After hours searching Leila's bedroom for fingerprints, lab investigators John Wagaman and Shelby Compton finally got a hit. On the interior underside of the east windowsill, they discovered a pristine fingerprint. The strange location of the print underneath the sill indicated it was made by someone steadying themselves while entering or leaving through the window. So valuable was this one print, the entire windowsill was sawed out of the wall and delivered to the crime lab for analysis.

Dazed and broken, George Welsh was forced to compose himself when police arrived at the Fleming home to fingerprint every member of the family. They requested George return with them to the crime scene to speak with Chief Reed. In the living room where he had slept through the horrific event, George detailed Leila's last day to Reed, adamant he had seen nothing unusual leading up to the murder. The name Richard Funk was prominent in his hour-by-hour account of the previous day, and Reed hastily summoned the young man.

By the time Funk arrived at Rockhill, he had already spoken with Helen Fleming, who brought him to his knees with the news of Leila's fate. As he entered the home, Richard was immediately embraced by George in a tight and desperate grip. No words were exchanged. What could be said? Reed asked Funk and Welsh for their cooperation downtown at KCPD headquarters, where he could continue gathering crucial information about Leila's inter-actions and movements. George would eventually be released at 11:00 P.M., after nine hours of questioning.

Soon after George left, the crime lab investigators rushed to find Chief Reed. They had successfully lifted the fresh fingerprint from the excised windowsill. It had been run through the state-of-the-art Battley single-print identification system, which came back nega-tive for any matches. Reed's disappointment was palpable. The fail-ure to match among the tens of thousands of names in the system eliminated anybody who had a violent criminal record, depressing hope for a quick identification of the killer.

His distress was short-lived. John Wagaman breathlessly declared that, nonetheless, they had made a match. The fingerprint found on the underside of the windowsill had thirty points of iden-tification, leaving no doubt to the certainty of the match. "Chief, you're not gonna believe this." Wagaman held a moment, signal-ing Reed should brace himself. "The fingerprint belongs to George Welsh."

CHAPTER 4

AN AWKWARD BUT FIENDISH AMATEUR

Amid the long and sordid history of American political machines, Kansas City's Pendergast organization remains unique in its nearly unparalleled power. For half a century, "Boss Tom" Pendergast and his brother before him united German, Italian, and Irish immigrants with the city's Jewish and Black citizens to form an invincible voting bloc that would send the rival Republican Party into electoral exile.

To maintain loyalty, a citywide system of patronage, kickbacks, and special favors was doled out by the machine from its Main Street storefront, a deceptively modest headquarters in which the fate of not only Kansas City but also the state of Missouri was decided. Each morning, lines formed around the block to kiss the ring of Boss Tom. When it was time to place bets on the horses or sidestep Mafia members looking for their cut, Pendergast would escape through a secret passage running from his office next door into the Hotel Monroe, which was machine-owned and operated.

As the political and criminal tendrils of the Pendergast network grew across the state, they eventually reached the seat of power in Jefferson City, where in 1932, the machine installed Guy Parks in the governor's mansion. At Boss Tom's behest, Parks promptly unwound the state's control of the Kansas City Police Department, returning it to local, and thus, Pendergast control. Guy Parks would not be the only chief executive that Pendergast elevated to power. In 1934, former haberdasher Harry S. Truman would be selected by the machine to run for one of Missouri's U.S. Senate seats after a successful career of Pendergast-backed judgeships. With law enforcement under firm machine control, the courts, the city, the state, and even federal representation of Missouri was decided by one man.

Seemingly unassailable, Pendergast's dominance would be first threatened not by outside challengers, but from within. With his hand comfortably gripping the governor's desk, Tom Pendergast selected loyalist Lloyd Stark in 1936 to replace Governor Parks. But the ambitious Stark had his eyes on an even bigger prize: Harry Truman's Senate seat. When Boss Tom made it clear that Truman would remain in Washington, DC, Stark began plotting. The opening he sought soon appeared when allegations of voter intimidation, ballot stuffing, and falsified returns surfaced in local Kansas City elections, arousing federal investigators whom Stark not only tolerated but encouraged. A cascade of trials and subsequent indictments flooded the machine, sending 287 men to prison and severely weakening Tom Pendergast's rule.

By 1938, all-out war was declared between Stark and Pendergast, with the fiercest battle waged over control of the powerful Jackson County Circuit Court. With the Kansas City Bar Association's backing, Pendergast was able to stave off Stark's attempts to purge the court of machine-backed judges. In 1939, Governor Stark struck back as the state retook control of the Kansas City Police Department. It was at this fiery moment that Lear Reed ascended into the state-appointed role of police chief and reformer John Gage was elected mayor.

While Gage rid city government of Pendergast patronage positions, Reed began his campaign against the criminal elements lining the machine's coffers. The year 1940 would prove the undoing of both combatants as Tom Pendergast was imprisoned for federal tax evasion and Lloyd Stark suffered defeat in his bid for Harry Truman's Senate seat. Shattered but still grasping for power, the Pendergast machine ached for an opportunity to reconstitute itself.

On March 9, 1941, it found that opportunity.

Rockhill Road was crawling with detectives and police lab technicians on order from Chief Reed to scour every inch of the Welsh home for the minutest trace of evidence, with the latest in FBI technology on its way to KCPD headquarters to assist. Orderly, sober, and professional, they were a well-choreographed team. But tension gripped them the moment Jack Gibbs and four other Jackson County Sheriff's deputies approached the home.

Ignoring the police cordon and a protective line of officers, the interlopers sauntered into the Welsh house as if every present member of the police department were invisible. They had been sent by newly installed Sheriff Granville Richart with strict orders to begin their own investigation into the Welsh matter, the police department be damned. They were to treat all evidence, all witnesses, all information as theirs and theirs alone.

Gibbs was no stranger to police officers. Chief Reed had personally fired him from the KCPD for his association with key Pendergast figures. Gibbs was quickly hired by the sheriff's department, which, along with the Jackson County Circuit Court, was the last vestige of Pendergast control in Missouri. As he walked the crime scene, Gibbs seemed to revel in his disregard for his former police colleagues. His loyalty now lay with Sheriff Richart, who had taken an unusually keen interest in the Welsh murder the moment it hit his desk.

Just as Gibbs's tour of the home ended, another commotion disrupted the pressing work of the police. Reporters gathered on the front lawn to hear Chief Deputy Sheriff Jacque Purdome announce that the sheriff's department already had a good clue in the murder case. The police were stunned by the announcement, the first salvo in an unprecedented battle they neither anticipated nor were prepared to wage.

The unrevealed clue deputies had uncovered was a one-sentence passage in the bestselling book *Out of the Night* by Jan Valtin, in which murder is proposed by a blow to the head and cutting of the neck. Sheriff's deputies sprang into action, demanding libraries turn over names of those who had checked the book out. Stakeouts quickly followed of these individuals' homes, though no suspects ever evolved.

With few leads, sheriff's deputies squeezed the extended Welsh family for any information that could break the case open. George Welsh was grilled for eighteen hours in his first encounter with the sheriff, nearly collapsing when finally released. The next day, two men showed up and escorted George away again. Worried, the Welsh family called the sheriff's department to ask that George be allowed to rest. But the sheriff denied sending any men for George that day. To the family's relief, George was deposited at his uncle's home later that night. The mysterious men were never identified.

Not only did George suffer through interrogations with the sheriff's department, but he also spent interminable hours with the police. Detectives did not disclose to him that they had found his fingerprint on the east windowsill, and they would continue to gather evidence and probe his movements leading up to the murder before considering any charges. Reed, however, remained skeptical of George's guilt. When asked whether he spent time in Leila's room, George told investigators he often chatted with Leila while he sat on the east windowsill and smoked cigarettes, throwing the butts into the backyard as there was no ashtray in the room. Surely, his hand would have gripped the underside of the sill, leaving a fingerprint. However, debate raged within the department as police fingerprint expert Gorman Raney claimed the print was less than twenty-four hours old. George had not entered Leila's room in the twenty-four hours before the murder, or so he claimed.

Drained of life, George shed no tears at Leila's funeral. His ashen face was a desert of emotion, showing nothing but pain and soul-consuming emptiness. Marie sat next to him, dry-eyed and hollowed out. Behind them sat a thousand people who had arrived at Stine-McClure Funeral Home to pay their last respects, including hundreds of University of Kansas City alums. There were friends and family members from near and far and strangers who had never known Leila Welsh but were drawn by mystery or spectacle. Leila's great-uncle, Reverend James McKee, led an emotional sermon and astutely noted, "No one could know her without loving her." Hidden among the crowd were plainclothes police officers scouring for any telltale sign the murderer was sitting among them. Detectives would extend their surveillance to Leila's gravesite at her family's plot sixty miles away in Carrollton, Missouri, where for weeks they would note every visitor and license plate number.

Tensions between the Jackson County Sheriff's Office and the Kansas City Police Department ran to a boil over the sharing of evidence. The railroad track hammer used to strike Leila Welsh was central to the investigation, and identifying its origin could reveal the killer. The sheriff wanted the hammer—badly. Chief Reed refused to allow deputies to take possession or even examine it. Similar requests for the crime scene photos were also starkly denied by Reed. Sheriff Richart was furious.

The behind-the-scenes tension threatened to leak into the press, raising the stakes for both law enforcement agencies. Any hopes of keeping the quiet war between the sheriff and the police out of the public eye were quickly dashed. Several days after the Welsh murder, a young couple, Jeanne Harvey and boyfriend James Persons, left a Kansas City nightclub and entered their car when mentally ill, handicapped fugitive Oliver Bridges slipped into the back seat, pushed a gun to Persons's head, and demanded he drive. For six terror-filled hours, Bridges directed them through rural Kansas roads, making frequent reference to the Welsh murder. A chill ran down Jeanne Harvey's spine when the car passed a mental institution and Bridges muttered, "Right here is where I belong." Bridges ordered the car back to Kansas City, abandoned his kidnap victims, checked himself into the dimly lit New Viaduct Hotel, and committed suicide. When a traumatized Jeanne Harvey revealed Bridges's comments about Welsh, Sheriff Richart smelled a suspect and jumped into action. Deputy Jack Brice was sent to interview the young couple, but was denied access by the police. Richart had enough.

The next day, Police Officer Winifred Dickerson was tasked with driving the couple back to their homes after a final debriefing with police. As she pulled close to Jeanne Harvey's house, they spotted a phalanx of men in double-breasted suits standing on the front porch. Harvey also noticed a car was following them. "Don't stop! Keep driving! Drive away!" she shouted at Officer Dickerson, who swerved back onto the roadway and raced across a checkerboard of suburban streets while the pursuing vehicle gave chase.

Dickerson screeched to a halt in front of the downtown police garage, honking the horn to alert fellow officers as the chase car pulled up within inches of her own. Sheriff's Deputy Jack Brice scrambled out of the rear vehicle, ran toward Dickerson, and reached inside to grab her keys out of the ignition. He slid into the back seat and demanded Harvey and Persons answer his questions.

Chief Reed and a group of officers rushed outside and pulled the trapped passengers out of the car to safety. Harsh words were exchanged as Reed threatened to arrest Brice. Officers stepped toward the enraged deputy but froze when he drew his gun, instantly triggering a wave of riot guns and revolvers drawn back at him. Undeterred, Brice waved his gun across their faces, daring them to step forward. Just before he finished the last word of his threat, officers lunged for the weapon, wrestling him to the ground and risking an accidental discharge. Finally disarmed, Brice was ordered inside.

When Reed admonished him, stating, "You had your finger on the trigger," Brice barked back, "I'm sorry I didn't click the trigger." Instead of receiving an apology from Sheriff Richart, Reed was told in no uncertain terms that Brice had every right to question the couple and to expect no letup in the aggressive rival investigation. Richart concluded, "The laboratory is the domain of police owing to your better equipment, but in all other aspects of this case, my men will be right in there with yours."

Reed recognized the threat posed by Sheriff Richart's campaign. It had all the earmarks of Pendergast ambition behind it, but true to form, no hunger for truth or justice. With his job hanging in the balance, Richart's mission was to find someone—anyone—likely to have committed the crime, get them in front of the Jackson County Court, and ensure a quick trip to the electric chair. Whether the convicted person was the real killer was an afterthought. This was business. If the fading Pendergast machine could no longer control the police department, they now had the opportunity to hobble it and replace it with the sheriff's department, which they did control. All they had to do was beat Reed to a conviction.

Chief Reed would not attempt to beat them at their own game. Certain an arrest of someone was days, even hours away, he was determined to find the real killer. Twenty of the department's best detectives had been assigned to the case around-the-clock. Failure was not an option. The eyes of not only Kansas City but also the entire nation were upon them. The day after the murder, headlines had exploded in newspapers across the country, proclaiming the tale of the beautiful heiress mysteriously mutilated in her bedroom just steps away from her family. The press, the mayor, the governor, the FBI, and even the nation would expect constant updates and a quick resolution to ensure the faceless monster responsible for this atrocity was no longer a threat to decent citizens. Events an ocean away were spiraling out of control. Kansas City could not fall prey to similar barbarity.

After detectives and the police lab crew had finished their exhaustive canvass of the Welsh home, Lear Reed paid one last visit, this time alone. The house was eerily quiet in the nighttime, the line of cars and their gawking passengers nearly gone. He scrutinized the worn Oriental rugs in the living room, the rose satin couch on which George had slept and its green throw pillows, the mahogany library table and the radio atop it. Hanging on the wall was a framed photo of Leila in a pink bridesmaid's dress taken months earlier at the wedding of her friend Mary Ann Peeler. Upstairs in George's small second-floor bedroom hung a peculiar inscription above his narrow bed, a verse from the tomb of William Shakespeare:

Good friend for Jesus Sake Forebeare
To Digg the Dust Encloased Heare
Blese Be Ye Man Ty Spares Thes Stones
And Curst Be He Ty Moves My Bones

Leila's room was by all appearances unremarkable. And yet there was a strange sensation inside. On the north wall was a framed photo of UKC's Cho Chin sorority taken in 1936. A picture of the Madonna hung on the east wall. Her bed was old fashioned, rural, and simple. It had been brought from the farm, the bed she had slept in as a child. The bloodied mattress upon which she was slain was gone, having been dragged into the backyard and burned. Her clothes still hung neatly in the closet, a new spring hat in a cellophane box. On her vanity, precious items sat in a neat array. Nothing had been stolen or rummaged through. The killer had no interest in theft beyond stealing the life of the young woman.

As Reed walked the room, he realized he was plainly visible through the open east window, and yet he aroused no suspicion. Kansas City had gone into a panic since the murder, guns had been sold at a record rate, and locks, bolts, and gates had been installed across neighborhoods that had routinely left doors unlocked at night. Yet no sound of alarm came from outside.

He would test the Welsh neighborhood further, making noises in the room, moving furniture. He turned a flashlight on and paraded the beam across the dark room. He stepped through the east window into the backyard and back into the room. Still nothing. Among the neighboring homes, he counted thirty-six windows that had an unobstructed view into Leila's room. And yet nobody stirred. Walking through neighboring backyards, he spotted people undressing through open windows, heard the sounds of families chatting and plates being washed. He even walked into garages. Nobody saw the strange figure lurking in plain sight. Not even the dogs barked.

The next morning, Chief Reed and the head of the Homicide Bureau, Thomas Farley, assembled their investigative team to detail and discuss everything they knew about the case up to that hour. While Reed smoked his ubiquitous pipe, Farley stood and reviewed aloud the timeline and narrative of the murder based on the evidence the department had gathered. He began at midnight on March 9.

A discarded newspaper had been found that bore an imprint of the hammer the killer had brought. Tests proved the hammer had been wrapped in the newspaper, standard packaging for a hard-ware store purchase. Around the top of the hammer's handle was wrapped a seven-inch piece of string with a minute piece of newspaper clinging to it. The killer had unwrapped the hammer while he waited in the dark.

Cigarette butts had been found in the backyard, suggesting the killer had smoked while he awaited Leila's return home in the thirty-two-degree weather. Near the east window, three faint heel prints had been identified in the soft ground. Plaster molds had been cast of the prints, revealing a medium-sized shoe, half-soled with a rubber composition. The open east window of Leila's room was only forty-two inches off the ground, an easy entry for a taller person.

Holding the T-shirt rag, the butcher knife, the two-tined fork, and the hammer in his left hand, the killer had lifted his left leg over the windowsill and into Leila's room, steadying himself with his right hand on the raised window. The cotton gloves he wore prevented identifying fingerprints. A muddy footprint had been found inside the room by the east window, showing the position of the left foot as it first stepped in. The killer then dragged his right leg up along the outside wall, leaving a small mud stain. The police lab determined the stain had been made with a downward motion, meaning the right foot had slipped before it crossed over the windowsill into the room.

Once inside, the killer approached the bed and raised the nearly five-pound railroad hammer over Leila Welsh's head. Her autopsy revealed a significant amount of adrenaline, a glandular hormone that is released when one is in great fear, agitation, or excitement. The police concluded that Leila had suddenly awakened in the final moment before the hammer rained down. The first hammer blow struck her right forehead close to her ear, cracking open a hole in the skull. Blood poured out, followed by a second hammer blow that did not penetrate the skull. The two impact points sat within a two-to-three-inch depression in her forehead, now gushing a significant amount of blood.

Marie Welsh was awakened at 3:00 A.M. by the sound of two thuds. She claimed the first thud was louder than the second and they were seconds apart, consistent with the two hammer blows. She rose, opened her door, walked into the living room, and turned off the light, which the killer must have heard. A small chair that had sat at Leila's vanity was placed against the door, likely the killer's attempt to bar it or to serve as an alarm should anyone in the house try and enter her room.

Several more minutes passed while the head wound bled out, with no activity and no sound in the pitch-black room but the stream of blood pouring off the mattress and pooling on the floor. Despite the trauma she had suffered, Leila Welsh was still alive. Holding the white T-shirt in his left hand, the killer placed it over the victim's neck and plunged the butcher knife through the rag and into her neck. The T-shirt blocked the blood spray from the neck wound, keeping the killer clean of splatter.

Over the next several minutes the killer hacked, sawed, and gouged through the neck, severing the jugular veins, carotid arteries, trachea, and esophagus. The knife made two gashes extending from the center of the lower neck toward both ears, creating a V-shaped opening. Having nearly decapitated her, he left only the vertebrae intact. Notches made by the butcher knife were found on the thick bones of the cervical spine along the neck, evidence that the killer put great effort into completely severing her head from her body but was unsuccessful.

When finished, he cleaned the knife of blood. Reed compared this singular act to the work of a butcher: "Straight, sharp smears in the folds of the bloody shirt revealed clearly that he had drawn his dripping blade through them as a butcher, after slashing the throat of a steer, would wipe his knife." With the knife cleaned, the killer thrust the blood-soaked T-shirt into the neck wound.

Coroner Leitch was certain the killer had struck with the hammer first owing to the presence of blood in Leila's ear canal. Had her neck been cut with the knife first, blood would have poured out of that wound, leaving much less blood to exit the skull and not enough to enter the ear canal. In addition, the pool of blood was centered directly beneath Welsh's head.

For the next thirty minutes, the body bled out, dripping between the floorboards into the coal bin in the basement below. No object in the room was disturbed, nothing stolen. The killer's singular, patient focus remained on the corpse of Leila Welsh. With the stream of blood now reduced to a trickle, the killer attempted to cut an opening in Leila's blue pajama bottoms at the right hip's junction with the buttock. He then stopped, cut the drawstring of the pajamas instead, and pulled them down to the thigh.

With her body resting on its left side and her right hip exposed, the killer introduced a new tool from his arsenal, a small razor-sharp pocketknife that would be used for the precision cutting to come. Carving a horseshoe-shaped trail in one smooth and rapidly moving stroke, he bore into the fatty flesh, then slid the knife underneath it to separate and pull away the inch-thick bloodless tissue. The five-inch-diameter memento was placed on the windowsill, leaving a telltale greasy stain. Amid the horror, Welsh's body showed no sign of sexual assault nor traces of spermatozoa.

It was now time to leave a signature. Pulling up Leila's right pajama leg, he dipped his gloved right forefinger into the blood and inscribed a bizarre mark on her calf: what appeared to be either a letter S or G, or a combination thereof. He pulled the bed comforter away from the calf, ensuring the four-inch-long blood-imprinted signature was "boldly exposed." He then dragged the blue comforter over Leila's body, shielding the horrific scene from view, and made his exit out the east window with the flesh in hand. Before he left, however, the killer inexplicably pulled down the window's pink curtains and hanging rod, leaving both dangling over the windowsill. Stranger still, the curtains had been "draped into folds, in an artistic manner as a person would arrange a plated corner decoration." Reed was convinced this was a second signature left by the killer, a message of vanity and egotism.

Once outside, the killer's foot left a tiny ball of an adhesive substance thought to be tar on the exterior wall. In it were found bits of yarn matching fibers from Leila's bedside rug. The killer walked several feet, then turned around to face the house and plunged the butcher knife into the ground at a forty-five-degree angle. The police knew he was facing the east window because of the shallow imprint of his thumb and index finger knuckles in the earth on either side of the knife.

He then proceeded north through neighbors' backyards, crossed 61st Street, and found himself in front of a garden fence on the opposite side of Mabel Murphy's yard. Having to scale the fence, the killer either purposely or accidently dropped the piece of flesh. Once on the other side of the fence, he discarded both gloves, which were completely clean of blood save for the stained forefinger. Though the gloves were a size small, the elastic on the cuffs had been overstretched by larger hands within them. The killer walked fifty feet further, where he washed blood away from either his clothing or a tool. No other trace of his escape route was found.

Coroner Leitch had put the murder no earlier than 2:30 A.M. and no later than 6:30 A.M. The official cause of death was "acute hemorrhage due to an incised wound of the neck" and "a contusion of the head with a fracture of the skull." Deft with a knife, the killer showed skills that drew comparisons to a butcher or doctor.

Commenting on the flesh wound, Reed conjectured, "It was a perfect curve, as though made by a surgeon. Had the slayer studied surgery, or read medical books and been interested in anatomy?"

The use of the rag to prevent blood spray demonstrated a familiarity with slaughtering animals. "Perhaps the slayer was experienced in killing chickens and hogs." In fact, the killer's full process mirrored that of the extensive Kansas City slaughterhouses: "He had prepared himself as if about to butcher a steer—a blow on the head, cut the throat, and remove the hide."

Despite the barbarity of the murder, Homicide Chief Farley defined the killer as deliberate and patient, his every move premeditated. The hammer blows were restrained, enough force to puncture a hole in the skull but not enough to shatter it. The killer had made no additional loud sounds in the room despite spending at least forty-five minutes inside. With a large pool of blood on the floor, the killer had cautiously remained on the bedside rug throughout the ordeal, keeping his shoes dry and never leaving a bloody footprint.

Even the gloves used to stab and hack and slice and rip were nearly free of blood, Reed noted. "These were no blood-soaked gloves from a dabbling, hasty, nervous perpetration of a crime in the darkness of the bedroom. On the contrary, few were the stains—remarkably few in the light of the manifest butchery. It was a planned crime, carefully and deliberately executed by one not pressed for time."

Though the killer had displayed remarkable planning and patience, Farley and Reed asserted this was the work of "an awkward but fiendish amateur." Why would an intruder bring a cumbersome five-pound hammer when a much lighter tool could have incapacitated Welsh and avoided making such a loud noise? Why bring a twelve-inch butcher knife when the smaller, more-precise pocketknife would have sufficed? Why risk exposure standing in the backyard for hours awaiting Leila's return home? Why risk entering first from the north window, which was easily visible from the street?

This was a murder of brazen and reckless risk for the killer. With so much premeditation, surely he was aware of these risks. Only someone with a burning, driving obsession with Leila Welsh would have taken this opportunity. Someone who took many days to plan the murder and assemble the murder kit. Someone who had staked the house out before. Someone who had been thinking about this for a very long time.

Two weeks after the murder, the police had interviewed five hundred potential suspects and former acquaintances of Leila Welsh. Both Richard Funk and Elery Boynton were thoroughly investigated and found to have rock-solid alibis from multiple witnesses. Homicide detectives were on sixteen-hour duty as hot leads came and went. The hammer that had been left at the side of Leila's bed bore traces of lime, leading to a nationwide search of quarries and railroad yards that even extended into Mexico. Nobody recognized the well-worn hammer, even with its distinctive marks.

Every and any suspicious character was hunted down and interrogated. In Nevada, Missouri, a gas station employee reported a customer who had left in a hurry when the radio announced news of the Welsh investigation. Reed sent men to find and interrogate the quick-footed stranger, who was soon cleared. A young blond man entered a store with three bandaged fingers and was immediately reported to the police. All known sex offenders were brought in for questioning, as patrol cars scoured schools for "exhibitionists and degenerates." Officers patrolled the streets day and night and set up traffic stops on highways to flag suspicious motorists entering or leaving the city. And yet, every morning Chief Reed went before an anxious national press to report no arrest was imminent.

Each day that passed seemed to bring greater anxiety in Kansas City, which was sure the beast would strike again. Parents forbade their daughters from seeing boyfriends. Housewives refused to answer their doors, leaving delivery drivers and water meter readers unable to perform their duties. Motels outside town refused rooms to traveling salesmen from Kansas City. The only topic of conversation was the murder as newspaper sales skyrocketed. In a city that had become numb to a decade-long conveyer belt of murder and violent crime, the Welsh case was proving to be a watershed moment. Overnight, Kansas City turned from a patchwork of communal Midwestern neighborhoods into a fortified metropolis of locked doors and windows.

Lear Reed, who at the outset had been certain the case would be quickly solved, now kept secret his growing doubt. Not one solid suspect had emerged. It was as if the killer had just vanished into thin air. All his FBI training, the state-of-the-art microscopes, fluoroscopes, and ultraviolet detectors had failed him. As the case entered a gray zone, Reed had eminent criminal psychologists brought in to analyze the case and issue a report. It pinned the killer's age the same as Leila, twenty-four years old. Neither a stranger nor a close friend, the killer likely was someone she had known peripherally for a long time, the report concluded. The suspect list could run hundreds of names long and would require significant resources to investigate, but if her killer had, indeed, known her, it would be just a matter of time before the police would find him.

Just as Reed and his team of investigators were about to flood Leila's known contacts, a dramatic identification of the killer's identity roared into the investigation.

CHAPTER 5

REVENGE OF THE MACHINE

One of the laborious and thankless tasks police officers were forced to grind out in the wake of the Welsh murder was a citywide canvass of every hardware and kitchenware store in hope of finding the source of the murder tools. Officer Alex Stewart had visited hundreds of locations and in return had received just as many blank stares of confusion. He was expecting the same when he entered a battered, cluttered hardware store at 1123 18th Street, the business and home of Joseph Louis Alport and his mother, Lena.

Stewart lifted a well-worn photograph of the hammer used in the Welsh murder and muttered the just-as-well-worn question, "Did you sell this hammer?"

"No," Alport replied, "but I did sell the knife used in that murder."

Stewart stammered and asked if he was sure.

"I'm positive," came the reply.

Officers converged on the store, where Alport showed them three more knives just like the one he had sold and then recognized when newspapers printed photos of the murder weapons. Suddenly the most important man in Kansas City, Alport was hustled down to KCPD headquarters at 6th and Locust, where he detailed his encounter with the most wanted man in America.

On March 6, 1941, at 4:30 P.M., a short man approximately five feet, five inches tall and between the ages of thirty and forty with auburn-tinted hair had walked into Alport's hardware store wearing a green hat and a dark overcoat. He perused the well-stocked aisles of new and secondhand tools, arriving at a showcase behind which Alport stood. With his head held suspiciously low, the stranger asked for a knife. Alport obliged with an impressive specimen that carried an equally impressive price tag of $1.50. The man told him that was far too expensive, so Alport pulled out an older, dulled butcher knife that was well priced at 35 cents. The man offered 20 cents.

Alport agreed to the sale, but the stranger demanded that he sharpen the knife on the emery wheel behind him, a brand-new grinder Alport had just purchased and a real investment in the business. The notion of breaking it in with a twenty-cent purchase gnawed at Alport, so he offered the stranger a common file instead. For the next half hour, the man expertly sawed and filed the knife to a fine point while Alport furtively kept his hand on a weapon in case the dubious customer attempted a holdup. He breathed a sigh of relief when the customer placed the knife in his pocket and walked out.

Police called Alport's description of the stranger "sketchy," but he swore he would recognize the man if he ever saw him again. With George Welsh's windowsill fingerprint fresh on their minds, detectives decided to give him that opportunity.

As a ruse, George was hastily called to the county jail to undergo further questioning while Alport was shuffled in through the back by Officers Alvin Hymer and Wayne Gibson. While George and his uncle Edgar Fleming waited in the hallway, Alport walked slowly past and scrutinized the face of the young man, as instructed. Taken to a private room, Alport emphatically denied George was the man who bought the knife. He was too young and too tall, no doubt in his mind.

The activity surrounding Alport grabbed the attention of the sheriff's deputies, who were also present at the county jail. Officer Hymer had developed a good relationship with the sheriff's office, so when Deputy Sheriff Jacques Purdome called him up to inquire about the commotion with George, Hymer was happy to share all he knew about Alport.

One month later, Police Chief Reed received a highly unusual message from Joe Alport: he wanted a second look at George, just to be sure. An important witness, Alport needed to be accommodated, so Reed sent Hymer and Gibson to pick him up in a patrol car. Blocks from KCPD headquarters, Alport was ordered to lie down in the back of the car to avoid being spotted as they drove into the building's basement garage. He was brought up in a secure elevator and placed in a private holding room.

Reed entered with George Welsh and asked if he recognized Alport, to which George answered *no*. Alport coolly responded, "You should know me because I'm the man who sold you the knife." Speechless, George was escorted away as stunned officers pressed Alport to explain his about-turn. He claimed he had always known George was the mystery customer but wanted to think it over first, aware of the serious implications.

Hymer and Gibson protested, reminding Alport he had been shown hundreds of photographs of local criminals for a possible match to the knife buyer and had always picked out short, thin, middle-aged men with light hair. He had also been driven around town by the officers and again pointed out men who looked nothing like George. Just a month earlier, he had been certain George did not fit any of the criteria for a positive identification. Alport shrugged off their objections with an arrogant nonchalance.

Reed had seen this before. Someone had gotten to him.

Alport had single-handedly changed the game, and the sheriff's department was ready to pounce. A motive for the murder was quickly established: with Leila gone, George stood to gain financially by having to split his family's inheritance with only one sister rather than two. If George refused to confess to that motive, the sheriff had special methods to break his will and extract what was needed.

Under intense pressure from the Chamber of Commerce and city business leaders, Reed was forced to hand over all physical evidence, including the hammer and knife, to Sheriff Richart. All crime scene photographs and reports were to be shared with the sheriff's office, all interview subjects to be made available. The distraction of Alport's positive ID forced the police department to slowly abandon the ongoing widespread investigative track they had been on and focus all efforts on ascertaining George's innocence or guilt. With the sheriff now gunning for George's arrest, the Welsh investigation had suddenly become the rushed, reckless footrace that Reed had desperately tried to avoid.

Less than two months after the murder of Leila Welsh, the man who had cleaned up the most wicked city in the United States and had transformed the worst police department in the country into "the best" submitted his letter of resignation to the board of police commissioners on May 1, 1941. Reed claimed he had asked for a salary bump that was denied and could no longer live on a police chief's wage. Still, most assumed the untouchable FBI G-man with a stellar pedigree had met his match in the Welsh murder and simply did not have the fight to continue. Others argued the rebuke he received just days earlier from the police board for unapproved promotions and hirings had been the final straw for Reed.

But there was something else the chief had kept hidden that threatened to unravel his regime. Missouri Governor Forrest Donnell had been inundated with allegations of police brutality against

Kansas City's Black community throughout Reed's nearly two-year reform campaign. Severe repression and harassment had followed in the wake of Reed's appointment, and civil rights leaders in the city had waged a concerted campaign for justice. Reed had grudgingly agreed to hire more Black officers, but months later the entire police force had only six Black employees. In an early and rare victory for the emerging civil rights movement, the state did not dismiss the campaign for change.

Stung by the governor's forthcoming investigation and facing an emboldened sheriff's department, Reed was finished. "Failure," he concluded, "was the self-imposed verdict upon myself." Reed would remain in a titular position for several more months but relegated most of his duties to Captain Harry Anderson, who would become the next chief of police. Having won the battle against the police department, the sheriff's department and its Pendergast backers now intended to win the war. All they needed was the conviction of George Welsh.

Through every interminable interrogation, the sheriff's department browbeat George with accusations, yelling, sleep deprivation, threats, and psychological torture to once and for all extract the confession they so desperately sought. He was even taken to a riverside cabin in the Ozarks, where he was grilled day and night with no food or water. Dragged to the edge of the raging river, he was threatened with drowning if he did not confess, his head dunked and held underwater. George never deviated from his story. A lie detector test was administered, and he passed. George then requested a second test, which he passed, and a third, which he again passed. He then demanded to be questioned under the influence of truth serum, which was denied. There was no need, he was told—he had passed three lie detector tests.

With the professional, state-of-the-art police investigation all but frozen, the sheriff's probe into Leila's murder had changed significant course as George became the lead suspect. The baffling preponderance of tools and clues left behind by the killer was now viewed as a deliberate trail of false leads planted by a brilliant mind to throw off suspicion. The hammer left on the bedside rug, the curtains and hanging rod arranged on the windowsill, the knife plunged in the ground, the gloves, the flesh—all had been left as a misdirect to draw attention away from the Welsh home, where the real killer plotted the terrible deed and assembled his murder kit.

However, all of the police and FBI laboratory evidence contradicted the new narrative. The knife had traces of cotton and rayon fibers that matched Leila's pajamas, and the blade tested positive for blood. The gloves also tested positive for traces of Leila's blood, and the flesh was undoubtedly matched to the wound in her hip. The evidence left behind was proven to be directly connected to the murder and not planted as a ruse. With George refusing to confess and no acquaintances turning against him, the sheriff's investigation stalled. Feeling the heat dialed down, George left Kansas City in the summer of 1941 for Los Angeles, California, where he worked as a bookkeeper for a drive-in restaurant. But Kansas City wasn't done with him yet. With Sheriff Richart coming up short, forces were at work to take matters in their own hands.

Radio station WOR, 710 on the AM dial in New York City, was airing the Brooklyn Dodgers/New York Giants football game at the Polo Grounds when the Mutual Broadcasting System interrupted transmission at 2:36 P.M. Three minutes later, the NBC Red network cut away from a live broadcast of Sammy Kaye's Orchestra from Chicago. One minute after that, NBC Blue would cut short its program *Great Plays*, the same moment CBS was going live.

Within minutes, the crackle of transoceanic static spread across the nation as a lone reporter from Honolulu's KGU radio station climbed to the top of the nearest three-story building with a microphone and a telephone in hand. An audibly distressed voice announced: "I am speaking from the roof of the Advertiser Publishing Company Building. We have witnessed this morning a distant view of a brief, full battle of Pearl Harbor and the severe bombing of Pearl Harbor by enemy planes, undoubtedly Japanese. The city of Honolulu has also been attacked and considerable damage done. This battle has been going on for nearly three hours. One of the bombs dropped within fifty feet of KGU tower. It is no joke. It is a real war."

The nation was forever changed in the terrifying, confused hours that followed the announcement of the bombing of Pearl Harbor on December 7, 1941, and the subsequent declaration of war by President Franklin Roosevelt. But in Kansas City, even Pearl Harbor couldn't forestall the outbreak of a very different war.

Judge Marion D. Waltner had been one of Tom Pendergast's most reliable judges, and hence a fat target of the reform campaign that had wreaked havoc on the old guard political machine. He had outlasted every attempt at purging the court of the Pendergast influence and knew to whom he owed his survival. Presiding over the Independence Division of the Jackson County Circuit Court, he was named by the judges en banc as criminal judge for the next term of court beginning in the fateful month of December 1941.

Based on the positive identification of George Welsh by hardware store owner Joseph Louis Alport, Waltner's first act was to empanel a grand jury in the matter of the failed Welsh investigation, which he had determined was of grave importance. One day after President Roosevelt declared war on the Empire of Japan, the grand jury was empaneled, the first in the Independence Division in fifty-three years. Taking a swipe at former Police Chief Reed without naming him and his dismissal of Alport's dubious claims, Waltner referred to "a certain dime novel detective who said two days afterward that he could reach out and put his finger on the perpetrator. Then he proceeds to destroy the evidence."

In his instructions to the grand jury members, Waltner dictated their mission: "The time has ceased to be when we can boast of a fine Police Department as long as this case remains unsolved. I don't know what the grand jury can do but it may be there are things you gentlemen can look into." Judge Waltner had made crystal clear the results he expected: the grand jury would not only indict George Welsh but also undermine and destroy the reputation of the police department.

Any hope of impartiality among jury members was quickly swept aside. Leaving nothing to chance, the twelve-man jury had been stacked with nine Pendergast precinct captains who had been long loyal to and financially reliant on the machine. Quirk Bernard was a top Pendergast organization leader. Garrett Smalley was the Pendergast-approved chairman of the state boxing commission. Shannon Douglass was the former city election commissioner responsible for the pad of eighty thousand fraudulent votes in the 1936 elections. George Millard had run and lost as the Pendergast-backed judge in the 1940 election for presiding judge of Jackson County and ran the Pendergast mouthpiece *Independence Sentinel* newspaper.

The man appointed to lead the lockstep squad was jury foreman Sheriden Ferrell, the raucous "Mayor of 12th Street," who managed the Hotel Phillips, where Leila and Richard Funk had their last drink together, and who would soon be appointed a city councilman with Pendergast support. Ferrell had proven himself a reliable soldier while serving as foreman for the 1940 grand jury that Judge Waltner had called to probe Chief Reed for "oppression in office" over his program of fingerprinting and photographing of suspects not charged with a crime. Waltner was impressed with Ferrell's unquestioning fealty, despite his failure to deliver an indictment in the matter. The judge would not allow a grand jury to fail him again, and Ferrell could be counted on to do what was needed to be done.

-《《◆》》-

The fix was in.

Sheriden Ferrell was a man of action and immediately moved to build a war chest for his total offensive against George Welsh. His first act was a request of two thousand dollars from the court, which was quickly granted. Next, Ferrell hired two private investigators, Arthur Brock and Thomas Higgins, former policemen and Pendergast stalwarts who had been indicted in 1934 for perjury, having ordered subordinates to lay off the Union Station Massacre investigation.

Higgins had survived the indictment, rising to chief of detectives, but was demoted when Police Chief Reed arrived. Like many disgruntled policemen who had been demoted or fired by Reed, Higgins remained in good stead with the machine and would be used time and time again for any dirty work that was required. Higgins and Brock were sent to Los Angeles to dig up dirt on George and keep tabs on him. They repeatedly showed up on his doorstep to question him further.

When George boarded a train for Kansas City on December 23 to visit his mother, Marie, for their first Christmas without Leila, Higgins and Brock wired his travel details back to Sheriden Ferrell. Sheriff's Deputy Jack Brice, who had pulled his gun on Chief Reed and a cohort of officers back in March 1941, was sent to Lawrence, Kansas, to board the train and serve George the grand jury's subpoena as soon as the train crossed the border into Missouri. Marie and other family members greeted a solemn George at Kansas City's Union Station. He held aloft the distressing piece of paper with news he would not be returning to Los Angeles anytime soon.

The grand jury went after George with a vengeance. Two hundred relatives, friends, acquaintances, and coworkers were subpoenaed. One grand jury member traveled out of state posing as a detective to falsely inform witnesses they were required to testify, even against their own will. On the stand, witnesses were told George was a known dope fiend, habitual marijuana smoker, and member of an underground perversion ring. When they denied any knowledge or firsthand experience with these alleged vices, they were screamed at, insulted, called liars, and threatened.

Richard Funk had recently enlisted in the air corps but was granted leave to give testimony to the grand jury. He was called a "God-damned liar" within minutes of taking the stand. University of Kansas City President Clarence Decker and Dean Glenn Bartle were accused of lying. Even Marie Welsh had abuses hurled at her as she steadfastly stood by her son. But the worst abuse was reserved for George, who endured the torment of interrogation all over again. Photographs of Leila's slaughtered body were pushed in his face for hours, sickening him.

One session that began at 2:00 P.M. ended at midnight when George collapsed on the stand. He passed out during other sessions, infuriating his interrogators, who doubled their attacks. Sheriff's deputies had to help him stand and walk out at the end of one interrogation. He was routinely stripped and searched for needle marks. He was accused of carrying on an indecent relationship with Leila, accused of exposing himself in movie theaters, accused of molestation—all with no evidence or witnesses to support the claims.

Throughout George's ordeal, the grand jury convened each day over bottles of whiskey that were carried out in crates. Also seen drinking with the jury were deputy sheriffs and members of Missouri Attorney General Roy McKittrick's office. When not drinking, jury members paid personal visits to friends and acquaintances, whom they recruited as "witnesses" in the case. Jury member Garret Smalley's business sat next to a hardware store owned by George Ehrnman, who suddenly recalled that he had sold George Welsh the cotton gloves used in the murder after Smalley paid a visit and

jarred his memory. Other witnesses emerged who had distinct recollections miraculously form in their minds ten months after the
murder.

With enough witness testimony in hand, the grand jury completed its final report on January 28, 1942. Its recommendation:
the indictment of George Welsh. Going even further, the report
slammed former Police Chief Reed as hopelessly corrupt and suggested he had colluded with the Welsh family for a large bribe.
Echoing Judge Waltner's December 1941 justification for the grand
jury investigation, the report stated, "It is the sense of this body
that the identity of the murderer was known to the then Chief of
Police within a short period of time thereafter. It has been proved
that that official caused a very important statement to be taken from
the police files and placed in a locked drawer known only to him
and one other."

The report referred to Reed, once again, as "a dime novel
detective" and blasted the police department for failing to arrest
George Welsh. Within an hour, a warrant was issued for the arrest
of George Welsh for first-degree murder. Shortly after 11:00 A.M.,
sheriff's deputies arrived at 5547 Charlotte Street, home of Welsh
family friend Katherine Jones and the new home of George and
Marie. Deputies stationed themselves at corners surrounding the
house. Drawing their guns, the deputies inched closer, covering all
exits from the home.

Chief Deputy Sheriff Jacques Purdome and Deputy Jack Brice
walked to the house and knocked. When George opened the door,
his heart sank. Purdome had been waiting for this moment for
nearly a year. "Come on, George, we want you." Marie walked into
the room and grasped what was happening. Purdome solemnly
instructed, "You'd better get your coat." Marie spun George around,
gripped his face in her hands, and whispered, "Be brave, George."
She watched as he was handcuffed, placed in Purdome's patrol car,

and driven away to Independence, where he would face Judge Walt-ner for the first time.

Having endured ten months of unbearable pain, Marie had become a shell of herself, unable to leave the home her family friend had so graciously provided her. Just blocks away stood her own empty house, but she had refused to step foot in it again. Her world had been reduced to a solitary bedroom, her life frozen in a block of pain. When she saw George hauled off by brutes who had tor-mented him for months, she felt an emotion that had disappeared with Leila: anger. A fire surged inside her that would not extinguish itself until George was free. She would not lose another child. She would gather every considerable resource she had to ensure that justice was served. The Welshes had built Kansas City. And now they would burn it down.

CHAPTER 6

FRONTIER JUSTICE

It was 10:55 A.M., January 28, 1942, when grand jury foreman Sheriden Ferrell entered Judge Marion Waltner's courtroom, already in session with another case. Waltner halted the proceedings to ask Ferrell, "Does the Jury have anything to report?" Ferrell replied, "Yes, your honor. We have an indictment to return."

Like clockwork, Waltner signaled, and Ferrell stepped forward with a folded piece of paper in hand, the true bill signed by county prosecutor Michael O'Hern and Missouri Attorney General Roy McKittrick. Waltner unfolded the paper and perused it. Satisfied, he placed it into an envelope and waited. Thirty-five minutes later, George Welsh entered the courtroom, escorted by Jack Brice, Jacques Purdome, and Sheriff Richart himself. Waltner was surprised by George's lack of emotion. He had heard of the young man's frustratingly calm demeanor, but the blank stare before him gave not a clue to George's mindset.

The large oak doors flung open as Welsh family attorney August Behrendt strode in. Sheriff Richart tensed—Behrendt was more than just a threat in the courtroom. He had run against Richart in the 1940 sheriff's race on the reform ticket, and the two had remained bitter enemies ever since. Having won a Purple Heart and French

Legion of Honor in World War I, Behrendt had fought to the death in much tougher circumstances than Judge Waltner's courtroom.

George nodded at his family's lawyer but did not recognize the man he brought with him. The former prosecutor of Jackson County, Forest Hanna, had sent more people to prison in two years than the rest of the state had in five. Hanna, like Behrendt, was a leader in the People's Commission, which had led the revolt against the Pendergast machine, and was now the newest member of the Welsh defense team.

As soon as the indictment was read, Hanna stepped to the bench and attacked the legitimacy of the grand jury's highly irregular investigation. He demanded a dismissal of the charges, but Waltner refused and further denied Hanna's request for bond. A plea of not guilty was entered, and George was escorted away to a holding cell in the detention block on the eleventh floor of the courthouse.

Later that night, Marie arrived with August Behrendt. She had brought a care package for her son: cigarettes, a pack of cards, a toothbrush, pajamas, a shaving kit, *Reader's Digest*, and a copy of *The Sun Is My Undoing* by Marguerite Steen. Sheriff Richart denied Marie a visit with George, telling her, "He will be treated like any other prisoner." The implications were ominous. Marie would not stand idly by. This was war, and the defense team needed a leader who would strike fear in the hearts of their enemies.

Former attorney general of Missouri, speaker of the Missouri House of Representatives, city counselor for Kansas City, and special assistant to the attorney general of the United States, John T. Barker was nationally recognized as a brilliant and fiery lawyer "with a caustic pen and tongue." Having beaten the powerful railroad and oil monopolies in the U.S. Supreme Court, Barker's stirring, evangelical oratory skill was acclaimed and much feared. As lead defense counsel, he selected the most experienced and aggressive lawyers to join the Welsh team: former United States attorney for western Missouri Charles Madison and former special judge of the Jackson County Circuit Court Rees Turpin. But his secret weapon was a former prosecutor turned trial lawyer named Roy Rucker, whose specialty was aggressive cross-examination.

For the next three months, George remained in a cell while his legal team gathered evidence of the grand jury's vast abuse of power, coaching of witnesses, intimidation, and illegal multistate investigation. On May 4, Circuit Judge Emory Wright had heard enough. Assailing the grand jury's actions as "utterly shocking" and "wrongful and unauthorized and its conduct illegal," he dismissed the indictment in dramatic fashion.

The Welsh family was not given a moment of relief, however, as county prosecutor and Pendergast loyalist Michael O'Hern was at the ready to strike back, filing a first-degree murder charge in a justice of the peace court. Half an hour later, George was arraigned and placed back in a cell. A criminal trial now seemed all but inevitable.

Reporters rushed to Edgar Fleming's home for a statement, and he laid bare the family's agony: "This family thought they had suffered the limit of grief from Leila's death, and this preposterous charge against George, coming on top of it, is almost more than they can bear." Fleming bemoaned the final nail in what had once been a promising investigation. "We feel, too, it closes the door to following up clues and the real solution we have always hoped for." Hounded by the press, Marie stated, "I do not have anything to say at this time."

On May 18, 1942, Soviet tanks make a massive breakthrough against German lines in the Ukrainian city of Kharkiv, turning the tide on the Nazi push into the East. Stirring hourly updates would capture the attention of the nation, but not in Kansas City, where the hottest ticket in town was a seat in the Jackson County Courthouse for the preliminary hearing in the George Welsh trial. Judge

J. J. Dougherty would preside over days of testimony and then render a decision whether the prosecution's case was strong enough to move forward to trial.

Crushing crowds poured out of the Jackson County courthouse property onto the sidewalks and streets. People stampeded for the doors to the courtroom as constables of the court tried to hold them back, with little success. Guards were swept to the ground and trampled, extra benches were carried in through the swell of bodies, people climbed into trees to get a glimpse through the windows, banging was heard on the courtroom doors throughout the day as people demanded to be admitted inside.

When George arrived, throngs of spectators tried to touch him, grab him, and pull buttons from his coat as souvenirs. Four of the huskiest sheriff's deputies covered him, one in front, one behind and one on each side, pushing through a rabid crowd. When a throng of women spectators rushed toward George, deputy Jack Delahunty was ordered to hold them back but was overwhelmed. He called out, "I've played football but never hit a line like this!"

Fearing a mob scene, sheriff's deputies snuck George around to the Oak Street side of the building, where he climbed through a window into a clerk's office and was escorted through the judge's chambers into the courtroom itself. A change of clothes was provided to disguise his exit at the end of the day.

The entire Welsh family was present in the front rows as Judge Dougherty began the proceedings. Sixty witnesses would be called to give testimony, with some proving to be explosive. Former KCPD fingerprint expert Gorman Raney stunned the courtroom when he revealed that not only had one fingerprint been lifted from Leila's east windowsill, but two palm prints had been found on top of the sill and two entire sets of left- and right-hand fingerprints had been detected underneath the sill. Though the other prints were not as clear as the one previously identified as George's, Raney was confident they all belonged to the defendant. Even more ominous was Raney's assertion that the prints were made less than forty-eight hours before the murder was committed.

Though George had sat on the windowsill many times in the past and likely left fingerprints, he had no recollection of sitting on the sill in the two days before the murder. But lead defense counsel John Barker was prepared for Raney's dire revelations. Opening up one of the windows in the courtroom, Barker proceeded to sit on the windowsill and steady himself with his palms atop the sill and his fingers gripping the underside. Raney conceded that this seated position was likely the only way the prints could have been left, throwing into doubt whether the killer would have taken off the gloves and sat on the windowsill facing into the room. With no prints found anywhere else in the room or on any of the myriad items left inside or outside the house, the killer would have had to display unthinkable carelessness to leave an entire set of palm and fingerprints on such an exposed surface.

With the windowsill having been sawed out of the room's east wall and now sitting in a cardboard box on the witness stand, Barker asked Raney if the fingerprints were still detectable. Raney affirmed they were. How then, Barker asked, could Raney claim the fingerprints were less than forty-eight hours old at the time of the murder when they were perfectly preserved fourteen months later? Raney reiterated his vast experience handling over three thousand fingerprint samples. Despite his credentials, the damage to his testimony had been done.

The prosecution called Joseph Smith, supervisor of the KCPD technical unit, who had made plaster casts of the three faint shoe prints found in the mud outside the Welsh home. Smith had compared the killer's shoe size to that of George and stated that the results "compared favorably." Defense counsel Barker leapt into his cross-examination of Smith with an experiment. First announcing he was considerably taller than Welsh, Barker dramatically pulled off his shoe, held it aloft, and plunked it directly onto the plaster cast. "Would you say that's comparable?" Barker asked. Smith swallowed his pride and affirmed it was. Barker then asked random men in the courtroom to remove their shoes and place them over the plaster cast, all of which proved to be comparable. The plaster casts were never to be seen in the courtroom again.

Throughout the days of testimony, Marie Welsh was exposed to the brutal details of her daughter's murder. During the testimony of Officer Lawrence Ober, who found the flesh excised from Leila's hip, a mason jar filled with liquid was produced by Prosecutor O'Hern. A dark object floated within. O'Hern asked Ober if this was the piece of flesh he had found on March 9. Ober took a good look and confirmed it was.

The jar was then passed around the courtroom, without a thought to the mother of the victim present in the first row. George and Marie bowed their heads and closed their eyes as the jar passed directly by them. It was then placed on the witness stand for the remainder of Ober's testimony. When Coroner Cecil Leitch testified to the disturbing details of the murder scene, Marie excused herself to wait outside the courtroom. When Leitch finished, Marie reentered, sat next to George, and held his hand in her lap for the remainder of the session.

The defense team had done an extensive examination of the evidence left behind at the crime scene and picked away at the prosecution's case with a litany of glaring inconsistencies. The police had determined the killer was right-handed, but George was left-handed. Muddy shoeprints had been found in Leila's room but nowhere else in the house, and no trace of mud had been found on any of George's shoes. In order to have reentered the living room after the murder, George would have had to open Leila's door or reenter through the front door, and yet the killer had barred Leila's door with the vanity chair. Marie was an extremely light sleeper and would have heard and been alarmed by the sound of the front door opening.

The defense claimed George's motive in the murder was a larger share of the family inheritance, yet when that share was paid out in early 1942, George refused it. No trace of blood was found on any of George's clothes or anywhere within the home outside of Leila's bedroom. A spot of blood had been found on the doorjamb of Leila's bedroom, which the prosecution claimed could only have been left with the door open. The defense quickly pointed out that multiple people were in and out of the blood-soaked room in the twenty-four hours after the murder and that any of them could have carried a minute trace of blood that landed on the jamb.

On May 28, 1942, after seven days of testimony by over sixty witnesses, Judge Dougherty shocked the courtroom.

Ruling that the prosecution's evidence would not convince a jury of reasonable people beyond a reasonable doubt that George had committed the murder, Dougherty dismissed the charges. Crowds both within and outside the courtroom burst into applause, Marie wept tears of joy, and George allowed a tired smile to break over his famously stoic face.

Once again, freedom was fleeting for the Welsh family as Michael O'Hern announced he was marching back up to the fourth floor of the courthouse, where new murder charges would be filed. With the crowd visibly upset and reporters shouting questions, O'Hern boasted he could refile charges before any of the eight county justices of the peace as long as he saw fit. With George still in the courtroom, spectators refused to leave when deputies attempted to push them out of the building. Lead defense counsel John Barker gave O'Hern a short window before he would escort his client away.

Forty tense minutes later, the nightmare roared back to life as charges were filed before Judge James Hurley. George was rearrested and taken back to his cell as all hell broke loose in the courthouse. Barker thundered against the malicious prosecution of his client, accusing O'Hern of breaking the law and abusing his power. He filed an aggressive writ of prohibition with the Missouri Supreme Court, accusing the prosecution of acting outside its jurisdiction, a potential kill shot to O'Hern's case and a nuclear button move in what was becoming full-scale war.

On June 4, George was released from his jail cell after four months of incarceration on a ten-thousand-dollar bond. Barker urged him to take the week off, mow the grass, and gain some weight. George spent afternoons on walks throughout the neighborhood with his mother, while passersby stared and debated in hushed tones whether he was the victim of a malicious prosecutor or a vicious killer freely roaming the streets.

After five months of legal wrangling, the Missouri Supreme Court denied Barker's writ of prohibition, confirming that the dismissal of charges first by Judge Emory Wright and then by Judge J. J. Dougherty did not bar O'Hern from further prosecution. With the preliminary hearing completed and the Supreme Court's greenlight of the first-degree murder charges, the case would now go to trial—again.

Barker and the defense team gathered as a war counsel, their overwhelming experience in prosecutors' offices key to forecasting O'Hern's strategy in the battle ahead. With the prosecution's questionable evidence fully exposed in the preliminary hearing, Barker would now plot his counterattack. But success depended on a jury that was impartial. Considering the twisted path the case had taken thus far, Barker had his doubts. Despite Judge Dougherty finding insufficient evidence to move forward, Michael O'Hern was hellbent on getting the case before a jury. His confidence unnerved the defense team. Did he know something?

O'Hern wasn't Barker's only concern. Having been sent to the Criminal Division of the Jackson County Circuit Court, the case landed in the lap of Judge Albert Ridge. Backed by the Pendergast machine, Ridge had been a target of Governor Lloyd Stark's 1938 campaign to rid the court system of machine influence. Ridge had survived, as had his association with Pendergast allies like Judge Marion Waltner, architect of the discredited 1941 grand jury. But if Ridge had enemies in high places, he had friends in even higher places. Having served together in an artillery battalion of Battery D in World War I, Ridge had cemented an unbreakable bond with Senator Harry S. Truman, who also enjoyed Pendergast support and showed no sign of wavering, even from Washington, DC. With a Pendergast-allied prosecutor, attorney general, and now judge arrayed against them, George Welsh's defense team couldn't help but wonder if they were walking into a trap.

The stakes could not have been higher. O'Hern was seeking the death penalty for George and would select jurors willing to make the weighty judgment he sought. With Marie Welsh now facing the potential deaths of both her children, the trial opened on April 7, 1943. She would not be given a seat at her son's tribunal. Over the defense's strenuous objections, the prosecution had lobbied Judge Ridge to deny her access to the courtroom, and the judge had obliged. The opening salvo in this war did not bode well for the defense team.

The prosecution presented a formidable team: O'Hern was joined by Missouri Attorney General Roy McKittrick, Assistant Missouri Attorney General Vane Thurlo, and Assistant Prosecutor John V. Hill, all seasoned and menacing in cross-examination. Tall, stern, and grave, with slicked back "iron gray hair," Prosecutor Michael O'Hern would be the defense's most formidable adversary. Barker had studied him well. His interrogation style was controlled, cool and emotionless, though hints of a temper could be detected. Barker and his protégé Roy Rucker would use O'Hern's steely coldness against him, using humor, drama, flair, and showmanship to undermine the prosecution's sober presentation. If spectators wanted a show, Barker would give them one.

One of the most daunting challenges facing the defense was the looming issue of the fingerprints found on the east windowsill of Leila Welsh's bedroom. During the preliminary hearing, police fingerprint expert Gorman Raney again testified that a set of George's fingerprints found on the windowsill had been left less than forty-eight hours before the murder was committed. The question was still open as to how George's prints had appeared so close to the murder.

While the prosecution relied on Raney to restate his expert opinion in the aging of the prints, defense counsel John Barker now had an ace up his sleeve. Shelby Compton and John Wagaman of the police crime lab both testified that many conditions such as atmosphere, temperature, oil, and sweat composition on the skin can affect the aging of a fingerprint and that there was no scientific basis for Raney's forty-eight-hour window. Defense counsel Forest Hanna closed in for the kill, asking Wagaman, "But your testimony still is based on the fact an opinion as to the age of a fingerprint is very risky."

"Yes," Wagaman replied.

With his fingerprint evidence dissolving before the court, Prosecutor O'Hern desperately cut in. "Now wait a minute. Isn't fingerprint study a science?"

Wagaman shot back. "Anyone who would give such an opinion is giving a pure guess. Any of a number of things can happen."

With Gorman Raney's credibility in ashes, the defense next trained its sights on George Ehrnman, the store clerk who had a sudden "vision" in January 1942 that he had sold George Welsh the gloves used in the murder ten months earlier. Nervous and jittery, Ehrnman fumbled with his hat on the stand and averted George's gaze. He would be an easy target for Roy Rucker, the specialist in cross-examination whom Barker had personally recruited for the defense team.

Ehrnman testified that the gloves he had sold George were pulled from a drawer and were lightly stained. Rucker asked, "How many dirty gloves do you sell?" To which an embarrassed Ehrnman stuttered, "None."

Rucker then asked the red-faced hardware clerk, "Did you ever sell anything to me?" which Ehrnman denied. Rucker slowly leaned into Ehrnman, who was squirming in his seat. "Now, let me refresh your memory. Didn't I buy an oven thermometer from you last March twenty-third?"

Ehrnman stammered, "Yes, I remember now."

Rucker then sprung a trap he had laid a year earlier at the preliminary hearing. He turned to the defense table and asked lawyer Eugene Brouse to stand. "When did you sell Mr. Brouse a pair of gloves?" Rucker asked.

Ehrnman replied, "It was some time the latter part of March or the first part of May [1942]."

Rucker coolly retorted, "And at the preliminary last May, you didn't remember selling Mr. Brouse gloves. What have you had about this, a vision?"

Ehrnman's credibility in tatters, the defense moved on to the state's most important witness, the man whom Attorney General McKittrick called "the crux of the whole case," knife-seller Joseph Louis Alport.

Police Officers Hymer and Gibson had testified that Alport repeatedly denied George was the knife buyer a month before he changed his mind. Once on the stand, Alport brushed off his change of heart as just buying time to wrestle with the weight of condemning a man. He testified that once he had come to terms with the burden upon him, he had contacted the police to reveal the truth—the knife buyer was George.

Attorney General McKittrick handed the knife to Alport and asked him to identify the customer who purchased it from him. Alport raised the knife, pointed it at George, and said, "That man." But if the prosecution expected Alport to deliver the slam-dunk testimony they were now in need of, they would soon have cause for concern. Throughout his testimony, Alport made jokes, winked twice at Attorney General McKittrick, passed notes to the prosecution team, snapped in anger when questioned by the defense, and pulled out pages of notes to remind himself of the "right" answers. The courtroom stirred when Alport mistakenly identified defense lawyer August Behrendt as George's uncle, Edgar Fleming.

The real fireworks arrived with the cross-examination by defense lawyer Roy Rucker, who attacked Alport's claim that George had filed the knife for half an hour. Rucker brought forward testimony from an expert who stated that no knife could be filed for that long. Declaring that any knife could be sharpened by hand in five minutes or less, Rucker stunned the courtroom when he pulled out a file, instructed Alport to "time me," and proceeded to file the knife used in the murder. Judge Ridge was outraged by the assault on the state's evidence and demanded he immediately halt, just as Rucker had anticipated.

The most consequential damage to Alport's testimony came after he left the stand. Lead defense counsel John Barker had one more ace up his sleeve, an old friend of Alport's named Ralph Bullock. One week after the murder, Bullock testified, Alport confided in him that he hadn't paid any attention to the knife buyer because "he was just another customer." Unable to recall what the man looked like, Alport wasn't even sure he had sold the murder weapon. Bullock's testimony had demolished "the crux of the whole case."

Through every day of gut-wrenching testimony, George remained sphinxlike in his steely gaze, listening intently and never displaying frustration or despair. As the case built to its crescendo over two weeks of roller-coaster testimony, court spectators' sympathy began leaning toward George. Even newspapers' description of him waxed eloquent. "His eyes are the most striking part about his features. They're pale blue and deep-set, capable of being as hard as blue granite one moment and lighting up with laughter the next."

Each day, the courthouse filled with growing crowds who had intently followed the drama in the news. To the surprise of many, those crowds were increasingly comprised of women. On April 15, 1943, the courthouse was overflowing in anticipation of perhaps the most important witness in the case, Marie Welsh. Terrified of the moment in which she now had to rise in defense of her son's life, Marie summoned what was left of her waning strength. Having been denied a seat in the courtroom, she would now face the eyes of the jury for the first time.

Arrayed in a simple brown crepe skirt, straw hat, and cream-colored blouse, she walked down the hallway to secure not only George's but also her own fate. As the heavy courtroom doors swung open, she was astonished by the crowd before her. It wasn't the number of spectators that surprised her. It was the spectators themselves. Nearly every single member of the courtroom audience was a mother or a daughter, each looking upon her with reverence, pity, and immeasurable sympathy. Silence filled the room as Marie walked to the witness stand.

For forty-nine minutes, the plain-spoken mother from Kentucky choked back tears as she described the unbreakable bond between her daughter and son. "It was about the closest brother and sister you ever knew," she said, her voice trembling. "He watched over her as a father or older brother. He was careful about the boys she went with. They had played together since babies on the farm. They went to the little country school together and high school. They used the same car; we only had one. They double dated together. They entertained friends together. I gave little dinners for them. They were close."

Barker approached the stand and lowered his voice for the final, defining question: "Did you really love your daughter?"

Marie looked into his eyes. "More than anything else in the world."

The *Kansas City Star* summed up Marie's moving testimony in eleven simple words: "a mother's love standing Gibraltar-like in defense of her son."

At 9:30 A.M., on April 17, 1943, the case went to the jury. Court watchers expected a verdict—up or down—within an hour. But by 12:00 P.M., no verdict had been reached and Judge Ridge called lunch. George and Marie were ashen, each minute that passed an eternity. George's sister, Mary Turner, and husband, Jack, fidgeted with worry, as did myriad other Welsh family members and friends arrayed in the second row. Lunch came and went. Each hour that passed signaled an ominous direction in the jury's momentous deliberations.

Two years, one month, eight days, and twelve hours after Marie Welsh awoke to the sound of two thuds in her home, two buzzing sounds under Judge Ridge's bench signaled that a verdict had been reached. A jolt of electricity surged through the courtroom as Marie gripped the arms of her chair, her knuckles strained white with fear. Foreman Meredith Collier entered the room and handed a folded sheet of paper to Judge Albert Ridge. Ridge passed the paper to a clerk, who then read aloud the verdict.

CHAPTER 7

TO HELL AND BACK

I t took the jury five ballots to reach a unanimous decision. The third ballot had been nine to three. The fourth ballot had been ten to two. The fifth and final ballot closed the deliberations.

Court clerk J. R. Duff slowly read aloud, "We find the defendant, George W. Welsh, Jr., sometimes known as George W. Welsh II, not guilty."

Kansas City Star reporters had arrived at 6109 Rockhill Road within two hours of the discovery of Leila Welsh's body on March 9, 1941, and had been a constant presence in the saga to the bitter end. On April 17, 1943, Kansas City's newspaper of record would capture the moment that followed the announcement of the verdict: "Mrs. Welsh's eyelids fluttered. She turned and her son's arms folded about her as she buried her face against his coat collar. Above his mother's suddenly drooping shoulder, Welsh's face brightened into a broad smile. As the mother and son broke the close embrace, Welsh's hands lingering tenderly, Mrs. Welsh dropped her head forward on her arms folded on the counsel table. A nervous shudder rippled her cream-colored blouse. She sobbed quietly. Behind the mother and son on a bench inside the enclosure, were seated the other members of the Welsh family and close friends. They sat a moment, overwhelmed by their emotions. They paused another instant, as though to give the mother and son the first instant alone, and then surged forward, some smiling and others bursting into tears. Mary Frances was there first, and husband Jack Turner was deeply moved, patted Mrs. Welsh's shoulder and walked over to shake the jurors' hands. George whispered to his mother to sit and smile. He tugged on her arm, but she could not smile. She was pale, eyes glistening with tears. 'Come on, smile,' he said to her. But she only stared helplessly into his face."

The courtroom electrified after the verdict was read. Spectators climbed over seats to try and reach George. Deputies struggled to hold back the surging crowd. Judge Ridge rapped his gavel to no avail. The news spread rapidly across the city and then the nation. At that moment, six hundred Allied planes were attacking Mannheim, Germany, in the biggest air raid of the year. Flying fortresses were devastating Palermo Harbor in Sicily, while the British First Army battled Erwin Rommel's forces at the gateway to the Plain of Tunis. But at 12th and Oak Streets in Kansas City, the war was over.

George Welsh was looking forward to his army induction at Fort Leavenworth on May 14. When asked, Marie told the press that if George left her for the army she wouldn't know what to do. Nonetheless, George eagerly entered the service but was soon causing waves among his fellow inductees. He suffered dramatic nightmares in his sleep, a result of the trauma he had endured before and during the trial.

Medical experts at Leavenworth determined another cause: George was diagnosed with narcolepsy, the neurological disorder that disrupts sleep and wake cycles. Stress and excitement often cause narcoleptics to instantly fall asleep during daytime hours. Suddenly, it all made sense—his physical collapse upon hearing the news of Leila's death, the repeated passing out during the sheriff's department interrogations, his twelve hours of sleep on the family couch the night Leila was murdered.

The disruptions were too much for his fellow soldiers, leading to his sudden discharge from the army. Back home, he pivoted to night classes at the University of Kansas City, where he studied radio engineering in hopes he would eventually join the radio section of the air corps. Neither Marie nor George would ever step foot inside 6109 Rockhill Road after March 9, 1941.

After the verdict, George had stated to a reporter he was thinking of leaving Kansas City, but Marie dispelled that notion, admonishing him for saying such things. They had so many family members and friends in Kansas City and such history. In time, Marie would see things differently. Despite the acquittal, Kansas City would never shake its uneasy feeling about George Welsh. Too many people were too unnerved by the disturbing details of the murder that had been printed in the papers throughout the ordeal of the trial. Suspicion, rumors, gossip, and dirty looks followed the Welshes through the years.

Marie would eventually realize there was no way to go home again. In the late 1940s, she and George made a quiet exit for Texas, where folks simply didn't know or care about the Welshes' past. Marie Welsh would pass away in 1965, never having returned to Kansas City.

In 1934, a crowd of onlookers witnessed a miracle when Richard Funk sent a model airplane made of wood, paper, and rubber bands flying so high it disappeared into the clouds. Nine years later, he entered military service and was assigned to the 854th Bomber Squadron, 491st Bomber Group stationed in England, where he served as copilot of a B-24 Liberator heavy bomber. On a mission over Germany on June 28, 1944, the plane was struck by antiaircraft fire, sending shrapnel directly into Funk and killing him instantly. He was the only crew member to not survive the ordeal. Upon landing, a member of the crew immediately called his family to let them know he was gone. Awarded the Purple Heart, Funk was buried in Cambridge, England—4,627 miles from Carollton, Missouri, where the love of his life was buried.

Elery "Gabby" Boynton married his high school sweetheart, Muriel Leyshon, nine months after the murder of Leila Welsh. He served in World War II, and returned to the Knoxville, Illinois, area, where he remained his entire life. He pursued his passion for student athletics, becoming a beloved coach and teacher at Princeville Community High School and Knox College. He was a devoted father and husband, and widely respected in the community.

Judge Marion Waltner, responsible for the discredited grand jury investigation, would be removed from office by voters in 1942, the only judge in Missouri to suffer such a fate for the next fifty years. Sheriff Granville Richart left office in 1944 and became the land trust commissioner of Jackson County. Two years after his death in 1956, criminal court cases revealed he had been receiving illegal bribes and payoffs throughout his tenure.

Deputy Sheriff Jacques Purdome was elected Jackson County sheriff in 1944 and served for eight years until a U.S. Senate committee on crime chaired by Senator Estes Kefauver uncovered a vast Mafia enterprise in Kansas City that was aided and abetted by the sheriff. Uncovered by the Kefauver Committee was Mafia crime boss Charles Binaggio's partnership with Purdome, who had handed out sheriff's badges to local racketeers and allowed them to operate red lights and sirens on their cars. Illegal gambling and liquor operations had been ignored in exchange for blocks of votes or kickbacks. Purdome's reputation was so stained by the Kefauver Committee that the "Rabbit faction" of the Pendergast organization, which had long backed him, actively campaigned against him.

Jackson County Prosecutor Michael O'Hern was voted out of office in 1946 when the Pendergast organization turned against him. Defense attorney John T. Barker was called up to the attorney general's office in Washington, DC, at the request of President Harry S Truman. He served as a special assistant before publishing his memoirs, recounting his fifty-year career as a lawyer in Kansas City.

Fellow defense lawyer Roy Rucker suffered illness in the years following the Welsh trial, but with immense pride, he watched his daughter Jane marry Alben W. Barkley, the vice president of the United States under Truman, on a kinescope television set from his bedside in 1949. Welsh family lawyer August Behrendt left Kansas City soon after the trial to serve as a lieutenant colonel in the Allied Supreme Headquarters during World War II.

After his resignation, Police Chief Lear Reed moved to Chicago, where he served as general auditor for the Montgomery Ward company. He held a position in the State Department for several years and returned to Kansas City to open a school for investigators. He would eventually move to Compton, California, several miles south of Los Angeles, where he served as managing editor of the Compton Journal. Haunted by the Welsh murder to his last days, Reed stated, "In seventeen years of law enforcement work, I had the duty of investigating and helping to investigate crimes and criminals in many states of the union . . . . But as I look back over many experiences and puzzling cases, I can honestly state that in none of them did I find as many inconsistencies, baffling circumstances, and theories that formed clearly and faded swiftly, as I did in the Welsh case."

By the late 1970s, almost every major actor in the Leila Welsh saga had passed. Just one man remained alive. He had outlasted them all. If you happened to live in Dallas, Texas, in 1978, you might have driven out to the suburbs to visit Wynnewood Village, Dallas's first open-air shopping mall. Between the big brand-name stores and the food court, you might have stopped by a generic-looking record store. Maybe you'd think of buying Blondie's *Parallel Lines*, or *Outlandos D'Amour*, the debut album of a new band called the Police. You might have even asked the man behind the counter for his advice, though his age at nearly seventy years old meant you probably wouldn't have trusted his thoughts about Van Halen.

You likely wouldn't have asked about the locket the old man carried around his neck and, more importantly, what was inside the locket. If you had asked him, he might have opened it for you to reveal a tiny photograph of a boy and his beloved sister. And he might even have told you who she was.

When the trial of George Welsh ended, so too did the investigation into the murder of Leila Welsh. The Midwestern values of Kansas City demanded that the years-long trauma of the Welsh case be quietly laid to rest. Rather than continue what was once a promising police investigation, city leaders chose to let the case simply wither and die. Having faded into obscurity, the cold case would appear in the rare magazine or newspaper article but would be quickly forgotten again as the city looked to a brighter future in postwar America.

But the case would not die. In February of 1947, the Kansas City Police Department received an important call from Los Angeles, California. The LAPD detectives urgently requested the Leila Welsh murder case files as well as information regarding a former University of Kansas City classmate of Leila's. The request was related to an ongoing investigation that was of critical importance to the police and the city as a whole. Having dominated headlines in every major newspaper across the country, the KCPD needed no introduction to LA's famous new case—the murder of a woman known as "the Black Dahlia."

PART II

ELIZABETH SHORT

CHAPTER 8

THE MYSTIC RIVER

I t was early afternoon when Phoebe Short heard a knock on the door of the third-floor railroad apartment she shared with her daughters. The voice on the other side frantically called for her to hurry. Phoebe rushed to open the door and discovered her neighbor with news that a long-distance call from Los Angeles was holding for her. Phoebe did not own a telephone. It was not unusual for callers to use the neighbor's line to reach her. But a call from Los Angeles? Nobody ever called long-distance, much less from across the country.

Cradling the receiver against her ear, Phoebe heard a man's baritone voice announce itself as Wain Sutton from the *Los Angeles Examiner* newspaper with the good news that her daughter Elizabeth had just won a beauty pageant. Phoebe wasn't entirely surprised. Twenty-two-year-old Beth, the third of her five daughters, had always attracted attention for her good looks and poise. Her natural beauty had drawn her to Hollywood, where beauty pageants would be in no short supply. Mr. Sutton wanted to know all about Beth, and Phoebe was happy to gush about the effervescent young lady who had shown so much independence and initiative, traveling to California all on her own at the age of eighteen.

Sutton thanked Ms. Short and hung up. Moments later the phone rang. It was Sutton again, perhaps with a question he had

forgotten to ask. But the tone of his voice had shifted. He was halt-
ing and nervous. Phoebe sensed something terrible. At first she did
not believe the news. It was impossible, a mistake. Her daughter
was safe and alive and would soon be sending her weekly letters
from San Diego. Beauty pageants be damned, she wouldn't speak
anymore with Mr. Sutton.

Within an hour, reporters from the *Boston Globe* were mean-
dering outside the clapboard apartment building at 115 Salem
Street in Medford, Massachusetts, trying to find the unit occupied
by the Shorts. Neighbors were cornered and asked about the beautiful young woman who had once attracted so much attention and
would now do so again. Consistently, neighborhood acquaintances
told the reporters how beautiful Beth Short was and how elegantly
she dressed.

Soon after, Phoebe was visited by Medford police officer Sergeant William Ryan. A Los Angeles police detective named Harry
Hansen had contacted Medford PD and confirmed Elizabeth Short
was the murder victim found in an empty weed-strewn lot and now
making international headlines. Phoebe's resistance withered away.
She now knew it was true.

On January 17, 1947, Phoebe took the first airplane flight of her
life, from Boston's Logan Airport to New York's LaGuardia Field.
Reporters slipped onto the flight and showered her with questions
while she attempted to read the details of her daughter's murder in
their very own newspapers. A connecting flight from LaGuardia
delivered Phoebe to Los Angeles Municipal Airport at 8:10 A.M.
Greeting her on the tarmac was a crowd of reporters and photographers from all over the nation, clamoring for comment from the
broken mother they would label as "graying but attractive" in the
next day's papers. She was desperate to keep her composure, and her
voice trembled only when asked about her daughter's slayer, saying,

"If I ever get my hands on him, I believe I will kill him myself." Asked what was ahead for her, she replied with a washed-out smile. "I have suffered deeply, but the worst is yet to come."

As she stood on the tarmac, her eyes drifted northward toward the horizon, where long ridges of mountains walled off the city. Beyond them, plumes of black smoke rose into the air, hundreds of trails forming a dark cloud over the San Fernando Valley. The smoke arose from thousands of smudge pots lit to keep vast citrus groves from freezing over in the thirty-one-degree weather. To Phoebe Short, it looked like hell.

For days, the press and police would pepper her with shocking questions about Elizabeth's lifestyle in Southern California. Was she a prostitute? Had she cavorted with gangsters and lowlifes? Why did she squeeze unsuspecting dates for money? Had she posed in the nude for pornographers? Why was she constantly moving around? Why had she escaped to San Diego? Beth's many letters home had been cheerful and optimistic. She had found work and made friends and was excited about the future.

Phoebe didn't know what to believe anymore. All she knew was something had gone terribly wrong for Beth in Los Angeles. The papers called her a "man-crazy adventuress" and had even given her a horrifying name—the Black Dahlia. What in hell had happened?

Everything changed in 1930. The Depression had bitten every family Phoebe knew, but its fangs tore into her husband, Cleo Short. He had found success building miniature golf courses outside Boston, allowing the family of seven a modicum of comfort. And then the bottom fell out, and so did Cleo. His car was discovered abandoned, with the keys left inside, in a Sullivan Square parking lot three miles south of Medford in Boston. Just steps away was the Malden Bridge, a suitable height from which to jump into the abyss of the Mystic

River. Others speculated Cleo had been robbed and murdered for the five hundred dollars he was carrying at the time. Either way, he was gone.

Now on her own, Phoebe found work as a bookkeeper and moved her five daughters into a tiny apartment where privacy would become a luxury they could not afford. Middle daughter Elizabeth, born July 29, 1924, suffered from asthma, and frequent doctor's visits would become the norm. Often stuck inside to avoid the havoc wreaked on her lungs by the cold weather, Beth soaked up radio shows from the NBC and CBS studios in Hollywood, a bright world away from her dismal circumstances.

As she grew into her teen years, Beth attracted attention for her beauty and natural grace, which belied her youth. Adult men took notice and misinterpreted her maturity for eroticism. Folks in Medford did not venture much further than Boston, but everyone agreed Beth was going places. Destiny came calling at the Medford Square Theater, where she thrilled to the fantasy world of the movies and dreamed of escaping her dreary, working-class town. Hollywood was a castle in the sky, while people in Medford stood in line for hours waiting on handouts from aid societies.

Burdened with asthma, Beth's lungs had become infected with pneumonia, and surgery was required, leaving a three-inch scar on her back. The heavy, cold air of winter along the Mystic River made the asthma worse, and so in 1940, Phoebe sent sixteen-year-old Beth to sunny Miami, where she would stay with family friends. She went to work at Mom's Restaurant, spending her money on a few fashionable articles of clothing.

Once back in Massachusetts, Beth found work at a restaurant in Harvard Square, where she met Marjorie Graham, a tall blonde with a broad smile and a taste for fun. Beth balanced a second job at the Metropolitan Theater with her classes at Medford High School, where she remained popular and much noticed for her fashion. At home in the cramped apartment, Phoebe struggled with Beth's mood swings, later stating "She was of the manic-depressive type. . . . She was ambitious and beautiful and full of life, but she had her moments of despondency. Sometimes, she would be gay and carefree one moment—then in the depths of despair another."

Beth would often cry inconsolably during her manic-depressive episodes, which would come and go for no apparent reason. In her book *Childhood Shadows: The Hidden Story of the Black Dahlia Murder*, Mary Pacios interviewed Joe Sabia, who, like Mary, grew up in Medford with Beth Short. "I think of her as beautiful, but a very private person with a sadness about her—a void, something missing. She seemed older than her years, more mature." Amid her family's Depression-era struggles, there was one lingering injury within Beth that never healed.

In the traditional Irish Catholic neighborhoods of Medford, divorce was rare and suicide even more rare. Cleo's death had dramatically affected Beth, his absence an open wound. Phoebe was a devoted, loving mother, but her time was spent working, cleaning, cooking, and caring for five daughters. Beth had practically raised herself and pined for her missing parent.

In 1942, the Short family was rocked again when a letter arrived from Vallejo, California—sent by Cleo Short. He admitted to faking his own death twelve years earlier in a fit of financial despair. He had long regretted his abandonment of the family and wanted to make amends, starting with a reunion. Phoebe and daughters Virginia, Dorothea, Elenora, and Muriel were adamant that no rapprochement would be forthcoming. Cleo was dead to them no matter how alive he might still be.

Beth found hope in Cleo's offer, a chance to love and be loved by the father she so desperately needed in her life. She began a correspondence with Cleo and eagerly accepted his offer to pay for travel to his home in Vallejo. Phoebe had to let her go. Beth was independent and strong-willed, the choice hers and hers alone. And so, in December 1942, Elizabeth Short boarded a Greyhound bus for the long trip to Northern California to close the wound Cleo had ripped open years earlier.

Beth arrived in Vallejo to discover Cleo was renting a room in the home of Ernest and Patricia Yanke and their five-year-old daughter, strangers with whom she would now be living. Ernest and Cleo's days were spent working at Mare Island Naval Shipyard, an enormous facility tasked with building the Pacific Fleet's next generation of warships after the attack on Pearl Harbor.

Seeking freedom outside the packed house, Beth explored the city of Vallejo and met a man with a criminal record. Cleo bitterly complained about her choice of dates and demanded she stay in the home to cook and clean for him. Beth hadn't traveled thousands of miles to serve as her father's maid, and the relationship turned tense.

An opportunity to restart came when the Yankes left Vallejo for Los Angeles, with Cleo and Beth in tow. The group moved into the home of Mary Booth, Patricia Yanke's mother, making living conditions even more cramped for Beth. With the University of Southern California just a block away, she yearned to escape her household duties, and the bickering between father and daughter started all over again. Bitter that Beth quickly spent what little money he gave her, Cleo ordered her to leave. Beth had been lured to California with the promise of a joyful reunion with the father who had abandoned her, only to find out it was strictly on his terms. He had used her.

The painful lesson burned in her a deep aversion to trust. But she wouldn't allow herself to return to Medford in shame. She would prove herself to Phoebe, the one person left she could trust, and make good on all the happiness life could bring . . . somewhere, somehow.

Situated on thirty-five thousand acres of prime coastal California ranch land, Camp Cooke had been rapidly built in 1941 to train thousands of army recruits in anticipation of the United States' entry into World War II. Elizabeth Short arrived from Los Angeles in January of 1943, looking for more than just a paycheck. Doctors had warned that her bronchial condition risked tuberculosis in the cold air back East, and she now desperately needed a way to stay in California.

Inez Keeling served as manager of a post exchange, the general store of the sprawling base just north of Santa Barbara. Beth wasn't the ideal job candidate, but she tugged at Inez's heart. "I've got to have a job, because I'm out here on my own—for my health. Won't you give me a chance?" Keeling would later recall Beth pleading. "I was won over all at once by her almost childlike charm and beauty. She was one of the loveliest girls I had ever seen—and the most shy."

Beth was hired and became a model employee, though she soon learned the post exchanges across the camp, known colloquially as PXs, offered more than just clothes and rations. The *Camp Cooke Clarion* newspaper enthused, "The topic of discussion this week was not the slacks at HQ but the blondes at the PX. Boy, oh boy, do they stand out, and do the boys stand around." But Inez Keeling took note of Beth's autonomy. "It was customary for all the girls at the various PX's to date these lonely servicemen, far from their homes ... but not Elizabeth. She never visited over the counter with any of the boys and always refused to date them. She was one of the few girls in my employ who didn't smoke or occasionally take a drink. She lived in the camp and never went out nights."

A month later, Beth finally accepted a date with a Filipino lieutenant, a member of the Army 2nd Filipino-American Infantry Regiment that trained at Camp Cooke before joining the battle to reconquer and occupy New Guinea and then the Philippines. They went out several nights in a row, but Beth soon returned to quiet evenings alone in her barrack. Privacy wouldn't last long, though, when the *Camp Cooke Clarion* printed her photo on February 26, 1943, alongside a dubious accolade. "A main reason for the steady increase of business at PX-1 is this week's Camp Cooke Cutie, Beth Short. Beauteous, Boston Beth has been in camp just one month, making her one of our newest, as well as nicest attractions. She is 18 years of age, five feet five inches tall, and weighs 125 pounds. Likes dancing, skating, and horseback riding."

Military officers flocked to Post Exchange 1 to meet the camp's star attraction, but by early summer Beth had quit Camp Cooke and moved in with friend and post exchange employee Mary Stradder and her husband at their home on the Tompkins Ranch in nearby Casmalia.

In mid-September 1943, Beth moved into a bungalow court three blocks from Cabrillo Beach in Santa Barbara with friend Vera Green. A week later, nineteen-year-old Beth and Vera spent the evening drinking with five soldiers at the El Paseo Restaurant. The group left just as employees called the police to report the girls for underage drinking. When cops arrived at Vera's bungalow court apartment, they found Beth and one of the soldiers in the living room and Vera and another soldier in the bedroom. Vera protested that the soldier was her husband, but the police discovered her actual husband was overseas.

Beth was arrested by Officer Mary Unkefer and hauled downtown, where her mugshot and fingerprints were taken at the Santa Barbara Police Department in the basement of City Hall. With no money and no home, a despondent Beth was released on probation by the juvenile court. Mary Unkefer took pity and offered up her own home, which Beth heartily accepted. Unkefer found an ideal guest in Beth, whose unflaggingly pleasant demeanor and compulsive neatness with clothes and hygiene surprised her. She was even more surprised by the appearance of a tattooed rose on Beth's left thigh, which she often casually displayed. After nine days, Beth was given ten dollars from the Santa Barbara Neighborhood House and a bus ticket back to Medford. Mary Unkefer saw her off at the station, and a grateful Beth would send her periodic letters for months to come.

Back in Medford, Beth kept the truth of her arrest from Phoebe. She soon left for Miami to ride out the winter months. She would waitress at the Rosedale Cafeteria along Collins Avenue and stay at the El Mar Hotel for as long as her money lasted. Weekends were spent with friend Marge Dyer at the beach. Miami was a routine tour of duty she had done before and would do again. But this trip would unexpectedly change the course of her life.

As she turned twenty, Beth's aversion to dating began to soften. Miami presented no end of servicemen with money to burn in the many nightclubs, bars, and restaurants. Most dates were uninspired and uneventful, with overeager boys facing redeployment days or weeks away. But Major Matthew Martin Gordon of Pueblo, Colorado, was no boy. He was a genuine flying ace, counted among the top aerial dogfighters of the Pacific Theater. Having shot down tens of Japanese Zeros and Mitsubishi 97 bombers in the China-Burma-India Theater of Operations, Gordon had already received the Silver Star, Distinguished Flying Cross, and Bronze Star medals by the time his L-5B Bird Dog recon plane crashed on Feb 25, 1944, while he was attempting to rescue a downed pilot.

Recuperating in Miami, Gordon was days away from a return to combat, where his much-lauded skill and courage would once again wreak havoc on the Empire of Japan. But for now, he was dating. Elizabeth Short was radiant the night he took her out for dinner and dancing, a perfect evening that found the two strangers enamored of each other's company. Gordon would ship out days later, but the one solitary date had cemented a bond that would grow through a series of passionate letters overflowing with desire.

Beth had found her answer to all of life's impossible challenges in Matt, a dream she would hold on to at any cost: "My sweetheart: I love you, I love you, I love . . . . Darling, those are the words of a new song in the States and believe me when I say that it suits me just to a T. . . . Just dreaming and hoping for a letter and now you are going to be mine."

Matt was overwhelmed by Beth's complete surrender to him as letter after letter swore her undying love. He would write back promising his heart in return, leading to more waves of letters from Beth. So overflowing was her commitment to him that Matt questioned whether it was genuine, even writing his mother for advice. "Mom, do you think she really loves me? It kind of looks like she does. In 11 days she wrote me 27 letters."

In Spring of 1945, Matt asked for Beth's hand in marriage, despite not having seen her in person since their first date. Beth's dream had come true, and her outpouring of joy and love oddly included a reference to having seen other men since his departure from her. "Yes, I have dated since I have seen you last. But most of them disgusted me. Naturally, there are exceptions, but you are the only one that interests me." She then pledged her undying loyalty, swearing off all dates with other men now that that they were engaged. She finished the letter with the promise that she would never lie to him.

Matt wrote his mother with the exciting news that he might bring home a bride-to-be from Medford, Massachusetts. But wedding plans would soon be halted. On August 10, 1945, four days before the end of World War II, Major Matt Gordon's airplane was shot down while flying over West Bengal, India, crashing near Kalaikunda. A wedding band and engagement ring were found in his personal effects. Twelve days later, Beth received a telegram from Frances Gordon, Matt's mother, informing her Matt was dead.

For a year, Beth's obsessive dream had been nothing but Matt Gordon, and in an instant it was taken from her. Just like everything good in her life. The Depression had taken her family's modest comforts, leaving them destitute. Her father had disappeared, forcing Phoebe to work and worry, taking her away from Beth. Asthma had taken Beth's childhood. Cleo had reappeared and taken advantage of Beth. The Santa Barbara Police Department had taken her chance to stay in California.

Now the war, whose end was being celebrated around the globe, had taken one last victim—the love of her life. Everything had always been taken from her, and if she ever got something good again, it was sure to be taken as well. It was all so unfair. Something broke within Beth. She could count on nothing anymore but the slim hope of finding happiness somewhere, someday, somehow. But to get there, she would stop being taken and start doing the taking herself.

CHAPTER 9

VIVID WOMEN

Before meeting Matt Gordon, Beth had met another air corps pilot in Miami who had quickly fallen for her. Gordon Fickling had grown up in rural North Carolina just outside Durham and then moved to Charlotte, where he worked as a newspaper route carrier. The war turned him into an air corps pilot, reaching a high rank of lieutenant colonel. Tall, thin, with strong angular features, Fickling looked the part of a fighter pilot. He and Beth had gone on dates that had left him yearning for more, and he continued to inquire about their relationship from overseas as she was awaiting Matt Gordon's return.

Weeks after Matt's death, Beth began to communicate with Fickling again, and a reunion in Miami proved to be electric. Fickling was soon sent overseas again while Beth returned to Medford in early 1946, but their letters continued. This time, Beth would not surrender to love, leaving Fickling confused and anxious. One letter would find her pining for him, the next would refer to him as a friend and casually mention dating in his absence. Fickling bristled at the thought of her seeing other men. "Your devotion is my most precious possession. . . . Darling, how many lips have joined with yours since ours last met? Sometimes I go crazy when I think of such things."

A letter from Fickling arrived in Medford in April 1946: he would be in Long Beach, California, by July and wanted Beth to join him. But he cautioned her to come west for the right reasons. "You say in your letter you want us to be good friends, but from your wire you seem to want more than that. Are you really sure just what you want? Why not pause and consider what your coming out here would amount to."

At long last the opportunity arrived to return to California. Beth had seen little of Los Angeles in 1943. The central coast had been rural, remote, and uneventful, save for the bitter arrest and one-way ticket out of town. She would take the offer despite Fickling's challenge to consider her motivation. But she would not wait until July. With the little money she had saved up waitressing at Claire's Restaurant in Boston, Beth brought a trunk of clothes and other possessions to a Railway Express Agency office on June 1 and had it shipped out to follow her route. She then boarded a bus for Indianapolis, where she spent a week, and then moved on to Chicago.

While Boston was conservative and staid and Miami more like a military garrison, Chicago was bursting with energy. It was also brimming with men who would do and spend anything to be on the arm of a beautiful, young woman they believed was out of their league. With her small but well-curated collection of form-fitting fashion, elegant manners, and enticing gait, Beth appeared as a woman of refinement and exoticism. The formerly shy, retiring girl Inez Keeling once knew at Camp Cooke had transformed into a postwar bombshell who turned heads and hearts.

One of those heads belonged to upholstery businessman Jack Chernau, who over the course of three weeks saw her fifteen times. They stayed at the elegant Blackstone Hotel together, while newspaperman Slig Diamond spent many nights with her at the Park Row Hotel. Her many dates soon discovered there was something different about Beth. She had become obsessed with the recent unsolved Chicago murder of six-year-old Suzanne Degnan, which had sent shockwaves through the city. Beth's only interest was in discussing the case, and she pressed Lou Paris, feature writer for the *Chicago Daily Times*, for every behind-the-scenes detail. Beth told John Giampe of the *Chicago Herald American* she knew a detective on the case. She even told her date Freddie Woods she was a reporter from Massachusetts covering the case. Woods thought she was beautiful, but her fixation on the murder of a six-year-old girl gave him pause.

Beth picked up extra money modeling for a hat manufacturer. By late July, Gordon Fickling had landed in Southern California. Beth jumped on a Greyhound bus to meet him. Gordon awaited Beth's arrival at the bus station in Long Beach, a moment he had imagined time and time again. His breath was taken away as she stepped off the bus and jumped into his arms. Fickling drove her through downtown Long Beach, an energetic port city not big enough to rival metropolis Los Angeles twenty miles north but big enough to dazzle a wide-eyed twenty-two-year-old transplant from the East.

Gordon's car arrived at the quaint Washington Apartments, just blocks from the water, where the couple would register with manager Fred Smelser on July 22, 1946. Beth took to Long Beach's relaxed tempo, sunning herself on the beach and walking up Linden Avenue to David Lander Drugs in a two-piece bathing suit baring her midriff. Heads once again turned as Beth's daring fashion choices drew attention, and folks at the pharmacy counter would strike up conversations with the mysterious new arrival with the jet-black hair puffed up like a flower. Just a block away, at the West Coast Theater on Ocean Avenue, the latest Veronica Lake sensation was drawing big crowds. It was a film called *The Blue Dahlia*.

Gordon had imagined an enthralling reunion with Beth, and their date nights proved romantic enough. But during the day, Beth was flirtatious with other men and would disappear for unexplained stretches of time. Gordon and Beth would sit on green vinyl stools and order Coca-Colas at the Lander Drugs soda fountain, but she also met a Navy sailor whom she would bring by the pharmacy, causing Fickling no end of jealousy. He grew resentful and the couple bickered. Beth pleaded she was faithful and had even written her mother declaring her love for him, but Fickling was increasingly doubtful.

On August 3, the couple moved out of the Washington Apartments owing to a county law limiting the length of hotel and rental stays. They would pass through various Long Beach motels, including the Sunset Motel, and finally the Brevoort Hotel, where they registered as husband and wife, despite the relationship worsening in each new location. Beth continued to pledge her love to him, but a chance encounter soon derailed what was left of their fading liaison.

Elizabeth Short was perusing a store on August 25 when she happened to run into Marjorie Graham, the tall blond waitress she had worked with in Boston's Harvard Square back in 1941. Both women, with their Bostonian accents, screamed out in glee, ecstatic to find each other in such a strange, faraway place. Marjorie's husband was in the Navy, and she had come west to be closer to him. She was working nights to raise money for the trip back east.

Beth told Marjorie she was engaged to an air corps lieutenant who was in the hospital in Los Angeles, and she was looking for a place to stay in the meantime. Marjorie got a quick read on her old acquaintance, later recalling, "In some ways she was strange, but for all her strange ways, she was good-hearted and good-natured." She made a split-second decision and offered Beth a novel solution. She was living with a roommate at the Hawthorne Hotel apartments in Hollywood. They were in need of some help with the rent and had space for a third roommate.

Hollywood. The castle in the sky. Destiny had come calling. Beth spent the next two nights at Marjorie's hotel apartment. On August 27 at 11:30 P.M., Gordon Fickling checked out of the Brevoort Hotel and caught the last train for the East Coast.

Norma Lee's earliest memory was her half-sister screaming. It wasn't just the sound of glass breaking or the site of flailing bodies that stuck with her. It was the terror she felt at just four years old. Her parents gone, she had been taken to Minnesota as a baby to live with her much-older half-sister and her common-law husband, who was usually drunk and just as violent. Her sister was always nervous, often crying, and had tried committing suicide many times. When her sister was taken to a mental institution, Norma was taken to a train station. At the end of the line was her maternal aunt, who brought her to the family farm in Washington State, where Norma bonded with her cousin.

Three better years passed by before the family could no longer afford to care for her. She was sent to a reform school for one year and was then adopted at nine years old by Fred and Marion Meyer of Port Orchard, Washington. During the adoption proceedings Norma would learn she had a brother and two sisters. The revelation shook her deeply and lit an obsession with finding her biological family and her true home—wherever home was. Norma told anyone who would listen, "If I could find them, I'd have somebody who really belongs to me." Until then, she would have to suffer her adopted family.

Soon after Norma joined the family, the Meyers moved to Long Beach, California, where John served as a chief quartermaster in the U.S. Navy and was gone for long stretches of time, serving on the USS *Floyds Bay*. Norma was left alone with Marion, who physically and mentally abused her. Norma was forced to sleep in the unfinished garage and was berated for "stealing milk out of the ice box." Neighbors called the police in alarm at the sounds they heard coming from the Meyer home, which in turn would lead to more beatings for Norma. The police would come and Marion would promise to reform, but the cycle would begin all over again.

A year later, at eleven years old, Norma Lee Meyer was arrested for stealing a blouse from a department store. At twelve, she ran away from home, returned, and then ran away again at thirteen with a girlfriend. The pair were arrested by the pier at Long Beach's Pike, caught in the middle of sexual activity with two merchant marines. Norma ran away again, this time to El Paso, Texas, where she married a soldier, quickly divorced, and returned to Long Beach. The courts deemed the Meyer home "unfit." Norma was sent to the El Retiro School for Girls in the San Fernando Valley, which she called "the happiest thirteen months of my life." She was eventually released back to the care of the Meyers, but ran away at fourteen in October of 1945, this time for good.

Norma Lee Meyer changed her name and identity, surfacing in Hollywood as twenty-two-year-old Lynn Martin. She earned twenty-two dollars a week waitressing at the Palace Garden BBQ. Her earnings barely covered rent and expenses. She received plenty of offers for dates, which meant a free meal and a chance to not go hungry, but sex was always expected in return, and sometimes she had to comply to survive.

On August 25, 1946, Lynn Martin's roommate Marjorie Graham brought home another girl from Boston who could help with the rent. Lynn later explained the rules in Hollywood. "Girls pick each other up in a store or a bar and start rooming together like old friends. It doesn't matter if they don't know anything about each other. It's somebody to talk to and share the rent with."

From the moment Lynn met Elizabeth Short, she didn't like her. Lynn had seen more in her fifteen years than most people would see in fifty. Life had taught her to read people instantly, who they were and what they wanted, and she saw in Beth a wannabe. With her phony high-class ways, self-importance, and desperate attention-seeking from men, Beth was just another Hollywood gate-crasher with delusions that she could handle all the angles. Lynn knew better.

In Lynn, Beth found a petulant kid with a chip on her shoulder. Lynn may have been in Hollywood longer, but Beth had more worldly experience and could handle herself just fine.

The Hawthorne Hotel was aging and musty, but it had a certain charm and the location was fabulous, just two blocks from all the action on Hollywood Boulevard. Shady characters passed through the halls, but there were also other young women and men, many fresh from the war, who were eager to let loose in Hollywood. For those with money or the right connections, there was the glittering Sunset Strip, dotted with ritzy clubs like celebrity-studded Ciro's, the always-in-trouble Mocambo, the glamorous but fading Trocadero, and the debauched Chateau Marmont. For those who didn't have the money or prestige for the Sunset Strip, there was the east end of Hollywood, where the Earl Carroll Theater, the South Seas Café, and the Florentine Gardens offered a full night of dinner, dancing, and a floor show for $1.50. The Flamingo Club and Bradley's Five and Ten discreetly catered to a gay and lesbian clientele.

For the younger set, there was dimly lit Club Tabu, scantily-clad live floor shows at Ace Cain's, and Billy Berg's, with its blues and jump-and-jive "hipster" swing. And for the younger set with no money, there was the Pig Stand drive-in restaurant, where Marjorie and several of the other kids from the Hawthorne Hotel worked as carhops, serving pork barbeque sandwiches to customers in their cars. For real action, there was Carpenter's Drive-in restaurant at the corner of Sunset and Hollywood Boulevards, a raucous hangout for teens and twenty-somethings who raised holy hell in the crush of cars that filled the parking lot.

To Beth, it felt like every twenty-two-year-old in the city passed through the drive-ins, where friendship, feuds, and romance seemed to form in a flash and fade just as quickly. Lynn Martin was a constant presence, as was Chuck Finkelstein, who attended City College and drove a sporty convertible; Bob Granas, who had trouble attracting dates and lived in his parents' mansion in Los Feliz; surly George Bacos, who booked musical acts for clubs; flashy Mike Foster, who served as master of ceremonies at the long-running Blackouts musical revue, and Alex Constance, a forty-four-year-old hairdresser who gave Beth henna rinses to highlight her black hair. Bacos and Granas both dated Lynn Martin, unaware of her real age.

Free meals at the Pig Stand aside, Beth grew weary of the juvenile antics and high school crushes at the drive-ins. She gravitated to Hollywood Boulevard, where servicemen, navy sailors, and slick-suited businessmen crowded the sidewalks. Hollywood was aglow in neon, big band music poured out of open-air dining counters, and behind every other cigarette-littered storefront was a themed bar or exotic club.

Beth was attracted to Hollywood Boulevard's glamour-on-the-cheap and was the constant center of strangers' attention. When Marjorie and Lynn were invited up to Carpenter Drive-In regular Bob Granas's house, Beth would disappear with no explanation, secretive and mysterious. Not even Marjorie knew where or who Beth was with most nights, though she always returned by 10:00 P.M. Beth kept her social calendar private from everyone, especially from the many men who pursued her all at once.

Blond, six-foot-one, with dimples in his cheeks, Lt. Stephen Wollock was movie-star handsome and drove a cream-colored Chevrolet coupe. Beth fell for him on their first date and would pursue him when he came up periodically from Long Beach. When Wollock was unavailable, she had dates with Chet Montgomery, Victor Lewis, Jimmy Bifulco, and real estate agents Ralph Johnson and Brandt Orr, who messaged her a plea for love: "Don't you realize it now?"

Beth could walk down Hollywood Boulevard and get ten requests for dates in just as many minutes, but she remained haunted by the memory of Gordon Fickling. When she had him she had pulled away. Now that she had lost him, she wanted to pull back in. Beth poured her heart out in a letter to Fickling. Days later, his response arrived at the Hawthorne Hotel: "Loving you the way I do would make me do practically anything, I guess. I learn so many things about you every day, that it's a little confusing. You do things that irritate me and burn me up, but no darling. I don't want to leave you, as you seem to believe." Fickling had just left the military and had returned to North Carolina. Beth would stay in Hollywood for now but planned to take back the man she had recklessly lost.

Having been asked to leave the Hawthorne Hotel apartments, Beth, Marjorie, and Lynn moved into the Hotel Figueroa, a fourteen-story Spanish-themed colossus in downtown Los Angeles. Hollywood was just a short fifteen-minute trip away via Pacific Electric car trolley, but downtown offered its own thrills, from the seedy penny arcades on Main Street to the palatial opulence of the Biltmore Hotel. People of all stripes whizzed through the girls' lives with little time to scrutinize their motives or ethics.

Lynn befriended twenty-five-year-old Bill Darrin, who lived the high life out at his home on ritzy Carbon Beach. But it was his father who was the real superstar of the family. Howard "Dutch" Darrin was a legend in automotive design circles, having built super-luxury cars worth the price of a Hollywood mansion for European royalty and movie stars through his Darrin of Paris offices on the Sunset Strip. Darrin's specialty-built luxury cars were driven by Hedy Lamarr, Clark Gable, and Errol Flynn. He worked directly with Packard in the thirties and forties, designing their highest-end models, and had competed in a flying competition during the 1936 Olympics, receiving the bronze medal from Adolf Hitler.

Father and son used the glamorous cars for personal missions, as well, picking up girls like Lynn Martin, who invited the pair up to her apartment, where they met Marjorie and Beth. Howard lived with his wife in the fashionable Brentwood neighborhood but had a ramshackle second home in Laurel Canyon just north of Hollywood. He lured Lynn to the remote mountain house with vague enticements. As soon as she entered, he came on to her. When she refused his sexual advances, a furious Darrin pulled a knife and slashed her. Lynn managed to escape the house, later confiding in friends about the ordeal.

Beth and Marjorie met an orchestra leader of dubious reputation named Sid Zaid. When their allotted days at the Hotel Figueroa ran out, Zaid offered a novel solution. He could house them at his bungalow on Windsor Boulevard, just on the fringes of Hollywood. A free place to stay suited Marjorie just fine, what with Beth always broke and never good for rent money. Lynn was not included in the arrangement but found room and board at a decrepit movie theater called Old Time Movie on the seedy east side of Hollywood Boulevard, where silent-film westerns played for a third of the price of a first-run movie ticket. Lynn slept in a back room of the theater and worked concessions, selling boxes of stale popcorn, her days lived in near constant darkness.

Beth and Marjorie walked into Sid Zaid's "bungalow" only to discover it was a tiny unit within a bungalow. The arrangement became uncomfortable for all after several days. Zaid had an idea. There was a man he knew with a comfortable bungalow home all his own who often took in young women short on cash and in need of a place to stay. Beth and Marjorie traded skeptical looks, but if no rent would be due, then the girls were game. Zaid drove them just a few blocks north to see about the new arrangement. Instead of arriving at a house, he drove into the sprawling parking lot of a massive warehouse-style building fronted by Greek columns on Hollywood Boulevard. Beth and Marjorie recognized the name emblazoned on the façade—they had heard rumors about this place.

The Florentine Gardens entered Hollywood lore in 1940, when nightclub impresario Frank Bruni performed a miracle. Master showman Nils Thor Granlund had revolutionized New York City's live stage shows with his elaborate, scantily clad musical revues overflowing with tropical decor, feather boas, and lines of gorgeous chorus girls. Bruni had triumphantly secured N.T.G., as the daring musical director was called, to a multiyear contract at the Florentine Gardens on the east side of Hollywood Boulevard, which was decidedly a step down in the geographic hierarchy of the town. Celebrities attended for a while but were soon replaced with servicemen and working-class couples looking for a night of glamour doused in silver tinsel and gold lamé.

When the war ended, N.T.G. still reigned supreme but the crowds had thinned out. Nightly shows featured elaborate musical numbers populated with beautiful young women desperate to make their big break into the movies, as well as second-rate comedy acts like Billy Gilbert, who could sneeze in every language, and Eppy Pearson, "the little man with the big piano." The Florentine was filled with well-compensated "b-girls" who flirted with unsuspecting male customers and squeezed them for overpriced drinks, only to disappear once a wallet was emptied. The "grippers" worked the floor, while the "sloppers" worked behind the bar. Despite the dubious conditions and a revolving door of new dancers, many famous names got their start at the Florentine, including Gwen Verdon, Yvonne De Carlo, and celebrated burlesque dancer and stripper Lili St. Cyr.

Beth and Marjorie followed Sid Zaid into the cavernous space as employees scurried about preparing for the evening's dinner and dancing show. Zaid called out to a short man in a well-worn brown suit, who spun around and eyed the girls with the precision of a professional. At fifty-six years old, Mark Hansen's slicked back hair was graying at the temples, but he still retained some of the Danish good looks that had helped him become a legend in the nightclub circuit as co-owner and manager of the Florentine Gardens. Hansen's gaze caught Beth and held. These were the girls, Zaid told him. Maybe he could help them out.

Hansen's mind had been made up the moment he saw Elizabeth Short. His eyes ranged over her, hungrily feeding on Beth's well-practiced, sensual movements. He was hooked. Having seen— and bedded—hundreds of Hollywood's most beautiful women, Mark Hansen did not impress easily. Something about this woman made every other girl feel cheap and common. He had to have her, and with his connections among the elite of Hollywood, he would do whatever necessary to get what he wanted.

CHAPTER 10

THE CLIMATE WAS WARM. IT WAS THE PEOPLE WHO WERE COLD.

Mark Hansen gave Sid Zaid the nod, and Elizabeth Short and Marjorie Graham were immediately bundled back into Zaid's car and driven around the block to 6024 Carlos Avenue, Hansen's house directly behind the nightclub. The quaint 1920s bungalow harkened back to the recent past, when Hollywood was still a small town dotted with farms and film studios shot silent films in barns. It was dark inside, lined with mahogany paneling and decorated with Oriental rugs and mission-style furniture. The walls were filled with framed photographs of showgirls, celebrities, and Hollywood luminaries. A gate in the back of the property led directly into the Florentine Gardens parking lot but had rusted over from lack of use. Heaps of dead palm fronds littered the small backyard, which was walled in by overgrown trees that shielded the home and whatever happened inside from view. Marjorie eyed the well-stocked liquor cabinet while Beth explored the house.

Hansen arrived minutes later and poured drinks for the girls, though Beth refused the offer. Mark stared at her with a ravenous intensity that Beth returned with cold indifference, leaving him even more intrigued. The trio sat down for proper introductions. Hansen had a hell of story. Having only completed grade school in his native Denmark, he had arrived in the United States penniless and alone at eighteen years old. He found the end of the road in Plentywood, Montana, a remote outpost just a stone's throw from the Old West. In nearby Scobey, Montana, he found work as a saloon keeper and married Ida Nelson, a South Dakota farm girl.

After stints in the cattle business, a chance opening at a local theater presented itself, introducing Hansen to the world of entertainment, even if just for local ranchers looking for a night of excitement in the nearest settlement. By 1920, Hansen was the proprietor of his own movie theater in Williston, North Dakota, deep in Sioux country. Running worn silent filmstrips for rapt audiences, he sensed a real industry was emerging and plotted to get closer to the action. The closest he got was Oxnard, California, sixty miles from Hollywood. But he soon owned three theaters and was starting to make real money. In 1924, he made his move to Hollywood with Ida and their two daughters and promptly splurged on a $4,800 Cadillac. By decade's end, he owned twenty-one theaters across Southern California and stashed a million dollars in the bank, making him untouchable. Then came the Depression, wiping him out.

By the mid-1940s, Mark had held on to the Marcal Theater on Hollywood Boulevard, two houses with rooms for rent, his home on Carlos Avenue, a modest diner on Hollywood Boulevard, and co-ownership of the Florentine Gardens. In 1945, Ida and their daughters moved out of the Carlos Avenue bungalow after an argument with Mark related to "his actions towards his daughters' friends in which it was indicated their social life was not in the theater world." Hansen had vowed to rebuild his pre-Depression empire, and he still reigned supreme, though diminished, on Hollywood Boulevard's east side.

Hansen's story may have been an American Dream come true, but he had selectively left out the "Hollywood Nightmare," like the underage girls who always turned up at the club looking for work only to find out they would be the ones paying the price. Popular Florentine bandleader Muzzy Marcelino had fixed up the sixteen-year-old Stull sisters with Captain Morrison J. Wilkinson, a VIP at the club. Wilkinson drove Dean Stull to Universal Studios, where he sexually assaulted her in the parking lot. She ran all four miles home.

There was nowhere to run aboard the yacht of swashbuckling movie star Errol Flynn, who raped underage Florentine Gardens showgirl Peggy Satterle after introductions had been made. Frank Bruni and Mark Hansen told the police they took every girl's word they were of age and never checked birth certificates. They had even demanded that employees not fraternize with guests. Investigators soon learned that Sugar Geise, emcee and hostess of the Florentine's famous floorshow, was responsible for setting up new chorus girls with older male patrons. The owners of both the Florentine Gardens and its competitor Earl Carroll's faced trial for repeatedly hiring underage girls but were ultimately slapped with just a fifty-dollar fine.

Hansen also didn't mention the many chorus girls with no money and no home who had been graciously invited to stay with him before Elizabeth and Marjorie arrived. Rent was paid in sex, and any refusal would send a girl packing, not only from his house but also from her much-coveted job at the Florentine Gardens. He had even pried sex from a girl who had undergone surgery just days before. Many a Hollywood dream ended the moment a girl passed over the threshold of 6024 Carlos Avenue. All except for one.

Hansen's campaign to wine, dine, and seduce Beth was well under way the day after she moved into his home. After dining at the Hawaii Malt Shop, a restaurant he co-owned a block from the Florentine Gardens, Beth arrived with Mark at the Carlos Avenue house only to discover there was another resident, twenty-four-year-old Anne Toth. Having just returned from a short trip to San Diego, the sprightly brunette actress moved a mile a minute throughout the house, unfazed by the arrival of the new girl. Over the five months since she had moved in, Anne had seen girls come and go from the home and knew the rules with Mark. A Dane herself, she had the native strong will that Mark knew not to tangle with, and she remained off limits to any sexual advances from either Mark or his many male guests. Besides, Anne's boyfriend, Leo Hymes, was a good friend of Mark's who had connected the two. Anne did light housework in exchange for room and board and kept a veneer of respectability for Mark when girls were invited to stay at his home.

Beth was relieved at Anne's sudden appearance. With Marjorie working nights, another woman in the house would offer a measure of protection from Mark's advances. Anne was intrigued by Beth's joyful innocence, which seemed so out of place in the Hansen house. She wasn't like the other women who had stayed for two weeks and then disappeared. She didn't drink, didn't smoke, and was obsessively neat with her wardrobe, never borrowing or lending an article of clothing and always keeping a tight guard over her two suitcases.

Beth was also meticulous with her prized makeup bag, which she always kept close at hand. Her Boston accent charmed Anne, and the two stayed up late talking and laughing. Beth avoided sharing much about her own past but wanted to know everything about Anne's. Born Anne Dolores Johnson, she had grown up in the dusty agricultural town of Modesto, California, eventually leaving for New York City to pursue her dream of acting. Disappointment followed as acting roles eluded her, forcing her to rely on hostess work at the New Yorker Hotel in the Garment District and forty-dollar-a-week modeling jobs.

Anne soon grew homesick and moved back to Northern California, where she got into a bad marriage but gave birth to a beloved baby daughter. Her acting dreams still alive, she moved to Hollywood, not knowing a soul. On V-J Day in 1945, she was picked up in a hotel by "an extraordinarily wonderful man" who was very well-connected in Hollywood and secured bit roles for her in the movies. He proposed marriage, but Anne "had a bad time once upon a time before" and refused the offer.

Anne had since started dating Leo Hymes, who made and sold hats at Joseph's Hat Millinery Store on Hollywood Boulevard. Leo was a portly, gregarious thirty-two-year-old who didn't put much pressure on Anne to marry, which was just fine with her. Mark Hansen was a client of Leo's and frequently bought expensive hats as gifts for the chorus girls he courted. He had immediately ordered two hats for Beth, who was delighted when they arrived at the home. Eyeing Beth's love of fashion, Mark continued to shower gifts on her.

Dressmaker Mrs. Ardis and furrier Mr. Barron were frequently called upon by Mark to make bespoke items for the objects of his affection. The two were summoned to the Carlos Avenue home and introduced to Beth, whom Mark called the most beautiful creature he had ever seen. While Mark poured drinks, he announced that Beth would visit Ardis's dress shop for a fitting the very next day. Mark had also unwittingly gifted Beth one more item, which she had decided to take for herself from his desk: a handsome, three-and-a-half-inch leather address book embossed with his name and the year 1937. He had picked up the keepsake on a trip to Europe but had never used it. Beth would put it to good use to keep track of all the contacts she was making in Hollywood.

Having quickly bonded with Beth in a way she never had with past tenants of the bungalow, Anne eyed Mark's gifts with noticeable skepticism. She watched Mark behave differently around Beth than he had with the chorus girls he had dated. He seemed—if it was possible—smitten. A shameless playboy, he was never jealous of the girls he dated. Now he was possessive of Beth, keeping tabs on her every time she left the home. Beth felt Hansen's obsessive hold over her but wanted to continue dating the many men she had been seeing in Hollywood.

Lieutenant Wollock was back in town and picked Beth up for dates at the home on Carlos Avenue. She had instructed him, however, to remain down the block so that Mark wouldn't see her getting into a car with another man. She had also begun seeing Santa Monica College Spanish teacher Michael Otero, a slight, thin introvert who also picked her up for dates down the block in his small two-door black Ford sedan. Beth swooned over Wollock and began to wonder if he was marriage material. At the same time, her thoughts drifted back to Gordon Fickling. The day after she arrived at Hansen's home, she used the house telephone to long-distance dial Fickling in Charlotte, North Carolina. When Mark was alerted to the expensive call, he flew into a rage. Beth vowed to pay him back.

Try though he did to seduce her, Beth avoided Mark's advances, using Anne's and Marjorie's constant presence as shields. Beth had more than one reason to avoid sex with Mark. She had long battled an embarrassing, painful infection that had made sexual activity a challenge. The Bartholin gland lies on either side of the vaginal opening and secretes a fluid for lubrication. When the gland becomes blocked, the fluids collect internally, creating a cyst that over time can become infected and extremely uncomfortable.

In her travels Beth frequently had to find doctors who could lance the cyst and drain the fluids. It was a dreadful cycle that made walking and sitting painful and required days of recovery. Beth found Dr. Aage E. Brix, a former Olympic soccer star and prolific writer of Christian songs, at his offices on Lake Street in downtown Los Angeles, but when the cost for his services was mentioned, Beth thanked him and left. She found a more affordable doctor in the heart of Hollywood, Dr. Arthur Faught, who welcomed walk-ins off the boulevard. Beth saw him several times throughout the fall of 1946 for the recurring issue.

To keep Mark Hansen at bay, Beth told him she was a virgin. His sexual advances retreated, but his near obsession with Beth continued to hold him in thrall. Regardless, he cancelled the order for the dresses and furs she had been fitted for.

Anne was both charmed by and wary of Beth's cheery innocence, especially toward the many men who gravitated around her. In Hollywood, everyone had a hidden agenda, but Beth seemed to accept strangers and their motives at face value. World-weary Anne tried to warn Beth about her misplaced optimism and reliance on dubious people, to no avail.

Beth trusted two brash former servicemen she met on the street named Marvin Margolis and Bill Robinson, who lived together just blocks from Hansen's home. Margolis was especially cocky. With a bright future ahead of him, he was in medical school at the University of Southern California after having served in a surgical unit during the invasion of Okinawa. Fellow USC student Robinson owned a sporty tan coupe and frequently drove Beth and Marjorie around with Margolis.

Beth didn't dare bring her dates around Mark for fear of his jealousy but pushed the boundaries, inviting Margolis and Robinson into his home. To cover herself, she falsely claimed Margolis was her cousin, though Hansen was not impressed with either of the two men who talked too much and oozed overconfidence. Mark had to throw them out on more than one occasion. On October 10,

Mark Hansen reached his limit. Though Beth avoided alcohol, Marjorie had been helping herself to the liquor cabinet, sending Mark into a rage. After eleven days at the Hansen home, both girls were ordered to leave.

Bill Robinson was nervous when Beth and Marjorie showed up with their luggage at the front door of his and Marvin's apartment on the seventh floor of the Guardian Arms. The girls had been fun dates and letting them move in might improve his chance at intimacy with either of them, but he was walking a tightrope over a precarious living arrangement. His aunt and uncle, Fanny and Leo Kalish, managed the Guardian Arms and had allowed the boys to stay in an apartment rent free on one condition—no women were allowed in the unit. Beth pleaded they had nowhere else to go, and Robinson couldn't help but feel a little sorry for her. The girls moved in. Beth slept on the couch and Marjorie shared the bedroom, platonically, with Marvin and Bill.

While Marjorie worked nights at the Pig Stand, Beth eagerly attended live radio show performances at CBS and NBC studios, which had broadcast so much of the entertainment she adored as a child while stuck inside with asthma three thousand miles away. George Bacos from the Carpenter Drive-In worked as head usher at NBC and often interacted with Beth when she attended. Bacos was still seeing Lynn Martin, who had left her rooming arrangement at Old Time Movie and had moved in with Beth and Marjorie and the two men at the Guardian Arms apartment.

When Bacos stopped by one night to pick Lynn up for a date, he found only Beth present. In Lynn's absence, Bacos took Beth out instead. The two drove through the Hollywood Hills, eventually parking at a lookout site, where they talked about their shared pneumonia and asthma afflictions. George claimed he didn't want to "mess things up with Lynn" so he never made a move on Beth, but he was sure she wanted him to. An oddly embittered Bacos would later state, "I didn't think I wanted to kiss her because of all the 'goop' she used on her face. I'm used to nice, cultured girls . . . I wanted to stay as far away from her as possible. . . . To me she looked cheap and I couldn't afford to be seen with her; but I had no desire for her physically. The more I found out about her the less desire I had."

Bacos wasn't the only embittered man in Beth's life. Bill Robinson took Beth for a drive and tried to make a move on her. When she refused his advances, he slapped her and threw her out of the car and onto the pavement. Anne consoled Beth as she cried from the humiliation and pain. Marvin Margolis had appeared jocular and outspoken at first, but his mood darkened behind closed doors. He had suffered horribly during the war, tending to hundreds of maimed Marines in the battle of Okinawa. Under heavy Japanese bombardment, his medical unit had been forced to work in caves near the beaches. Taking a direct hit, Margolis's cave filled with mud that buried the twenty-year-old up to his neck. He endured twenty-four hours of live entombment before managing to escape, resulting in years of ongoing "battle dreams," extreme fatigue, and depression.

On October 21, Marjorie, Beth, and Marvin popped up at Mark Hansen's house for a visit. Doing all the talking for Beth and Marjorie, Margolis announced the girls were sick of Hollywood and would be returning back East.

The writing was on the wall. Los Angeles with all its strange, unpredictable characters was not the kind of place Beth wanted to stick around in much longer. Whether she didn't have the money for a train ticket or wanted to avoid returning to the East Coast in the winter, Elizabeth Short nonetheless made a fateful decision in the ensuing hours to stay in LA for just a little longer.

The next day, Marjorie was on a train back to Boston when Marvin Margolis arrived unannounced at Hansen's house with one of Beth's suitcases in hand. Margolis asked, "Can she leave this here overnight? She's going away tomorrow and would like to leave these until tomorrow." Hansen grudgingly agreed. At that moment, Beth's other suitcase was being thrown into the car of twenty-two-year-old photographer Glen Stearns, who had just met Beth on Hollywood Boulevard. They spent the day at Marshall High School in Los Feliz, where Stearns photographed her. Once the session was over, Stearns spent hours driving Beth around the city to try and find her a place to live. Sometime after midnight, the car arrived at Mark Hansen's house on Carlos Avenue. Beth knocked on the door and begged Mark for another chance.

Anne was surprised Hansen took her back. He had called Beth a tramp and cheap. Anne couldn't contradict Mark or she'd be the next one out the door, but the comments had stung. She and Beth had bonded and none of what Mark said was true, most of all the accusations that Beth had dated gangsters and suspicious-looking lowlifes. Mark was more irritable than ever under the immense stress of the Florentine Garden's financial problems, but in Anne's eyes nothing could justify his cruel words.

Now that Beth was back, Anne felt closer than ever to her. So many of Beth's relationships in Los Angeles had been born out of pity. Beth often told strangers that she had lost her fiancé, Matt Gordon, to an airplane crash. In some stories the two had been married, in other stories she had lost her husband and a child. Beth could elicit pity from nearly anyone she met, and acquaintances, strangers, and dates had all given her the money on which she survived. With Anne, the relationship had no agenda, no transaction. Anne was the one person with whom she could be herself.

Mark, however, was a different story. Anne noticed a change in his relationship with Beth from the moment Beth returned. No longer a one-way street with Hansen chasing after Beth, it seemed to Anne as if the two were now dating, even if it were only Mark's understanding: "Mark told Betty that he was going with her and she was going with him." Beth confided many private thoughts with Anne but never shared whether she had agreed to date Hansen. Beth feared anything she told Anne would find its way back to Mark, and she didn't plan on getting kicked out a second time. Beth and Mark's relationship had both matured and grown complicated. She took liberties she never would have before, like cleaning Mark's bathroom and throwing out hygiene products he hadn't used in ages. Hansen raged at her, but instead of retreating Beth argued back. Anne was awed by Beth's defiance of the man who did not allow himself to be challenged by women.

While tensions with Mark were growing, Beth continued to court Gordon Fickling's affections. She also courted his wallet, asking for financial help, which Fickling for the first time rejected. "Darling, your request impossible at this time, other obligations have me against a wall. Try to make other arrangements. I'm concerned and sorry, believe me." His growing insecurity over the long-distance relationship was not financial, however. Lingering doubts about her fidelity gnawed at him, and her failure to break a date with a stranger elicited an angry letter. "Just tried to call you for the sixth time since 11:00 A.M. I hope that you enjoyed your breakfast date which you seem to have kept despite the fact that you said you were not going to. If I am ever able to understand you, I'm going to consider myself quite accomplished. Will continue trying to call you and hope that you can say hello between dates."

Beth flailed about in search of "true love," shocking some of her dates with amorous proposals. Frequent suitor Lieutenant Stephen Wollock, who had since moved back to the East Coast, wrote her in late October. "When you mentioned marriage in your letter, Beth, I got to wondering about that myself. Seems like you have to be in love with a person before it's a safe bet. Infatuation is sometimes mistakenly accepted for true love which can never be." Another serviceman named Paul Rosie had written Beth, too. "Your letter took me completely by surprise. Yes I've always had the feeling that we had a lot in common and that we could have meant a lot to each other had we only been together more often." Just as she had with Matt Gordon, Beth came on strong with vows of love, but just as she had with Gordon Fickling, she would pull away when those vows were reciprocated. Beth seemed to want what she could not have . . . and did not want what she could have.

Though she had avoided Mark's advances in the past, when he came home with another girl on November 13, Beth saw what she could no longer have and flew into a rage.

CHAPTER 11

HE'S WAITING FOR ME

Beth often had to share Anne's bed when other bedrooms were occupied by houseguests. The two had just settled in for sleep on November 12 when they heard Mark enter the house at an unusually late hour, the voice of a young woman accompanying him. Beth pulled the sheets off and ran into the living room, where she found Hansen with a short, stocky, blond girl whom she had seen at the house several times before. Beth tore into the girl, accusing her of loose morals and demanding she return to her mother where she belonged.

Anne described Beth's unbridled rage. "She said in Boston they never did those sorts of things, or something. She had a lot of high ideas, that Betty, believe me, with her Boston family and all that stuff, and she got up and locked her suitcase, because she thought this girl was going to get into her suitcase, and she said, 'I don't want to touch your damn suitcase, I don't want anything in there.' Anyway, words were flying back and forth and there was almost a beef and a fist fight, and Mark stepped in between them and he ordered Betty to move the next day. She was right though, I'll tell you that."

Anne further explained Mark's motivation for kicking Beth out. "Because she insulted another girl, called her a bum. Later we found out she hit the nail on the head. But at the time she had insulted a guest in the house and the landlord had to ask her to leave. She had the right idea—they're all a bunch of phonies in this town."

The next morning, Beth desperately called around to various acquaintances and past dates, looking for a place to stay. Anne and her boyfriend Leo Hymes had been gifted the use of a Nash automobile by Mark Hansen, and they used it to shuttle Beth downtown to the palatial Biltmore Hotel, where she planned to meet with a stranger. The streets were clogged as cars struggled through a torrential downpour, a fitting backdrop for a distraught Beth, who was still fuming at the "cheap blond girl" who had ruined everything for her. Leo recalled Beth referring to TWA airlines several times on the drive to the Biltmore.

Beth was dropped off at the grand hotel, while Anne jumped into action for her best friend, securing a bed at the Chancellor Hotel apartments off Hollywood Boulevard and even paying the first week's rent of five dollars for her. Anne kept her plans secret from Mark, who wanted Beth reliant on him and would have been furious with her for helping Beth find her own living arrangement.

Beth entered Room 501 on the top floor of the Chancellor Hotel to find seven metal frame beds crammed together and stacked like bunkbeds. Her five or six or seven roommates greeted her, all living together in one room, smoking cigarettes, trading outfits, sharing makeup, and swapping stories of dates gone wrong. They included cocktail lounge server Sheryl Maylond, Rouge Room makeup artist Linda Rohr, telephone operator Marion Schmidt, and a hot dog stand server named Schell, who slept in the bed above Beth's.

Appalled by her new living arrangement, Beth took an immediate dislike to her roommates, who seemed cheap and experienced with life in all the wrong ways. She closely guarded her suitcases and refused any requests from the other girls to borrow her eye-catching fashion ensembles. To her roommates, Beth appeared haughty and unfriendly, using the room only to sleep and get ready for her many dates. At Mark Hansen's house, Beth had spent evenings at home with Anne, but conditions at the Chancellor Hotel now found her spending as much time away from home as possible.

Roommate Linda Rohr complained, "She was out early every night. She had a lot of telephone calls, mostly from her 'favorite boyfriend' Maurice." Beth had begun dating a Columbia Studios voice-over artist named Maurice Clement and continued seeing real estate agent Ralph Johnson of Inglewood. She also made several calls to a mysterious phone number in Beverly Hills with the telephone exchange of "Crestview," which had impressed Anne because of its posh location. (Telephone numbers into the 1950s were composed of an exchange name referring to the local area followed by a four-digit number. The exchange names eventually became the three-digit prefixes we use today.)

Beth was at Breneman's on Vine and other famous Hollywood eateries so often staff members became well acquainted with her. She attended radio shows at NBC and CBS alone nearly every night of the week. Jack Egger ushered at CBS Studios and along with the other employees was awestruck by the mysterious lone woman. "She was a striking girl, with that raven hair, blue sweater or pink sweater. She more or less became a legend." Bill Fowler worked the door at the lavish Pantages Theatre near Hollywood and Vine, where Beth stopped by several times to inquire about the films playing at the ornate palace. He was in awe of her beauty, grace, and fashion, all working to form a haunting image he could not forget.

As the days passed, Beth became increasingly aimless. She kept up the charade of going to a job every morning but would only wander the surrounding neighborhoods. Having gone missing for several months, her wardrobe trunk had finally been located by Railway Express Agency and arrived at downtown Los Angeles' Union Station. But with no clear plans to either leave or stay in

Los Angeles, Beth simply kept it in storage at the cavernous train station. Former flame Gordon Fickling's letters were increasingly cold, other men she had met ran away from her strong emotional attachments, fewer acquaintances were willing to loan her money, and winter was coming to most of the country. Beth was frozen, unable or unwilling to get a job or move out of the city, unable to establish real friendships or romantic relationships.

The stress of her precarious existence was growing and so was the shame. She told acquaintances and strangers increasingly elaborate lies about herself to shield the truth of her life. Desperate to prove herself to her mother, Phoebe Short, she painted a rosy picture in her letters back home. Anne saw Beth every day while she lived at the Chancellor, bringing her mail, even giving her money when she could afford it. Searching for a way out, Beth confided to Anne she was dating a pilot named Tim Mehringer who was stationed at an airbase in nearby Burbank. She was thinking of moving there to work and live in the dormitories, if Anne would join her. Anne never heard Beth mention the plan—or Tim—again.

As bad as Beth's circumstances were, Lynn Martin's went from bad to worse throughout the fall of 1946. After Marjorie and Beth left Bill Robinson's apartment, she found herself with no home and drifted around trying to find work and a place to live. Alex Constance, the forty-year-old hairdresser who had gotten to know the girls at the Hawthorne Hotel and Carpenter Drive-In back in September, knew a lot of people in Hollywood. Some of them could even get a pretty girl a few bucks in a pinch.

George Price lived in a tiny, ramshackle house high in the Hollywood Hills up a twisted dirt road called Jewett Drive. Access in or out of the isolated hillside bungalow was a challenging maze, which actually served Price's profession of photographing girls. His photos appeared all over the city, but not in magazines or newspapers. He produced erotic nude photography sets that were printed in the tens of thousands for under-the-counter sale at countless bars, liquor stores, and novelty shops across the city.

Alex Constance dropped Lynn Martin off at Price's combination studio and home. Reeking of cigarettes and sweat, the chubby photographer made small talk in an anxious effort to get her relaxed. He offered five dollars for a photo shoot that would require minimal nudity. The session went fine. Price dropped Lynn off in Hollywood and invited her back for more money.

The second shoot was different. Price demanded that Lynn pose fully in the nude. Scared for her safety, she complied. Price completed his snaps, and then sexually assaulted her. Lynn returned for another photo shoot—and another and another. Price reliably paying her five dollars at each session. Lynn also found work at Club Tabu on Sunset Boulevard, where she met a bunco-and-check-artist conman named Duke Wellington, whose real name was Bill Cochrane. With his marriage on the rocks, he offered Lynn a cheap motel room, with benefits.

One night turned into several nights. The pair got along well enough, but Duke was perturbed by Lynn's eagerness to chat up complete strangers. She pushed back, defiant that she always liked talking to new people. It was one of the reasons she liked working as a waitress. Burdened with loneliness, Lynn kept alive the dream of reuniting with her biological family and finally coming home "to her people."

Elizabeth Short became increasingly anxious to leave the Chancellor once her roommates made clear their distaste for her. Arguments often broke out, leaving Beth feeling attacked and ostracized. The final nail arrived when the police arrested two of her roommates for possession of marijuana, sending Beth spiraling with paranoia that she, too, would be charged for the crime, despite never having smoked dope.

Top LAPD detective Finis Brown would later surmise that the Chancellor marijuana bust was a setup because no smoked joints or "marijuana cigarette" butts were found, only two "sticks" of unsmoked marijuana, which should not have led to an arrest or investigation. Why the LAPD set up the specific roommates, two women from Texas, was never established. With memories still fresh of her 1943 arrest in Santa Barbara for underage drinking, in which she was the only member of her party not drinking, Beth feared a second arrest could spell trouble.

Desperate for money as she plotted her escape from the Chancellor Hotel, Beth went on dates with airplane mechanic Jimmy Harrigan on December 1 and 2. The first night was spent at Club Tabu, where Lynn Martin worked, for drinks, chatting, and dancing.

The next date "ended Harrigan's association" with Beth. As they drove back from the Sycamore Inn, where they had dined and danced, Beth's persona suddenly changed. Pleading with him, she explained she had to visit her sister in Berkeley, California, the following week but couldn't cash a check she had received for funds and was now urgently in need of money. Harrigan was put off by the ploy and gave her his business card instead. Beth tried calling him twice more in the ensuing days, but Harrigan wasn't available to take the calls.

By December 5, Chancellor Hotel manager Elsie Ringo was fed up with Beth's late payment on rent and took possession of her suitcases, to be returned upon receipt of five dollars. Desperate to get her suitcases back, desperate to avoid criminal charges, desperate to leave the Chancellor, desperate to leave Los Angeles, Beth was trapped and on the verge of homelessness. On the evening of the fifth, Anne invited a nervous, frightened Beth back to Mark Hansen's house for dinner and solace. While Beth despaired over her circumstances, Anne tried to soothe her nerves.

Mark arrived home to find Beth crying at his dining room table. "She was sitting there . . . about 5:30 or 6:00 o'clock—sitting and crying and saying she had to get out of there . . . she said there was bad company over there and she couldn't stand it." Beth then announced she would be leaving for several days to visit her sister in Berkeley, just as she had told Jimmy Harrigan. Anne, too, would be leaving soon for Richmond, California, to visit her daughter, which was not far from Berkeley. It would be a perfect coincidence and chance to see each other up north. Beth promised Anne she would share her sister's address and phone number with her. Strangely, she never did so. Even stranger, Beth hadn't seen, spoken with, or written to her sister in over two and a half years.

Anne couldn't help but notice Beth was cold. Then again, Beth was cold all the time. Anne gave her a tan coat that she could return when they met up in Berkeley. Mark insisted that he be the one to drive Beth back to the Chancellor Hotel, and when he returned, Anne found him in an agitated, excited state, bewildered over Beth's apparent independence in finding and renting her own place. Anne's mind raced—had Beth told him Anne had helped set her up at the Chancellor? Mark surely would have said something by now. She asked for Beth's sister's address and phone number in Berkeley, but Mark said she never got around to sharing them with him.

First thing in the morning of December 6, Anne called apartment 501 to get the address, but was informed by one of the roommates that Beth had disappeared that morning and had left her possessions at the Chancellor. Soon after Anne's call, Beth arrived back at the Chancellor with the rent money in hand and collected her suitcases from manager Elsie Ringo. Roommate Linda Rohr stated, "The morning she left she was very anxious. She said, 'I've got to hurry he's waiting for me.' We never found out who 'he' was. She was supposed to go live with her sister in Berkeley."

But Beth did not leave for Berkeley. Instead, she disappeared, making no contact with any friends or family. She was as close as ever to Anne, whom she had seen every day, but did not contact her, nor Mark Hansen or Gordon Fickling, nor anyone else. None of her regular letters were sent to her mother. In all her movements over the previous six months from hotels to homes to apartments, regardless of whom she was staying with, Beth had never been out of communication with those closest to her.

Her next verified location would come two and a half days later on the night of December 8 at the Hollywood Greyhound bus station on Cahuenga Boulevard, where Beth bought a ticket for a six-hour bus ride to San Diego, a city she had never been to nor knew a soul in. Over and over again, Beth had found herself without a home and scrambling to find someone who could help her. She had moved in with stranger Mark Hansen when Sid Zaid could no longer house her. She had knocked on Bill Robinson's door when Mark Hansen kicked her out. She had gone back to Mark when her stay at Robinson's ended. She called friends when Hansen kicked her out for fighting with another girl. But never had she inexplicably left in the middle of the night for a strange city bereft of any contacts.

Something had gone terribly wrong for Elizabeth Short when she left the Chancellor Hotel on the morning of December 6.

Beth's bus arrived at the Greyhound terminal in downtown San Diego at 6:00 A.M. on December 9. With two suitcases and two hat boxes in hand, she wandered eight blocks to the twenty-four-hour Aztec Theater, an aging second-run movie house that had once served as a meat market. The movie playing at the Aztec that week was *The Blue Dahlia*. When Beth had arrived in Long Beach the previous July, the newly released noir movie was going strong with crowds around the block. Five months later, the aging film was at the end of its run, relegated to the cheapest seats in town. Elizabeth Short settled into one of the Aztec's 564 cheap seats as *The Blue Dahlia* began to play.

Dorothy French was surprised to find such a pretty girl asleep in the near-empty theater, especially at such an early hour on a Monday morning. The twenty-year-old Aztec cashier and usher roused Beth from her sleep. Dorothy couldn't help but feel sorry for the poor girl, who had lost a child and a husband during the war and had nowhere to go. The home Dorothy shared with her mother and brother was cramped, but she couldn't just leave Beth on her own.

Dorothy's mother, Elvera French, allowed Beth a few days with the family while she got on her feet. Their compact, one-story home sat in the Bayview Terrace housing development in the Pacific Beach neighborhood, where thousands of units had been built during the war to house workers at the defense plants in San Diego. "Light, airy and cheerful," all Bayview Terrace government-issued homes came equipped with electric refrigerators, automatic water heaters, and combination kitchen sinks and laundry trays. Beth had caught one more lucky break.

The next morning at 6:00 A.M., Dorothy drove Beth to a telegram office, where she sent a message to an unknown person. This was likely Gordon Fickling, as his subsequent letters soon began arriving at the new address in Pacific Beach. Beth's first priority was maintaining communication—and hope—with Gordon.

While Dorothy maintained her job at the Aztec Theater, Beth spent her days in the French home—reading magazines, writing letters to her mother and Gordon Fickling, and chatting with Elvera, who noticed how little of her past Beth was willing to share. Beth lamented her deceased husband, Matt Gordon, but always avoided details of the marriage or the child she claimed to have lost. She especially avoided discussing her time in Los Angeles.

Beth was moody, happy one moment and then blue the next. She would gleefully bake a cake for the family then quietly retreat. While Beth had always swung between elated and depressed, Vera witnessed a new side of her. "Betty seemed constantly in fear of something. Whenever anyone came to the door she would act frightened." Anne Toth, who had lived with Beth for weeks in Hollywood, stated she was never afraid of anyone, never even expressed concern about anyone.

Beth spent days holed up in the French home, rarely venturing outside. Gordon Fickling responded to Beth's growing anxiety about the future with unusual bluntness. "Time and again I suggested that you forget me as I believe that's the only thing for you to do to be happy." On December 13, Beth poured her feelings out to Fickling as she never had before in writing. Gone was the flowery prose of her love-addicted heart, replaced now with raw emotion. "I would never be happy in a house alone. I want the kind of happiness everyone else has . . . I am so unsettled and discouraged."

Beth speculated whether Matt Gordon had truly been the only man for her, his absence the source of all her misery. She denied any regret in having joined Fickling in California, despite his cold shoulder to her, his indifference, and his seeming distraction by other matters. She admitted to missing him terribly but felt ready to move on, as he would never reciprocate her feelings. Finally, she declared her freedom from him. "I'll never be settled unless I find my own happiness."

Beth had bared her heart, letting the chips fall where they may. She postmarked and stamped the letter. And then never sent it.

Robert Morris Manley, who went by the nickname Red owing to his wavy reddish hair, grew up in the working-class town of Southgate, seven miles south of downtown Los Angeles. He had served in the Army Air Corps band, playing saxophone and clarinet, but was discharged as "mentally unfit for service" on a "psychopathic discharge," though he was found to be mentally "normal." Married to wife Harriet since November of 1945 and a father since the arrival

Leila Welsh.
Associated Press.

e one-room prairie schoolhouse
ar the Welsh farm that
orge and Leila walked to
ch school day.
*urtesy of Jackson County
storical Society.*

First Row: Patty Power, Lucile Cahill, Doris Jean Bramley, Jean Miller, Maureen Carlock, Mary Lou Stocks.
Second Row: June Cline, Mary Alice McKay, Barbara Jean Warner, Berniece Jewell, Lee Welsh, Josephine Duffy

Cho Chin sorority at the University of
Kansas City, 1938. Leila Welsh stands
in the back row, second from right.
Courtesy of Kenneth J. LaBudde
Special Collections and University Archives,
University of Missouri—Kansas City.

Leila Welsh refused to wear the
Enforcement Committee's mandated
blue and gold ribbons while on the
University of Kansas City campus.
Courtesy of Kenneth J. LaBudde
Special Collections and University Archives,
University of Missouri—Kansas City.

The heiress from the prairie farm grew confident and cosmopolitan at the University of Kansas City. *Courtesy of Kenneth J. LaBudde Special Collections and University Archives, University of Missouri—Kansas City.*

Leila's on-again, off-again boyfriend Richard Funk, who desperately wanted to tell her he loved her. He followed her in death only three years later. *Courtesy of Ted Funk.*

The last known photo taken
of Leila Welsh, just weeks
before her murder.
Courtesy of Ted Funk.

March 9, 1941: With neighbors
crowding around, Kansas City
Police Department investigators
examine the footprints left by
the killer outside the window
of Leila Welsh's bedroom.
Associated Press.

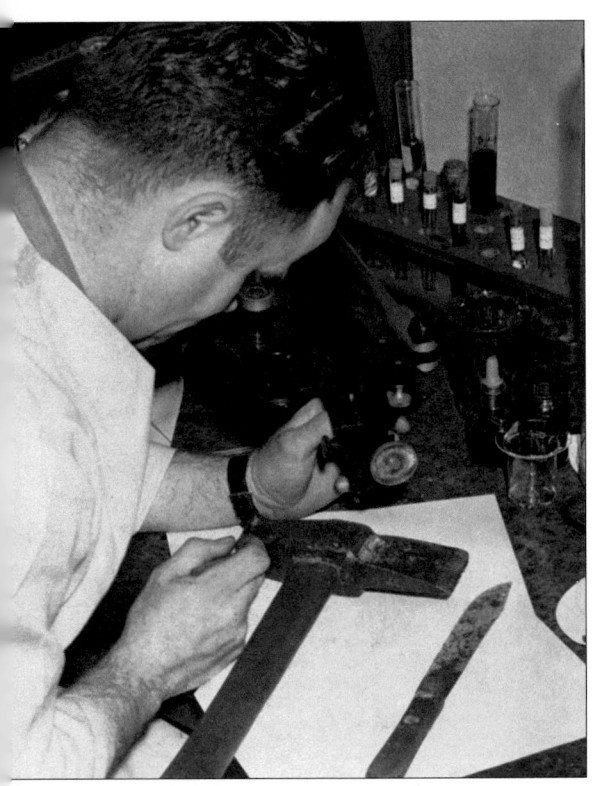

A Kansas City Police lab technician examines the tools used to slaughter Leila Welsh—a nearly five-pound railroad hammer and a butcher's knife. *Associated Press.*

The small but stretched gloves used by the killer throughout the murder—and inexplicably discarded in a nearby backyard. *Associated Press.*

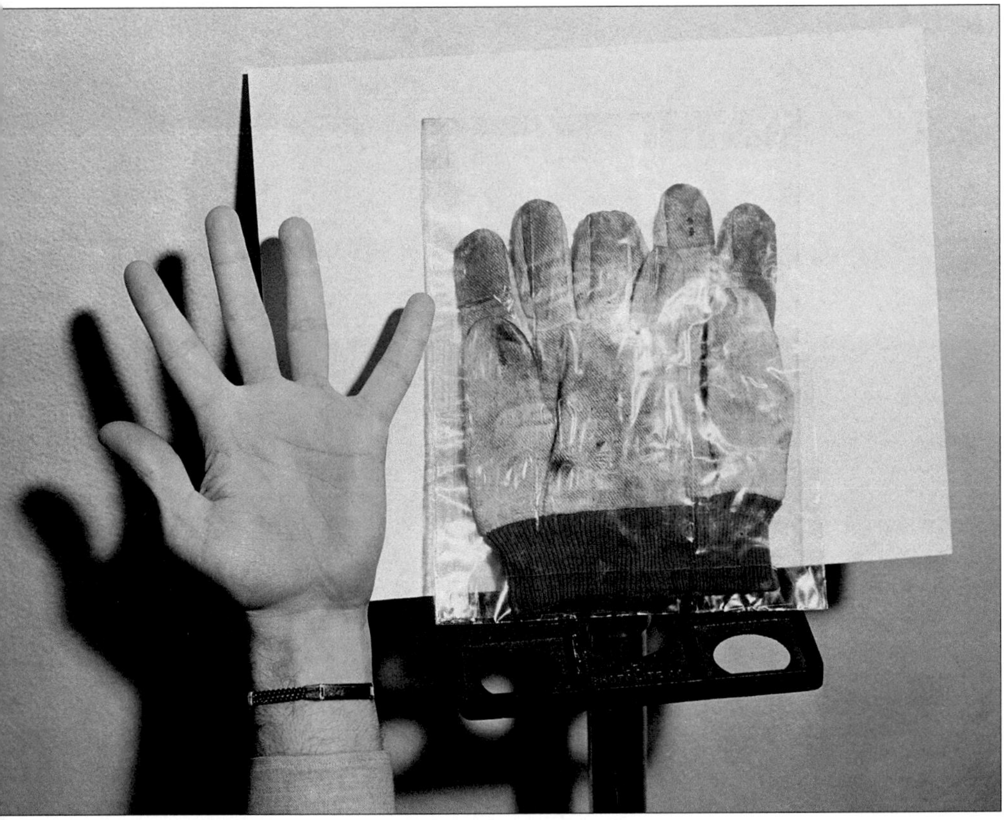

Kansas City police burn Leila's
blood-soaked mattress in the backyard
of the Welsh home.
Associated Press.

The trials of George Welsh: The crowds were
so thick at the Jackson County Courthouse
that George had to enter through a window.
Associated Press.

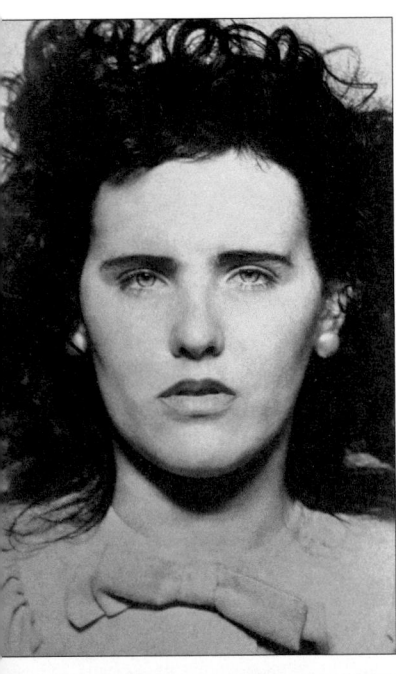

Elizabeth Short.
Historic Collection/Alamy Stock Photo.

...eth Short (left) and her best friend
...arge Dyer in Miami during World War II,
...here she meets fiancé Matt Gordon
...d future boyfriend Gordon Fickling.
...ssociated Press.

Betty Bersinger discovered the bisected body
of Elizabeth Short on January 15, 1947.
What she saw has been kept a secret by the
LAPD since that day.
*Herald Examiner Collection/
Los Angeles Public Library.*

Phoebe Short and her surviving
daughters trudge through the
Boston snow as she prepares
to fly to Los Angeles to identify
the body of Elizabeth.
Associated Press.

Dusting the envelope message sent
in by the killer of Elizabeth Short
for fingerprints.
Associated Press.

The Balsiger family at Lake of the Forest in 1927. A few months later, seven-year-old Elizabeth "Betty" Balsiger (far left) would drown under mysterious circumstances. Twelve-year-old Carl is second from right. *Courtesy of Karl Kanehl.*

The exact location at Lake of the Forest where Elizabeth "Betty" Balsiger's bicycle was found barely submerged in the water. Her body was discovered much farther in the lake. Just 200 feet away is the clubhouse, seen in the background. *Courtesy of Karen Tennant/Lake of the Forest Historic Preservation Society.*

The Balsiger home
where Carl lived
until forced to sell
after the divorce fr
Tabitha Teall in 19.
*Courtesy of
Christopher E. Wo*

Carl Balsiger at the University of Kansas City.
*Courtesy of Kenneth J. LaBudde
Special Collections and University Archives,
University of Missouri—Kansas City.*

Kegon

FRONT ROW: Funk, Oliver, Jarvis, Balsiger, Lockton, Webb, Charles Myers, Chaney.
SECOND ROW: Doolittle, Herndon, White, Harold Myers, Birkhead, Wherry, Teefey, Blomquist, Rouse, Bob Myers, Torbert.
THIRD ROW: Holland, Thompson, King, Bryson, Ready, Willits, Wickham, Cash, Geary, Husbands.

KEGON was founded October 15, 1934, by Bill Abernathy, Carl Balsiger, Bob Boand, Irl Oliver, Bernard Jarvis, Bob Myers, Charles Myers, Barry Renfro, Bob Torbert, Jack Redheffer, Gardiner Rapelye, James Webb, Wayne Wherry. It was organized for social purposes.

The men of Kegon fraternity, co-founded
by Carl Balsiger, who sits in the front row,
fourth from left.
*Courtesy of Kenneth J. LaBudde
Special Collections and University Archive
University of Missouri—Kansas City.*

Carl Balsiger (center right) among the elite Greek-system students at the University of Kansas City. Eyeing Balsiger to his immediate right is Phyllis Wetherill, best friend of Leila Welsh. *Courtesy of Kenneth J. LaBudde Special Collections and University Archives, University of Missouri—Kansas City.*

The big men on campus: Carl Balsiger (second from left) and his fraternity brothers traveled the Pacific Coast on bicycles in the summer of 1936. Student Council President John Chaney is at far right. *Courtesy of Kenneth J. LaBudde Special Collections and University Archives, University of Missouri—Kansas City.*

Quartermaster Captain Carl Balsiger among his field bakery units in the South Pacific during World War
Courtesy of Karl Kanehl.

The sleepy, pastoral town of Camarillo, north of Los Angeles, where Carl Balsiger
opened the successful Homecraft Bakery (far left) with Walt Thacher.
Courtesy of Pleasant Valley Historical Society.

The Candle-Lite Motel in Camarillo, California, where Carl Balsiger and Elizabeth Short spent the night of December 6, 1946.
Courtesy of Pleasant Valley Historical Society.

Jean Thacher and her son on the Thacher Ranch in Camarillo. She immediately cut all family ties with Carl Balsiger.
Courtesy of Dorothy Parris.

an Cleveland Thacher
Beverly Hills, wife of
alt Thacher, business partner
f Carl Balsiger at the time
f Elizabeth Short's murder.
ourtesy of Dorothy Parris.

Carl Balsiger in 1946.
Courtesy of Karl Kanehl.

SAN FRANCISCO. 1946

A three-minute drive from the star-studded
mansions of Beverly Hills lay the eerie
wilderness of Benedict Canyon,
where Carl Balsiger lived in seclusion.
A decade later, the winding country road
would be filled with homes.
*Herman Schultheis, Herman J. Schultheis
Collection/Los Angeles Public Library.*

A lifelong hunter, Carl Balsiger had skills with a knife and bleeding out his kills. *Courtesy of Karl Kanehl.*

CITY OF LOS ANGELES
CALIFORNIA

DEPARTMENT OF
POLICE
CITY HALL
LOS ANGELES 12
MICHIGAN 5211

OFFICE OF THE
CHIEF OF POLICE
C. B. HORRALL

IN REPLYING PLEASE GIVE
OUR REFERENCE

FLETCHER BOWRON
MAYOR

June 2, 1949

1.6.16

File   295 771 Elizabeth Short

Adjutant General's Office
Demobilized Personnel Bureau
Record Section
St. Louis (20) Mo.

Gentlemen:

Information is sought as to assignments of one H.
CARL BALSIGER, during his period of service in the
United States Army.

This man had the rating of Captain and was attached
to the Quartermaster Corps, stationed in California
in 1945 and part of 1946. It is believed that he
entered the service in 1941 or 1942, and was discharged in 1946.

He is described as white male American, approximately
thirty (30) years of age, six (6) feet tall, weighing
approximately one hundred eighty five (185) pounds,
brown hair and eyes. His parents live in Kansas City, Mo.

If possible, it would be appreciated if you could forward a photograph of the subject. Also, record of
service and assignments during his period of duty in
the army.

The purpose of this request is to try and eliminate
subject as a suspect in a murder investigation being
conducted by this Department.

Yours truly,

C. B. HORRALL
Chief of Police

W. J. BRADLEY, Deputy Chief
Director Detective Bureau

WJB:FJK:FAB:LS

A 1949 letter from Los Angeles Police Chief Horrall to the U.S. Army in St. Louis
requesting Carl Balsiger's military files. Two and a half years after the murder
of Elizabeth Short, the LAPD was vigorously investigating Balsiger.
Lead detective Finis Brown's initials are cc'd at the bottom of the letter.

of baby Steven four months earlier, Red suffered from stress and a crisis of faith in family life.

The handsome, trim Manley dressed sharply, had a sparkling set of teeth, and kept his hair in an understated but eye-catching pompadour that garnered much attention on his many out-of-town trips selling fixtures for Baker & Company, a pipe clamp repair business. He had been sent down to San Diego just nine days before Christmas to meet with prospective clients. Having finished his sales visits for the day, Red was kicking around downtown in his sporty 1940 cream-colored Studebaker with a rear window sticker that read HUNTINGTON PARK, his home base back in Los Angeles.

Around 5:00 P.M., he noticed the shapely figure of a young woman standing at a corner bus stop. Red pulled over to the curb and called out to her, but she pretended not to hear or see him. Red called out again, offering her a ride. She snapped her eyes at him and she asked, "Don't you think it's wrong to ask a strange girl into your car?" Red was taken aback by her blunt response and responded that all he wanted to do was give her a ride home.

When Red Manley and Elizabeth Short arrived at the French home back in Pacific Beach, he asked if he could take her out that night. She accepted and Red returned at 7:00 P.M. to pick her up. Beth introduced him to Dorothy and Elvera as an executive at Western Airlines, where she claimed to be working. The two sped off for a night of dining and dancing at the Hacienda Club, which a waitress had recommended to Manley.

At midnight, they left for a drive-in restaurant, where they sat in the car and ate. Red kissed her, but found her lips cold—no passion, no lust. Struggling with his choices, he confessed to Beth that he was married and had a child. She was understanding and opened up about the pain of losing her husband in the war. Beth saw Red for the next five nights. They dined at a restaurant overlooking the airport. On December 21, Red returned to his family in Los Angeles for the Christmas holiday, but he promised Beth to wire her a message when he was next in town. He made sure to sign her address book with an alias, Red Morris.

Christmas came and went. In Red's absence, Beth ventured out of the house more, going on trips into town with Dorothy and her brother, Cary French, and she dated local boys Sam Navarra and Frank Dominguez. She frequented Patrick's Café on Balboa Avenue, just a four-minute walk from the French home. She read and wrote letters and hung out at home, but as New Year's Day approached, Beth felt the creeping weight of Elvera's impatience. What had started as "a few days' stay" had turned into three weeks with no end in sight.

Anticipating the inevitable parting from the Frenches, Beth planned her next move. There was no doubt she would be leaving California, her contacts and options exhausted. She wrote to Gordon Fickling. "I want to go to Florida in the new year, and stay there. I honestly did believe that I would be well here or in the west. Time has proved differently to me."

In one of Fickling's December letters, he updated Beth on his post-army career as a commercial pilot for Twentieth Century Airlines, based out of Charlotte, North Carolina's Douglas Airport. He would soon be piloting the airline's new Charlotte-to-Chicago route. Beth had spent three splendid weeks in Chicago the previous summer before leaving for California to meet Fickling, but she had always contemplated a return to that magical city. A day after Fickling's letter arrived, Beth wrote Fickling back, informing him she had decided to move back to Chicago, where she would model hats again. "Do not write to me here. I am planning to go to Chicago to work for Jack."

Fickling's terse response followed. "Anything that will make you happy is all right with me. I trust that you'll be very happy, back in

Chicago modeling, doing what you like best. Time and again I've suggested that you forget me, as I've believed it's the only thing for you to do, to be happy." He was pulling away, but she was pulling him back in.

On the night of January 6, a strange incident occurred that left Vera French perplexed. While she was sleeping, a neighbor spotted a car pull up to the French home. Two men and a woman approached the house, knocked on the door, and waited for a moment. They then backed away, turned, ran back to their car, and sped off. The next morning, the neighbor alerted Elvera, who asked Beth if she had seen anything. Beth claimed she had heard the knocking and had peered out the window at the strangers but was too scared to answer the door. She was vague and evasive and avoided any more questions. It was clearer than ever to Elvera that it was time for Beth to leave.

Right on cue, a fateful telegram for Elizabeth Short arrived at the French home the next day, January 7. Red Manley was returning to San Diego on another sales trip. "Be there tomorrow afternoon late. Would like to see you. Red." Unusual for a telegram, Manley had not added the sender's name or address. Beth found her opportunity to get on the road and began packing.

If she was hoping to reach Chicago, Beth faced a monumental problem. The three-day journey by bus, which left from Los Angeles and not San Diego, was exorbitant at $36.85, approximately $550 when adjusted for inflation. She had not a dollar to her name. Beth had received money from her mother, Gordon Fickling, Michael Otero, Anne Toth, Mark Hansen, and others in the past, but only in small sums, which she had quickly spent. Any escape from California would require real funds now.

For weeks, Anne had wondered what happened to Beth and why she hadn't heard from her since arriving in Northern California.

They had seen each other every day for a month and then . . . nothing. Well, practically nothing. Beth had wired Anne in December asking for money, and Anne had promptly wired her twenty dollars. Then no word again. Anne couldn't help but wonder when Beth would return her prized tan coat. Mark Hansen had heard nothing from Beth, either—until January 7, when he finally received a long-distance call from her. Mark was shocked to hear that Beth had moved to San Diego. When he asked why, she revealed what had caused her bizarre and desperate move to the strange city.

CHAPTER 12

SWALLOWED UP
BY THE CITY

Surprised to hear that Elizabeth Short had turned up in San Diego, of all places, Mark Hansen asked why she had chosen to go there. He recalled her response: "She had met a screwball who had scared her, so she decided to go to San Diego for a while before going to visit her sister, after she arrived at the bus station." Just before midnight on December 9, 1946, Beth had arrived at the Hollywood Greyhound bus station and went south, in the opposite direction of her sister's home in Northern California, to throw off the screwball who had frightened her.

Beth now needed money to leave San Diego and asked Mark to help her. Anne Toth detailed what Mark told of her of the January 7 phone call from Beth. "He got a wire from her. And he said he got a telephone call from her and he said that she wanted some money to come back to Los Angeles. So, he said he didn't send her—he wouldn't send her any, and that he said if she did get up here that she could come to the house and stay for a few days and he said that she had intentions of bringing my coat back to me, and I imagine she mentioned it over the phone and so forth and I lent her some money, I imagine she mentioned that, and I [sic] was just about all there was to it . . . ." In need of money, Beth had pleaded with Mark once again but only received an offer to stay with him at his home. Hansen stated, "She never showed up after she called up and say [sic] she was in San Diego."

If Beth had been frightened by the previous night's incident involving the three strangers at the front door, it didn't stop her from going on a date that night to the theater with Sam Navarra, whom she had seen several times over the previous weeks. The next day, January 8, Beth sent her final letter—and plea—to Gordon Fickling. "Frankly darling if everyone waited to have everything all smooth before they decided to marry none of them would be together now. It takes two to make a marriage successful and it also takes time to have everything as you want it . . . I'm getting ready to leave now that the holidays are over. I'll need my fur coat in Chicago, I guess. It's going to be cold there. I know that you'll be happy someday soon darling."

On the afternoon of January 8, 1947, Red Manley drove through downtown San Diego in hopes of spotting Beth. He drove by the street corner where he had first picked her up, then showed up at the French home. Beth greeted him at the door and asked that he take her to a pay telephone to make a call. Red obliged, but once on the road she changed her mind and decided against the phone call. She then asked if he would drive her to Los Angeles that day, where she planned on meeting her sister at the Biltmore Hotel.

Just as she had before leaving Los Angeles in early December, Beth fabricated the "plan to visit her sister" as a smokescreen for her real travel plans. Virginia West hadn't heard from her sister Beth in over two and a half years. Beth had never even met Virginia's husband, Adrian West, whom she had married in February of 1945.

Red had sales calls to make and wouldn't be able to return to Los Angeles until the next day, but he offered to drop her off at the bus station later that night, which suited Beth. Manley drove back to the French house, where Beth said her good-byes to the family that had taken such good care of her the last month. Elvera had always admired the fashionable hats Beth had picked up in Hollywood, and for all her hospitality Beth now gifted her one. Penniless, she also asked for and received one dollar from Elvera for the trip.

Beth seemed free and happy as she placed her two suitcases and hat box into the trunk of Red's Studebaker at 7:30 P.M. The two drove around the corner to Patrick's Café, at the corner of Balboa and Pacific Avenues, where Beth went to a pay phone to make calls to an unidentified person in Los Angeles. When she returned from the phone booth, Beth had changed her mind about going to the bus station that night. She would return to Los Angeles with Red the following day. They traveled six miles south of Pacific Beach into Old Town San Diego, where Manley had booked a room at the Mecca Motor Lodge. "We didn't make love in the room. I washed and shaved. She combed her hair. To eat, we went again to the Hacienda Club."

Beth had a ball back at the Hacienda, dancing for hours with Manley and chatting up band vocalist Wayne Gregg, who slipped her his phone number. At midnight, she and Red picked up "a bag of hamburgers" and retreated to the Mecca. Once in the room, Beth's mood dropped dramatically. Quiet and withdrawn, she complained of feeling cold, so Red lit a fire to warm her. Ill from menstrual cramps, she sat on a chair as Red draped his coat over her, though he had doubts about her actual condition. "She asked me to get her suitcase out of the car. It was the one with her makeup and stuff in it. She didn't really seem to be sick." Beth spent the night sleeping in the chair while Manley slept in the bed.

On January 9, 1947, Red Manley awoke to find Beth propped upright on the other side of the bed. She claimed to have suffered chills all night. Manley hopped out of bed, got dressed, and left to make his business calls. At 1:00 P.M., he returned to the motel to check out and collect Beth. They drove a half hour to nearby

Encinitas, where Manley attended one more sales call for a water company, an important new account for his company. The manager was late for the meeting and kept Manley waiting for over an hour while Beth sat in the car. Manley noticed her chatting with a couple of men who passed by on bicycles.

They grabbed lunch in Encinitas and by 4:00 P.M. were back on the road. Manley spotted something odd with Beth as they passed Oceanside, a town fifteen miles north of Encinitas. She kept craning her neck to scrutinize every car they passed on the passenger side. He asked what she was staring at, but she dismissed his questions. At 5:00 P.M., they stopped in Laguna Beach for gas and then continued on. Beth asked if she could write him after they parted, and he shared his address, which she wrote in her address book.

The day before, Beth had told Manley she intended to meet her sister at the Biltmore Hotel, but on the drive back to Los Angeles she instead asked to be dropped off at the Greyhound bus terminal. When asked why, Beth stated she wanted to put her bags in storage at the bus station in the event her sister showed up late to the Biltmore Hotel, which was a full seven blocks and a half mile away from the bus station. Manley claimed Beth told him she had never been to Los Angeles before, and he worried that she was unprepared for the shady Greyhound terminal and, even more, its seedy surrounding neighborhood.

At 6:15 P.M., Manley's Studebaker pulled up to the corner of 6th and Los Angeles Streets on the edge of downtown Los Angeles's Skid Row. With buses running twenty-four hours a day, the Greyhound station lit up the sidewalk, crowded with commuters and unsavory loiterers. Manley double-parked and carried Beth's suitcases through the jostling crowds. The noise inside was deafening, the air thick with cigarette smoke, cheap cologne, and bad breath. Beth went to the temporary storage desk, where she checked her hat box and two suitcases, which held her all-important makeup bag. Beth told Red she would be fine at the bus station and tried to bid good-bye, but he insisted on taking her to the Biltmore Hotel, which would be a safer location to wait for her sister.

Manley's recollections of Beth's plans were contradictory and baffling. "She wanted me to drive her to Los Angeles because she was going North to see her sister, a Mrs. Adrian West, I believe, who lives in Berkeley. I drove her up and when we got to the Greyhound bus station in downtown Los Angeles, I let her off. She was going to check her bags there and was rather indefinite as to where she was going from there." At first, he states Beth had planned on meeting her sister at the Biltmore Hotel, but then states she was going North to meet her sister in Berkeley, and then states she was rather indefinite about where she was going next. Manley either ignored or didn't pick up on the conflicting statements she had fabricated to distract from her real plans.

One of the central and most conjectured mysteries in the Black Dahlia saga is Elizabeth Short's intended destination upon her arrival back in Los Angeles on January 9, 1947. Was she headed for Mark Hansen's home? Was she going to stay with a friend? Was she headed for the Crown Jewel Room & Grille just two blocks away, which Anne Toth and Leo Hymes frequented?

Beth Short's own words and actions distinctly spelled out her plans. What Beth had not told Manley but had made clear in her letters to Gordon Fickling was her plan to leave Los Angeles for Chicago. Now, at the bus terminal, she had two choices of routes that night, both of which would depart in four to five hours and take approximately sixty hours to reach Chicago.

The 10:30 P.M. bus taking the LA–El Paso–St. Louis–Chicago route.
The 11:00 P.M. bus taking the LA–Denver–Omaha–Chicago route.

Beth had made the bizarre excuse of storing her bags at the Greyhound bus station in the event her sister might be late to meet her at the Biltmore Hotel, knowing her sister would never actually arrive. Her bags were stored at the station because she intended to leave on one of the two Chicago-bound routes later that night. All she lacked was the $36.85 for the ticket. Beth had no money to her name. Elvera French had given her one dollar, which she had used for phone calls, and Manley stated he gave her no money. She would need the next few hours to get the money for the bus ticket.

Beth wanted to stay at the Greyhound station, but Red insisted he take her to the Biltmore. She had never been away from her suitcases and the all-important makeup bag. Her appearance was everything to her, her clothes always kept impeccably clean and organized, her makeup a critical component of her persona. She would never have spent the night somewhere without her clothes and makeup bag. They were kept at the Greyhound bus station because she intended to go back to the bus station that night and leave California for good.

Red drove Beth the eight blocks to the Biltmore hotel and escorted her into the opulent Renaissance revival masterpiece. Though Beth told him she was only meeting her sister there, Red recounted going to the front desk while Beth freshened up in the bathroom to ask if Mrs. Virginia West had checked in yet. Hotel reception informed him there was no record of a guest named Virginia West. Beth came out of the bathroom formally dressed for the evening, choosing an ensemble appropriate for a date or an important meeting: a black suit without a collar, a fluffy cream-colored blouse, white gloves, nylon stockings, black suede high heels, a black plastic purse with two handles, and Anne Toth's full-length beige topcoat. Red looked to make his exit. "I was anxious to get out of there. . . . I was just glad to get rid of her."

At 7:00 P.M., Elizabeth Short sat down alone in the Biltmore Hotel lobby fatefully named the Rendezvous Court. Surrounded by a Moorish wood-beamed ceiling, a resplendent Spanish baroque staircase, oak-paneled walls, and crystal chandeliers, Beth waited hours for someone. Guests in the lobby claimed they saw her walk to a bank of pay phones, though nobody definitively saw her making calls. No one would ever come forward claiming they had received a call from her on the evening of January 9.

At 10:00 P.M., with the first Chicago bus leaving in a half hour from the Greyhound terminal, Beth stood up. Bellboy captain Harold Studholme insisted she looked as if she had been signaled by someone on the outside of the hotel. In her unsent letter to Gordon Fickling, Elizabeth Short had written, "I'll never be settled unless I find my own happiness." Throughout a life of struggle and discouragement, she had pursued adventurous travel to find fulfillment—somewhere, somehow.

Beth's high heels clicked over the mahogany floor, echoing in the room. As Harold Studholme opened the Biltmore's massive solid bronze doors, she had all the hope in the world her next move would finally bring her a step closer to finding her own happiness.

Anne Toth was very unhappy when she stepped off the San Joaquin Daylight train at Los Angeles's Union Station on the night of January 10. Having been gone a month visiting family in Northern California, she fully expected boyfriend Leo Hymes to pick her up, but he was a no-show. Now Anne had to pay for a cab all the way to Mark Hansen's house.

When Anne entered, she found Hymes relaxing on a couch, and she let him have it, until Mark cut her off with news he had received a phone call from Beth Short three days earlier. He related that Beth had gone to San Diego and had asked him for money on the call.

She had also asked to speak with Anne, but Mark had informed her he didn't know when she would be back from her trip.

Anne was flabbergasted that Beth had turned up in such a strange location. "I said, 'well, that is like Wrong Way Corrigan,' headed for Berkeley and went to San Diego." She was also surprised by Mark's agitated state. "It was the first thing on his mind when I came back. It was the first thing he told me about. It looked like it was bothering him, because he was very anxious to tell me."

For the next five days, Anne and Mark carried on as usual, with Mark home by 10:00 P.M. each evening. And yet Anne's worry grew with each passing day and no word from Beth. She was dumbfounded that Beth hadn't contacted her yet, what with all the support she had given her. Certainly, she would have called Anne before calling Mark for help.

On the evening of January 12, Mark received a call on his house phone. Someone was on the other line but didn't speak. Mark hung up. Five minutes later, the phone rang again, with no voice on the other end. The calls continued. Each time Mark hung up, the phone would ring again. Over and over again for half an hour. Anne had gone to bed but was so perturbed by the incessant ringing that she picked up the next call and yelled into the receiver. When she stopped, she could hear breathing on the other end. Anne hung up and the calls ceased.

It was 11:19 A.M. on January 15 when Captain Jack Donohoe radioed the call car, a maroon unmarked Chevrolet sedan at 11th and Burlington Avenues. Harry "Red" Hansen and partner Finis Brown were awaiting the coroner at a dead body scene but were ordered to drop everything and head to Norton Avenue and 39th Street. Donohoe signed off with a stark warning, "It sounds bad, Red. Damn bad. It's going to be a rough one."

Hansen and Brown arrived at 11:30 A.M. to find a mob scene of cops, detectives, crime lab techs, reporters, a man who had been walking his dog, and eleven-year-old Bobby Smith on his bicycle. The two halves of a young woman's bisected body lay sprawled out inches from the sidewalk, a display of razor-wielded torture and postmortem surgery. Los Angeles had an unenviable history of shocking mutilation murders. Detective Lieutenant Paul Freestone had seen the worst of them and yet still claimed, "This is the most brutal example of a sex crime I have ever seen."

Hansen and Brown conferred with the radio officers who had first arrived on the scene, then squatted in the grass to scrutinize what was already becoming a press sensation. With flashbulbs popping and reporters taking notes inches from the body, the two detectives read the crime scene with the experience of a thousand murder investigations behind them. Nonetheless, they were as shocked and baffled as every other witness that day by the utter horror of what had been inflicted upon the unknown victim.

Officers had fanned out beyond the body and discovered a prominent set of tire tracks along the driveway curb cut just feet away, suggesting the killer's car had screeched to a halt onto the sidewalk. Reporters noted, "Tire tracks indicated the car came from the south and swung hastily to the curb. The corpse was either dragged or tossed out. Tire marks showed the car continued north." Neighbor Bob Meyer, who lived at the closest house, half a block away, reported that at 6:30 A.M., he looked out his kitchen window and saw what looked like a black 1936 or 1937 Ford sedan pause where the body was found and after three to four minutes' drive away. An anonymous caller phoned the police and reported, "The car, splattered with mud, turned into an alley near the scene, backed out, and continued on toward Norton Avenue, where the body was found."

More evidence arose with the discovery of a small bloody heel print. Lieutenant Paul Freestone theorized that either the heel or the sole of the shoe was blood stained. A drop of water-diluted blood was found on a discarded empty sack of cement, leading to theories the killer had used the bag to transport the two halves of the corpse.

Harry Hansen arose and looked around at the too-typical suburban landscape. Wildly overgrown and strewn with rusted bedsprings and bags of trash, the west side of Norton Avenue looked like it had been abandoned by the city, a forgotten blank space suddenly the center of the world. Beyond the two blocks of the trash-scattered lot was a sea of cookie cutter pre-war homes in all directions. Two-story gas storage tanks loomed just blocks away, industrial blight perched over the working-class neighborhood. In the distance looking west was heavily trafficked Crenshaw Boulevard, where a massive construction project was under way, the Broadway-Crenshaw Center, California's first open air mall. This was the uninspired location chosen to throw away the victim of a shockingly malevolent murder. Somewhere amid the endless sprawl was the one person who knew why.

Homicide Bureau chief Captain Jack Donohoe was already marshalling resources for a manhunt unlike anything seen in recent history. But law enforcement would have a worthy competitor in the hunt to unmask the identity of Jane Doe #1 and her killer. Reporters were already driving in and out of the crime scene to the closest pay phones, breathlessly calling into home offices what they had seen and heard.

Less than an hour after the discovery of the body, Los Angeles *Daily News* rewrite man Jack Smith received the first bulletin phoned in by the police beat reporters. Less than sixty seconds later, he had typed the first words ever written about the slaying: "The nude body of a young woman, neatly cut in two at the waist, was found early today on a vacant lot near Crenshaw and Exposition Blvds." Smith grabbed the page from the typewriter and ran to the desk of the city editor, who was anxious to get the fast-moving story into type. He read the two lines and, with no knowledge of what the victim looked like, added one word. The lead now read, "The nude body of a beautiful young woman . . ."

Los Angeles was a week away from its first-ever television broadcast, The Western Premier of Commercial Television, starring Bob Hope. The Hollywood Freeway, promising the end of traffic woes, was just months from opening. The UCLA football star Kenny Washington signed with the LA Rams, breaking the NFL's color barrier months before Jackie Robinson would do so in baseball. The city was fast becoming a national model of a safe and secure atomic-age future. At 6:00 P.M., when the evening editions of the newspapers would hit the stands, that narrative would be changed forever. All hell was about to break loose.

CHAPTER 13

FADE TO ZERO

Chief Autopsy Surgeon Dr. Frederick Newbarr, along with Assistant Chief Autopsy Surgeon Dr. Victor Cefalu, readied Room 100 at the Hall of Justice for a highly complicated and unusually important autopsy. Newsstands and radios stations had become engulfed with the fast-moving developments of the beautiful, bisected girl, and now all eyes were on Dr. Newbarr, one of the nation's most respected forensic pathologists.

Also present were lead detective Harry Hansen and Ray Pinker of the Scientific Investigative Division, a legendary pioneer of crime analysis technology. Hansen had gotten an eyeful of the mutilations back at Norton Avenue, but Newbarr's expertise promised to crack open the deepest secrets of what befell the victim on her last night, and perhaps the clues that could unlock the identity of her killer.

The findings would prove to be startling. There were three deep wounds over the right eye where the victim was slugged with a blunt instrument, likely causing a concussion. However, the blows to the forehead were not made with enough force to shatter the skull. They were controlled swings meant to fracture and incapacitate but not kill. A hemorrhage caused by the trauma to the head had led to a stroke. Blood had poured out into the space between the brain and its surrounding tissue. It had also flowed under the skin of the forehead.

Lacerations, deep cuts through the skin from razors or a blunt instrument, were found at the top of the head. Scores of tiny abrasions, made from the friction of a rough surface against skin, had been inflicted on the right side of the face and forehead. Dark lacerations a quarter of an inch long were found on either side of the bridge of the nose, as if a clamp or fastening device had been placed over the top of her nose to restrict breathing. Five lacerations made to the right upper lip were so deep they extended a half inch into the soft tissue.

Then came the startling feature that had shocked witnesses as much as the bisection. A three-inch gash had been torn open from the girl's mouth on either side toward each ear, creating a ghastly gaping wound stretching nearly the width of the face.

Newbarr pointed out a series of ridges and depressions across the body, evidence that the victim had been tied down and restrained with a complex ligature of rope or wire at the wrists, ankles, right thigh, and neck. An irregular abrasion on the back of the neck evidenced the buckle of a neck restraint. A circular ridge around the lower left leg evidenced a cuff having been used as a restraint. Traces of strangulation marks appeared on the neck. A three-inch-long elliptical piece of skin had been sliced out of the left side of the left breast to the nipple. The top of the right breast had also been sliced and torn out, with a square piece of skin, tissue, fat, and nipple missing. A four-inch diamond-shaped cut had been torn open just below the navel. A tic-tac-toe design had been carved into the victim's right hip junction with the buttock. Much of the pubic hair had been torn out by hand or with an instrument. The skin beneath the patches of pubic hair was slashed in a crisscross fashion, with cuts appearing to form the letters E and D.

A horseshoe-shaped piece of flesh with a flat bottom topped by a circle five inches in diameter and weighing one pound had been sliced, torn, and pulled out from the left thigh where the rose tattoo was. The inch-thick puzzle piece of skin, fat, and muscle was missing. The sides of the open wound, an inch deep, were barren of traces of blood. The circular cut with a flat base had been made in one smooth motion, leaving no evidence of hacking or sawing with the blade.

An abrasion was found on the lower half of the vagina's labia minora, but there was no evidence of spermatozoa or sexual assault. Inside the vaginal canal, Dr. Newbarr discovered the source of the labia's abrasion. He pulled out the missing puzzle piece of flesh that had been cut from the thigh, bearing the rose tattoo, over which a crisscrossing tic-tac-toe design had been carved. The anus had been dilated a quarter of an inch. From the anal canal, Newbarr pulled out the clumps of pubic hair which had been torn from her skin.

Most startling of all was the clean bisection that had separated the body neatly in two. The near-perfect carving hadn't disturbed any organs except for minor lacerations found on the intestines and both kidneys. The bisection had sliced between the second and third lumbar bones of the spine, an opportune location owing to the thicker spongy discs separating the vertebrae. The small intestines had been separated from the stomach at the connecting duodenum. Surprisingly, fecal matter and digested food was found in the intestines and stomach, proving Short had eaten dinner the night she was murdered.

Newbarr determined the victim had been alive during the mutilations and blows to the head and face, the slashes from the mouth, and the cutting of the right breast, and had likely passed away during the cutting of the left breast. The official cause of death was "shock and loss of blood from hemorrhage." All other wounds had been inflicted after death.

What lay before these experienced professionals was like nothing they nor any other autopsy surgeon had ever seen. Jane Doe #1 was the first murder victim to have been bisected and exsanguinated, or drained of blood, in American history. The killer seemed acutely avoidant of blood, having drained the body first with the slicing of the face and then the bisection. The killer then washed or soaked the body clean of any remaining traces of blood, followed by a meticulous scrubbing of the exposed areas. Cocoa fiber brush bristles were found clinging to the victim's skin, particularly in the open wounds, suggesting an obsessive desire to scrub away any remaining traces of blood.

Also clinging to the top of the body were leaves, grass. and dirt, which could have only resulted from the body being placed face down in the empty lot on Norton Avenue. Dr. Newbarr noted the extensive amount of blood that had settled down into the front facing, or supine, half of the body. Known as postmortem lividity, the settling of blood occurs from the heart's cessation of circulation as gravity pulls blood to the lowest point of the body. Newbarr's autopsy report stated, "There was a marked postmortem lividity on the top side of both parts indicating that the deceased had lain on her front side or face for some period of time immediately following death."

Rigor mortis, or the stiffening of the body's muscles and joints, sets in approximately ten hours after death. But when the police examined Short's body after 11:00 A.M., they found rigor mortis had not yet appeared, placing the murder after 1:00 A.M. that morning. With the postmortem mutilations and bisection likely lasting hours and the body loaded and driven to Norton Avenue by 6:30 A.M., the lividity could only have occurred after the killer placed the body face down in the weeds on Norton Avenue, where it lay until its discovery. Knowing the body had been left by the killer in such a position before it was moved by the first policemen on the scene— the "Key Question" that had been closely guarded among only a handful of LAPD officers—Detective Hansen would have quietly recognized why blood had settled down into the supine side of the bisected body.

Newbarr further surmised the murder kit had included a blunt, heavy object, which had been used to incapacitate the victim on the right forehead, and two specific blades. Homicide Bureau chief Captain Jack Donohoe stated, "We believe that a very sharp knife of the long bladed butcher or carving type was used to sever the body. It is also possible that the killer may have inflicted torture and mutilation with a straight razor."

While the coroner unraveled the mysteries of the unprecedented murder, the well-funded *Daily News, Herald-Express*, and *Examiner* newspapers released armies of reporters called "legmen" to seek witnesses and chase down leads ahead of the LAPD in the mad-dash race to identify the beautiful, bisected girl with the grey-green eyes. Legmen were specialists in finding and squeezing information from witnesses, suspects, and victims, though they did not write articles, a task assigned to desk reporters.

Many legmen would soon get caught up in the world of Elizabeth Short's female acquaintances and "disappear" for a few days, eventually calling into the office with vague excuses about the delay in their assignment. Far more disciplined desk reporters at the *LA Examiner*, who worked nonstop shifts in the early days of the case, hit upon a groundbreaking idea. The paper had use of International News Photos' state of the art Soundphoto system, which could transmit images via sound impulse through leased telephone wires. The FBI in Washington, DC, had the world's most extensive fingerprint catalogue, a room the size of four football fields in the former National Guard Armory filled with 104 million prints and an army of readers. *Examiner* editor Jimmy Richardson approached the LAPD with an offer: If the *Examiner* was guaranteed the scoop on the girl's identity, it could get the prints to the FBI immediately.

Within one hour of receiving the victim's fingerprints, the FBI had a match: Elizabeth Short, twenty-two years old, of Medford, Massachusetts. Her fingerprints from the 1943 arrest in Santa Barbara had connected the dots, starting a domino chain of revelations. The first to fall was the girl's mother, whom the *Examiner* newspaper located in Medford, Massachusetts, minutes ahead of the *Boston Globe* newspaper. Despite editor Jimmy Richardson's unethical ruse to get information from Elizabeth's mother, Phoebe Short, using a fake beauty pageant award, she revealed Beth had sent letters from the home of one Vera French in San Diego, and from Vera French were gleaned the details of Beth's mysterious sojourn in San Diego and her sudden departure with an unidentified red-haired man back to Los Angeles.

Beth's letters to Phoebe had detailed her love affair with Gordon Fickling, who was located in Charlotte and interviewed, detailing his time with Beth in Long Beach. Donald Leyes and Harold Costa had been friends with Beth and Marjorie Graham at the Hawthorne Hotel and were the first Hollywood acquaintances to come forward with information about her. They revealed there had been a third roommate named Lynn Martin, whom the police became determined to find. Bill Robinson and Marvin Margolis walked into the Hollywood police station to tell of their encounter with Beth. Within twenty-four hours of the FBI identification, the *Herald-Express* had pieced together a portrait of Elizabeth Short's life in a front-page article titled "Life Story of 'Werewolf' Victim."

Since writing the opening salvo in the press's onslaught of headlines about the beautiful, bisected girl, Jack Smith of the LA *Daily News* had been scrambling for a scoop. Hundreds of "ecstatically competitive" reporters were now roaming the city in search of the same. But destiny had a surprise in store for Smith. Since the discovery of Short's body, the press had referred to the case as "the Werewolf Murder," a title that would soon be replaced and forgotten with one far more spellbinding. A *Daily News* police beat reporter called in to Smith with a tip: Elizabeth Short had frequented a pharmacy in Long Beach near the Washington Apartments, where she had stayed back in August of 1946.

Smith opened the Long Beach yellow pages. Twenty-six-year-old Arnold Lander answered the phone at the family-owned David Lander Drugs. Sure, he remembered the girl who had frequented the pharmacy the previous summer. He and his three sisters—Frieda, Gloria and Hilda—all worked as clerks at the store and poured sodas for Elizabeth Short. Lander then casually dropped a bomb. "She used to hang around with the kids at the soda fountain. They used to call her the Black Dahlia—on account of the way she wore her hair."

Lander explained that Short's penchant for wearing her jet-black hair high made it look like a dahlia flower. With *The Blue Dahlia* movie playing just around the corner, the wordplay nickname was created. Smith recalled the jolt of electricity running through his body. "The Black Dahlia. It was a rewrite man's dream. The fates were sparing of such gifts. I couldn't wait to get it into type." On January 17, the *Daily News* was first to name the case "The Black Dahlia," launching Elizabeth Short into the national limelight.

The Black Dahlia slaying sent shockwaves of terror across the city. A "werewolf maniac" was loose and capable of repeating the horrors inflicted upon Elizabeth Short anywhere, anytime. Police Chief Clemence Horrall and the LAPD brass were under intense pressure to solve the case, with Mayor Fletcher Bowron demanding constant updates on their progress. Homicide Bureau chief Captain Jack Donohoe initially assigned ten detectives to the case, then twenty, then fifty, then a hundred.

In the first seventy-two hours, lead detectives Finis Brown and Harry Hansen did not sleep, go home, or change clothes. Officers visited every residence and business within a miles-long box surrounding the Norton Avenue body disposal site. While Captain Donohoe marshaled more bodies to the case, Chief Horrall issued an all-points bulletin ordering "all persons arrested on misdemeanor charges such as vagrancy, prostitution, offering, soliciting and resorting" to be photographed and investigated.

Within forty-eight hours, the Black Dahlia murder had become a citywide emergency. The reputations and fate of Donohoe, Horrall, the LAPD, and the mayor himself were on the line.

Lynn Martin was running on fumes. She had spent the last month living off and on with forty-five-year-old engineer-turned-con-artist Duke Wellington in various motel rooms, her money spent and work hard to come by. The latest flophouse was the Sun Motel on Sunset Boulevard's gritty east end. Duke had disappeared yet again, and Lynn couldn't cover another night's room charge. He had surprised her with a beautiful, white-tipped silver fox fur coat for Christmas, but she couldn't bring herself to pawn the one nice thing she now owned.

Having lost sleep from worry, she begged the hotel manager to let her crash in one of the rooms for a few hours, then she'd be on her way. He granted her a room for the afternoon, but as he walked by later he heard Lynn sobbing inside. The next day, she strode into the fabulously appointed Darrin of Paris luxury-car design offices on the Sunset Strip in her striking fox fur coat, her girlfriend Bobby at her side. Though Howard Darrin had once tried to rape her and cut her with a knife, Lynn was desperate for help. She didn't stay long at the car design showroom and was soon spotted getting into a cab on the other side of the Sunset Strip. Lynn Martin had no idea hundreds of police officers were looking for her.

Newspaper sales skyrocketed as each day's multiple editions kept Los Angeles on a knife's edge of fast-moving developments. The mystery man named Red with whom Elizabeth Short had left

San Diego became the target of a nationwide manhunt. Every paper at every newsstand around the country featured front page photos and large-font headlines blaring news of the Black Dahlia and the unidentified last man with whom she was seen.

Robert "Red" Manley was checking into a San Francisco motel with colleague Harry Palmer on Friday evening, January 17, when he picked up a newspaper. "Elizabeth Short's picture was splashed across the front page. Before I read much of the story, I turned sick inside." Sick as he was, Manley went about his business trip, avoiding any contact with the police. But the LAPD was one step ahead of Manley. Forest Faith, an autoworker who lived across the street from the Frenches in San Diego, remembered a portion of Manley's license plate from when he'd left with Elizabeth Short on January 7.

On Sunday night January 19, Manley drove back to Los Angeles with Harry Palmer, turned the car into Palmer's driveway, and was swarmed by police officers. As he was patted down, Red proclaimed, "Listen, I knew Elizabeth Short."

Phoebe Short was on the tarmac at Los Angeles Municipal Airport for only forty-five minutes before catching a connecting United Airlines flight to the Bay Area, where she reunited with daughter Virginia and her husband, Adrian West. The trio flew to Los Angeles as a united front to face the horrors to come. The first and worse of it all would be the identification of the body. Phoebe pleaded with officers, "I just can't do it. It would be too much for me to do. You can't expect me, her mother, to look at her now." Virginia fought back tears as Adrian tried to comfort her, flashbulbs popping all around.

Phoebe's resistance was futile. Detectives accompanied the Shorts to the coroner's office, but when they arrived, press photographers crowded around to record the moment the mother would lay eyes on her mutilated daughter's body. The Short family walked out in disgust, refusing to cooperate. Later that night, Sergeant Finis

Brown led them through a back door to the morgue, where Phoebe positively identified the body. After that, she became an ice block.

At the coroner's inquest, Phoebe took the witness stand and "without a trace of emotion" confirmed her identification of Elizabeth's body. But when asked when she had "first noticed her daughter died," Phoebe's eyes tightened. She rose from her chair and exclaimed in defiance, "She was murdered!" The police probed the family for information, but neither Phoebe nor her daughter Virginia nor her husband Adrian, who had never even met Elizabeth, could provide any known acquaintances of Beth's in Los Angeles. Her time in the city had been a black void to them.

LA Examiner city editor Jimmy Richardson sent reporters to scour San Diego. They quickly hit pay dirt: a detailed description of Elizabeth Short's luggage, which could yield valuable clues. Richardson made LAPD Captain Jack Donohoe an offer he couldn't refuse— the detailed description of the luggage in exchange for access to it once it was located. Two *Examiner* reporters and an LAPD detective began a painstaking search of bus depots across Los Angeles. Hours later they, arrived at the downtown Greyhound terminal and rummaged through storage until they found their prize.

Back at LAPD headquarters, *Examiner* reporters watched as police fingerprint expert George Wheeler and Lieutenant William Cummings delicately opened the two suitcases. Inside were the immaculate clothes that had made Elizabeth Short so noticed around Hollywood: the pink sweater, the baby blue sweater, the A-line wrap dress. Beneath the clothes lay a treasure trove of letters and photographs with servicemen and assorted dates over the years. Suddenly, Short's personal story came to life. But none of the men identified from the contents of the luggage emerged as viable suspects.

Short's wardrobe trunk was quickly discovered in a search of downtown's Union Station Railway Express office. A photo album inside the trunk stacked with two hundred photos of friends and romantic interests also failed to deliver on any suspected actors in the drama of Short's January 9 disappearance.

Elvera French told the police Beth had mentioned a friend in Los Angeles named Anne Todd, also the name of a movie star of the era. Investigators reached out to question the bewildered actress, but she denied ever meeting Elizabeth Short. Reading the papers, Anne Toth recognized the mistake French had made with her last name. She soon arrived at Room 42 in City Hall's Homicide Division offices with Mark Hansen in tow. Both divulged extensive information about Elizabeth Short's last months, filling in gaps detectives had been pondering.

When asked by loitering members of the press who he was, Mark grumbled he was only Anne Toth's chauffeur and refused to give his name. But Anne had a statement to make. While nearly every other friend and acquaintance of Beth either avoided speaking to the press or spoke of her disparagingly, Anne came to her defense. "We used to think the world of that kid. She was always well behaved and sweet when I knew her." Mark Hansen could breathe a sigh of relief. He had successfully kept his name out of the newspapers, especially important while he courted Las Vegas impresario Barney Vandersteen for an investment in the Florentine Gardens nightclub.

With his wife out of town, Bill Cochrane, a.k.a. Duke Wellington, reentered Lynn Martin's life. The pair checked into the M&M Motel on Ventura Boulevard in San Fernando Valley's Studio City. The oft-burglarized, tiny auto court provided three-hundred-square-foot units for eighteen dollars a week and plenty of anonymity, which Lynn would soon appreciate. While she was walking on Hollywood Boulevard, a stunned friend handed her a newspaper and muttered, "They're looking for you." It was the first Lynn had heard of Elizabeth Short's murder and the citywide search for the mysterious roommate named Lynn Martin.

Terrified of the notoriety, Lynn jumped in a cab back to the M&M, where Wellington greeted her with a copy of the same newspaper. He urged her to turn herself in. Four days later, Lynn still hadn't contacted the police and Duke was panicking. On the morning of January 21, Lynn awoke to find Wellington gone, leaving only a letter begging her to turn herself in. He added that he loved her and would be in touch. Hours later, motel manager Eleanor Baumbaugh led police officers to Lynn Martin's unit. Her time on the run was over.

A six-hour interrogation yielded little information from Lynn, until she suddenly cried out "I didn't think I could get away with it" and broke down in tears to divulge everything she knew. Detectives asked repeatedly what she meant by stating that she didn't think she could away with it, but Lynn would not explain. As her personal story unfolded, investigators began to suspect she wasn't twenty-two years old. The questioning was halted when Lynn admitted her real age was fifteen. Juvenile authorities were called in, a new suit was purchased for her, and the press jockeyed for position to get photos of the mysterious new entrant into the Black Dahlia saga.

Lynn's age sent shockwaves through Hollywood as former boyfriends and victimizers scurried into the shadows. Detectives announced at least ten men could be prosecuted for sexual relations with the minor, including some "prominent Hollywood personalities" whom the press shielded from naming. Newspapers had a field day with Lynn Martin and her sordid Hollywood story "in the backwash of Hollywood." The *Daily News*'s lurid headline VIVID WOMEN promised juicy details about the beautiful, broken girls on the fringes of the glamourous film colony who were willing to do anything for a role or a meal.

Red Manley was interrogated, strapped to a lie detector, and raked over the coals. He came up clean, with friends and wife Harriet confirming Red was playing cards on the evening of January 14 at the home of Don Holmes in Huntington Park. With flashbulbs popping, Red walked out of police headquarters, passionately kissing Harriet. His father also at his side, Manley addressed the assembled reporters. He had been facing a crisis in his marriage at the time he met Elizabeth Short. He had only used her to clarify his marital commitment. "I thought I'd make a little test to see if I still loved my wife." He admitted only to kissing Short and declared he was a changed man. Harriet held him tight.

With lead suspect Red Manley now eliminated, Police Chief Horrall poured every remaining resource into the case. Captain Donohoe drew a large circle around downtown LA, with the Biltmore Hotel at its dead center, and ordered officers to investigate every bar, nightclub, hotel, motel, theater, and lounge, spreading out all the way to the harbor twenty miles away.

Farther north, fifty detectives were assigned to question workers at every bar, restaurant, and café in Hollywood. The use of a butcher knife in the murder led to a citywide investigation of all butchers, slaughterhouses, and meat markets. All medical supply stores, knife stores, and barber supply companies were checked for suspicious customers. Every mortuary in the city was investigated, employees at every laundry facility questioned about bloody clothing.

By January 22, the entire homicide squad was assigned solely to the Elizabeth Short case, along with seven hundred police officers, sheriff's deputies, and state highway patrol officers. Police phone lines were flooded with tips and sightings, though none could ever be verified. Having grown into the largest investigation in city history, unparalleled resources were committed in a desperate drive to solve the case at any cost. And yet no suspects, no real leads emerged.

A thirty-year career officer who always stayed cool and kept his cards close, Homicide Bureau chief Captain Donohoe felt the squeeze, and his frustrations bubbled up to the press. "It is unbelievable how a person could be swallowed up by the city like the Short girl was during the week before her murder. If we can find anyone who can give us definite information placing the girl in the city after she arrives here January 9, we may be able to establish her whereabouts prior to the slaying." Increasingly, investigators came to believe Elizabeth had been held captive during the "Missing Week," likely drugged and bound. "The fact that the murdered girl failed to claim her clothes, which were checked for five days prior to her death at the Greyhound bus depot package room, pointed out the captive theory. She had only the clothes she was wearing when she arrived in Los Angeles on January 9 from San Diego and would conceivably have picked up the luggage had she not been prevented, it was believed."

Exasperated, sleepless, and under a threatening level of pressure, the investigators could not solve the twin mysteries of Short's three-day disappearance before she left for San Diego on December 9 and her six-day disappearance after returning from San Diego on January 9. With the public's faith fading fast and its frustration rising just as quickly, newspapers blared the desperation spreading across the LAPD: Clues in Black Dahlia Case Fade to Zero, Police Run Into Blank Wall.

"We're right back where we started. We've got nothing," publicly bemoaned lead detective Harry Hansen. The killer surely would have rested easy knowing the chances of an arrest were vanishing. But then, on January 23, Captain Donohoe announced a new theory in the case, which the police believed would turn the whole investigation on its head. "Some of the evidence points to a woman killer—a brittle, masculine type, who killed for revenge or sadistic pleasure, and who now, knowing the bewilderment of police officers, is trying to prove her superiority to men."

Evidence of a female killer was listed: The victim's eyebrows were bleached white, which only a woman would know how to do;

the victim's hair was hennaed black, which only a woman would know how to do; scores of cuts had been made where a woman "would be expected to inflict them"; the victim was tied up and bound because a woman would lack the physical strength to hold the victim down while inflicting torture; and the body was cut in half because a woman wouldn't be able to carry a 120-pound body.

Despite the press's enthusiasm for the new direction in the case, the evidence was glaringly weak. Elizabeth Short's eyebrows were not bleached, and hairdresser Alex Constance had been established as the person who had hennaed her hair. With the victim detained by the killer for over five days, surely a man would have restrained her as much as a woman would have. History provided ample precedent of female murderers with the physical strength to dispose of a fully intact human body.

The investigative pivot to a woman killer was born not of real evidence but of desperation. Or it may have been concocted as a trap. The killer had displayed a shocking hatred for women. Placing responsibility for the high-profile murder on a woman would challenge a male killer's ego and possibly lure him into a public response. If a psychological ploy was behind the LAPD's much publicized new profile of the slayer, the plan worked. But not in the way they intended.

CHAPTER 14

THE CITY DOESN'T PAY FOR GENIUSES. IT PAYS FOR DETECTIVES.

On January 24, the day after the "female slayer" angle was announced in the press, the killer emerged, delivering two bombshells onto the Black Dahlia murder investigation. One was an expertly devised and calculated move, the other a glaring amateur mistake.

Wilfred Barlow's Wilbar Café was a nondescript diner on an unremarkable stretch of Crenshaw Boulevard, a straight 2.7-mile shot north of the Norton Avenue body disposal site. Restaurant manager Robert Hyman had just arrived for work through a narrow alley to the back of the diner when he noticed a high-heeled black suede shoe and a plastic purse with two handles sticking out the top of an open trash can. Neither had been there late the night before. With a citywide emergency calling on all citizens to report anything suspicious, Hyman contacted the police.

By the time he got back to the trash can, it was being emptied into an LA By-Products trash truck. Hyman pleaded to save the suspicious items, but the trash collector only brushed him off—"We

find lots of things like this, and they never amount to anything"—
and drove away. Jess Haskins of LAPD's University Division sent
scores of detectives to the By-Products company trash yard, where
all work was halted so employees could load recently arrived refuse
onto a conveyer belt for viewing. Detectives sifted for hours until
the fateful items were discovered.

Red Manley was summoned and immediately recognized the
shoe with double heel taps affixed to the bottom. He had paid for
those taps in San Diego. The perfume smell inside the purse was
unmistakable. Manley was certain these were Elizabeth Short's
possessions.

Having walked down the Wilbar Café's sixty-foot alley on private property with a purse and a woman's shoe in the early morning
hours, the killer had taken an enormous risk. The building even
had a private-residence bedroom in the back where a man named
Charles Thompson lived. He could have easily spotted a stranger
rummaging in the trash just feet away.

Much like the sighting of the Norton Avenue body disposal by
neighbor Bob Myers, the killer had risked exposure with a clumsy
public appearance. But the bigger mistake was simply placing the
telltale possessions atop the trash can, sticking out for anyone to see.
These were not the actions of an experienced, calculated criminal.

Later that day, at 3:00 P.M., the killer was on the move again,
arriving at the Metropolitan Post Office at 719 Spring Street in
downtown Los Angeles, five miles directly east of the Wilbar Café,
five blocks from the Biltmore Hotel, and three blocks from the Greyhound bus terminal. He slipped a package into a mailbox, which
was sorted in the next two hours. At 5:00 P.M., the central mail
receiving office took possession of the envelope. Handlers paused at
the unusual item, which had opened at one end and reeked of gasoline. But most striking was the address and message on the outside
of the home-crafted envelope.

At 5:30 P.M., Chief Postal Inspector Judge Wood called the police and then called the five major LA newspapers with news that an alarmingly important package had arrived addressed to them. After nine days of a relentless thousand-officer search across the city, representatives of the press, Captain Donohoe, Lieutenant William Cummings, Postal Inspectors Wood and Green, and fingerprint expert Sergeant George Wheeler met the killer's response. On the outside of the cut, folded, and glued homemade envelope was a "crazy-quilt" message made of letters and words scissored out of recent newspaper.

> Los Angeles Examiner and OTHER Los Angeles PAPERS
> HERE! is 'Dahlia's' BeLONGingS
> LETTER TO FOLLOW

From the opened side of the envelope slid out a collection of contents from Elizabeth Short's purse: her social security card, an emergency contact card, assorted business cards she had collected, a Western Telegram message from Railway Express in Chicago regarding her lost trunk, the claim tickets from Greyhound, various snapshots of Beth and servicemen, and other assorted personal effects.

The star attraction was Short's address book, emblazoned on its cover 1937 MARK M HANSEN. Inside were the names of between fifty and seventy contacts Elizabeth had written into the book since early October 1946. Having once been filled with four hundred pages, it had since been reduced, with large intermittent sections missing. In some places, 2 pages were missing, in others, 125 pages were missing. The larger chunks were cut out with a knife or scissors, while the shorter sections were torn out by hand. The names and contact information Short had written were not alphabetized or added in any order. People she met earlier in her journey appeared throughout the book interspersed with the names of people she met later in her journey. Poring over the four-inch treasure, Donohoe was astonished at the roadmap the killer had provided.

The presence of gasoline was quickly recognized by Ray Pinker as a method to dissolve the minute traces of oil that form fingerprints. Pinker was impressed—relatively few people were aware of this method of destroying prints. The gasoline had only been applied to the outside of the envelope. All contents found inside were searched for fingerprints, though only smudges were found.

Even with the ingenious use of gasoline, the killer made amateur mistakes, betraying any professionalism or brilliance. The killer had walked into a busy public post office with an envelope reeking of gasoline. Any passerby could have been alerted to the smell and remembered the face of the person depositing the envelope in the mailbox. The gasoline had worked to unseal the end of the envelope, potentially spilling its precious contents in transit, and it could have then been discarded by a post office clerk.

The greatest mistake was made with the crazy-quilt letters. Pinker knew that the gasoline as well as the hands of mail sorters at the post office would have destroyed any fingerprints on the envelope. However, the back of the cut-out letters as well as the sticky underside of the Scotch tape used to affix them to the envelope would have picked up minute traces of the killer's sweat, dirt, prints, or other evidence. Starting with the large cut-out word "'Dahlia's'," crime lab chemists found one partial latent fingerprint, which was sent to the FBI on January 25. On February 6, J. Edgar Hoover responded to LA Police Chief Clemence Horrall, stating, "The latent fingerprint appearing in the photograph was searched through this Bureau's single fingerprint file, which contains the finger impressions of a number of individuals known to specialize in certain types of crimes, but no identification was effected."

The newspaper from which the word "'Dahlia's'," was cut was the January 20 Sunset edition of the *Evening Herald-Express*. The paper was four days old, suggesting the killer had been reading and saving newspapers related to the Black Dahlia slaying.

Within an hour of the discovery of the address book, LAPD officials went into a closed, two-hour emergency meeting as every cop and every detective assigned to the case was called back to work regardless of whether their shift had ended or they were on break. When the meeting ended, assignments were handed out to locate and thoroughly investigate every name found in the address book. Anyone without a rock-solid alibi would be brought back for thorough questioning. All assets and resources would be made available.

"This new material has given us so many leads we don't know where to begin," enthused Lead Detective Finis Brown.

"This is the big push," Captain Donohoe announced. "Our men are fanning out now to bring in the killer. We will bring in all sorts of people for questioning and eliminate them so long as they can eliminate themselves." Forty more bodies were added to the army of investigators blanketing the city for the big push.

Mark Hansen's plan to remain out of the public eye collapsed as his name took center stage on the cover of the address book. It couldn't have come at a worse time, with the Florentine Gardens in desperate need of more investment. Hounded by the press, Hansen twisted the truth to protect his reputation, creating myths about Elizabeth Short that would take hold and persist to the modern day. "Several girls rented rooms here at the house. But I never went out with them. She had lots of dates. There was a language teacher that I know of, and with other persons, mostly hoodlums whom I wouldn't even let in my house."

Risking her relationship with Mark and his home, Anne corrected him on the spot, denying Beth dated hoodlums. "She was a nice girl. She was quiet, she didn't drink and she didn't smoke and we ought to look on the good side of people."

Scrambling to avoid suspicion, Hansen twisted his story to the police and the press, directly contradicting earlier statements. When asked about Beth's phone call to him from San Diego on January 7, he claimed that she had asked to stay with him for several days and that he replied no, not until Anne came back. This directly contradicted what he anxiously told Anne when she returned to his home on January 10—that Beth had asked him for money, not to stay with him.

On January 26 at 5:30 P.M., the killer arrived at the Post Office Terminal Annex, the city's enormous central mail-processing center, and slipped a penny postcard into the mail. As it was being postmarked an hour later, mail handlers recognized its significance and contacted the police. This time, the message was not written in crazy-quilt cut-out newsprint. It was written by a pen. The postcard was addressed to LA EXAMINER 1111 S. BROADWAY. The message on the reverse side read, "HERE iT iS TURNiNG iN WED JAN. 29 10 A.M. HAD My FUN AT POLiCE." It was signed "Black Dahlia Avenger."

Shockwaves ran through the department upon word the slayer was voluntarily giving up. Caution was dictated, but the glimmer of hope felt like a Hollywood klieg light in an otherwise dark two weeks. Oddly, the killer had dug the pen into the card stock when writing the address line. The impression had imbedded so deeply that the letters of the address could be read in reverse on the card's opposite side. Even stranger, the pebbled effect of the ink suggested the use of a ballpoint pen, a rarity in 1947.

Detectives wondered if the use of a pen implied the killer was now more willing to reveal his identity. With hundreds of investigators out pursuing the names found in the address book, Donohoe and his officers awaited the Wednesday 10:00 A.M. deadline. The moment arrived . . . and passed. A follow-up crazy-quilt letter appeared soon after addressed to Captain Donohoe: "Have changed my mind. you would not give me a square deal. Dahlia killing was Justified."

Though no fingerprints were found, the killer had once again made a mistake using Scotch tape to affix the letters, with several dark hairs found underneath. A slew of other bizarre, taunting messages would arrive through the month of February, though only the original three could be scientifically linked and therefore attributed to the killer. No further message was ever sent.

After five days, Donohoe somberly announced that the long list of names found in the packet sent in by the killer had yielded no suspects or promising leads. But behind the scenes, detectives had located a suspect who had unraveled a central mystery in the case. One of the names discovered in the killer's packet wasn't written in the address book and didn't appear on a business card. It was written on a loose piece of notebook paper. When detectives found and questioned him, he admitted to picking Elizabeth Short up the morning of December 6, 1946. The mystery of the missing three days preceding Short's inexplicable escape to San Diego had suddenly been solved.

His name was Carl Balsiger.

Lead detective Finis Brown took charge of the Balsiger probe. The story began at a real estate office on Sunset Boulevard, where Carl claimed to have met Elizabeth Short the morning of December 6. He had business that day in Camarillo, a small town fifty miles west of Los Angeles in the vast, rich agricultural breadbasket of Ventura County. Short tagged along with him for the long car ride to Camarillo, where he made a sale of baking supplies to a local baker. He claimed to have also been a salesman for Marwyn Dairy Products, selling flour and syrup to various businesses around Southern California.

On the evening of December 6, Balsiger returned to Los Angeles with Short and a business associate named Walter Thacher, whom he first dropped off in Reseda in the San Fernando Valley. Balsiger then checked Short into a hotel on Yucca Street in the heart of Hollywood, where he signed his name in the register. The next day, December 7, he drove her to the Hollywood Greyhound bus station, as she claimed to be traveling to San Francisco to visit her sister. He insisted he never slept with her, that he just felt sorry for her.

Detective Brown recognized holes in the story. Short had taken a bus late the night of December 8, not December 7. Thirty-six hours were missing from Balsiger's story. Brown sent detectives to visit every motel and hotel on Yucca Street, none of which had any record or recollection of either Balsiger or Short. With Yucca Street only a block from the Chancellor Apartments and so close to Mark Hansen's house, it made no sense Short would be staying there for any length of time without contacting anyone.

Balsiger had claimed he met Short the morning of December 6 in a real estate office, but Brown knew she had disappeared that morning from her room at the Chancellor and returned with cash to pay her overdue rent, then stated to roommate Linda Rohr, "I've got to hurry he's waiting for me." What would she have been doing in a real estate office when she was in a rush to meet someone and had repeatedly stated her intention to leave Los Angeles? Short had not a dime to her name after paying the rent and was in no position to buy or rent a home or apartment from a real estate office.

Brown ordered an investigation into Balsiger's past. What the LAPD uncovered was unnerving. Balsiger had been stationed at Camp Cooke at the same time as Elizabeth Short in early 1943, during the war. An officer in the Army Quartermaster Corps, which was responsible for supplies and the feeding of soldiers, Balsiger would have been familiar with the PXs at the base where Elizabeth Short worked selling supplies and food.

Brown was next handed a report in which "it was established this suspect had on two occasions given different women vicious beatings apparently for no good reason." The unfortunate wording, "for no good reason," indicated that Balsiger had simply snapped when violently attacking the women, with nothing causing or leading up to the attacks. But the next item from Balsiger's background report set alarms ringing. "A young twenty-two-year-old woman by the name of Dorothy Welsh with whom he had attended a school in Kansas City was murdered in that city in 1941 in a similar manner as victim Short. The brother Claude Welsh had been tried for this murder and acquitted."

The LAPD possessed some institutional memory of the then-famous Kansas City murder of Leila Welsh, when in 1944 Kansas City Police Lieutenant Charles Welch had contacted the LAPD about the murder of Elizabeth Georgia Castaneda in a downtown Los Angeles hotel room. A nationwide manhunt had ensued for her suspected killer, Steven Josef Vernon, a.k.a. Alvin Arnsen. The Kansas City Police Department's interest was piqued by Vernon's use of a broken wine bottle to slash and slay Castaneda. They wanted to question him about his whereabouts in March of 1941, when Leila Welsh was slain. Lieutenant Welch requested a sit-down with Vernon if and when the LAPD ultimately brought him into custody.

Though Vernon was cleared of any connection to the Welsh murder, the KCPD had provided LAPD detectives with a description of the unusually gruesome Welsh slaying, which had left an impression. When Balsiger's background report revealed a connection to Leila Welsh, the similarities of her murder to that of Elizabeth Short became evident. But details of the 1941 slaying were lacking at the LAPD, and even the victim's name was incorrectly referred to as Dorothy Welsh, as well as her brother George's name as Claude.

Brown reached out to the Kansas City Police Department to request all information pertaining to Carl Balsiger, George Welsh, and the Leila Welsh murder case. At that very moment a major transition was occurring at the KCPD. Police Chief Harold Anderson, who had served under Police Chief Lear Reed during the Welsh investigation, was stepping down from the top post, representing a dramatic changing of the guard from the 1930s Gangster War generation of cops to the World War II generation that was modernizing the department as rapidly as the city itself.

New Police Chief Henry Johnson had been elevated from his position as superintendent of the Traffic and Safety Division. Singularly focused on improving Kansas City's traffic woes, he was unimpressed with a six-year-old murder case that had been botched by the police and the sheriff's department. Despite the LAPD's fervor to reexamine the embarrassing Welsh investigation, Johnson was looking to the future, not the past. Finis Brown was told the KCPD would send on what they had. But the documents never arrived.

Chief Johnson may have had another reason to withhold the crucial police reports from the LAPD. Carl Balsiger and his family were no strangers to the veteran police official. He and then–Police Chief Lear Reed had both sat on the Kansas City Chamber of Commerce Fire and Police Committee with Carl's father, Herman Balsiger, in 1940 and 1941, when the Leila Welsh murder and investigation occurred. Herman's longstanding relationship with the KCPD had made him an important, respected, and somewhat feared member of the business community, with influence in city government. Certainly, Johnson's cooperation in the LAPD's ongoing investigation into Carl Balsiger would not be looked upon kindly.

Brown could never establish whether Carl Balsiger had attended the University of Kansas City at the same time as Leila Welsh, much less whether he had ever met or knew of her, putting the theory connecting the Welsh and Short murders at a disadvantage. Further investigation into Balsiger located his one-room residence in a small apartment building at the corner of Sunset Boulevard and Gardner Street, between Hollywood and the

Sunset Strip. It was likely impossible a woman could have been held captive for six days and then brutally slain in such a small and public space.

Brown had hundreds of other names to investigate. He moved on from Balsiger, though suspicions would persistently gnaw at him and grow over time. Balsiger would remain in the LAPD's concealed crosshairs.

With the quick exhaustion of the address book's treasure trove of potential suspects, desperation was seeping through every corner of the investigation and dripping out into the press. More than 400 sheriff's deputies, 700 police officers, and 250 state officers had been assigned to the case. And yet, with 316 suspects, 50 arrests, and over 2,200 case documents filed by Homicide, no solid leads had turned up.

In a stunning admission, Captain Donohoe publicly stated, "All I know about the case I read in the newspapers." In its vigorous but scattershot effort, the LAPD expended enormous resources investigating dead-end clues. CBS Studios usher Jack Egger, who had witnessed Elizabeth Short attend radio shows throughout the fall of 1946, was certain she was at CBS the night of January 8, 1947, accompanied by a gray-haired Chicago police officer who had flashed his badge for identification. Despite the much-verified fact that Short had been at the Mecca Motor Lodge in San Diego that night, the LAPD acquired a long list of active and retired Chicago police officers present in Southern California that week and thoroughly investigated all of them, costing thousands of hours of precious labor and predictably yielding nothing.

Surgeons across the city were investigated, then suddenly "abortionists," then a pivot to embalmers, then morticians, chiropractors, butchers. The press zealously reported every frantic new twist to a terrified public anxious for any developments in the capture of the monster. With newspaper sales at unprecedented levels, the Black

Dahlia dominated headlines for three weeks, longer even than the attack on Pearl Harbor.

With hopes dampening, the narrative changed from finding the mad slayer to blame. Captain Donohoe sidestepped any fault on the part of the LAPD, bemoaning a chronic lack of staffing. With three thousand hours of overtime clocked by twenty-five homicide detectives alone, Donohoe stated, "Sleep is an unknown luxury in this department." His men were overworked, under-resourced, tired, and beaten up by the press and city officials. "This isn't any bunch of geniuses down here, you know," Donohoe said with a hearty laugh. "The city doesn't pay for geniuses. It pays for detectives."

The press avoided placing blame on the LAPD. Instead, it blamed the victim herself, with exaggerations and outright lies that persist to this day. Newspapers around the country painted Elizabeth Short as a cautionary tale, her murder laying bare the seedy underbelly of Tinseltown's gilded image, where young girls arrived in hopes of finding the Hollywood dream only to discover a nightmare. For a nation coming out of its own nightmare in World War II, the story of the ultimate unsolved Hollywood murder took on its own dimensions.

Jack Kofoed of the *Miami Herald* wrote, "Sometimes it seems girls deliberately stick out their chins and ask for it. It's pretty sure the Black Dahlia asked for it a lot of times. She finally got it, but good." The *St. Louis Globe-Democrat* opined, "Such a girl was 'The Black Dahlia' in 1946—a trapped, haunted, desperate girl who had blackened her record, aroused distrust in the men she sought, and proved herself unwanted anywhere." Scurrilous lies were fabricated to portray Elizabeth as a dangerous sexpot implicated in the fate that befell her. The *Los Angeles Herald-Express* concluded, "Romances had changed her, according to friends, from an innocent girl to a man crazy delinquent known as the Black Dahlia."

Jack Webb of *Dragnet* fame implied she was trading sex for money. "Two or three times, friends later remembered, she had hitched rides to the Sixth Street area when she was out of funds. After a day or so, she would reappear, mysteriously replenished. Where she got the money never was known." Webb blamed her for not working. "She was a lazy girl and irresponsible," and he blamed her for the many years she did work. "She ushered in theaters, she slung plates as a waitress. It was the kind of work where a girl too young and attractive would meet too many men."

Mark Hansen vocalized his own insults. "She's a little tramp. I didn't want her there, and I told her to leave." Famed mystery novelist Craig Rice, who had appeared on the cover of *Time* magazine, portrayed Elizabeth Short as an exotic flower that could only grow in darkness. "A black dahlia is what expert gardeners call 'an impossibility' of nature. Perhaps that is why lovely, tragic Elizabeth Short was tortured, murdered and mutilated because such a crime could happen only in the half-world in which she lived. A world of—shadows."

Elizabeth was painted as cheap and broken, the papers repeating ad nauseum that she used candlewax to fill holes in her teeth, never considering that during the Depression working-class Medford residents couldn't afford dental care. She was painted as sexually voracious, despite the fact that the police could only confirm three intimate partners across her entire life. Repeated endlessly was the myth she dated a new man every night of the week, when in fact she spent most nights alone, attending radio shows at CBS and NBC or movies at the Pantages Theatre.

She was accused of fabricating her engagement to World War II pilot Matt Gordon, when Matt's own letters verified he had asked her to marry him and had bought an engagement ring. She was labeled a desperate wannabe actress, even though she had never auditioned for or sought out any acting roles. She was called aimless, a drifter, and homeless, though she had exemplified the new freedoms of women in postwar America. In 1967, Short would have been considered a free spirit, traveling the country in search of herself. But in 1947, she was just a two-bit chiseler who refused to settle down and only "gave men a hard time."

The lone figure who pushed back against the new narrative was Anne Toth, who steadfastly asserted Beth didn't sleep around, never stayed out late, never drank, never smoked, never made a pass at any other girl's boyfriend. After Bill Robinson hit on Beth, slapped her, and threw her out of his car, Anne stated, "I don't think anyone else tried anything." Anne proclaimed, "Betty was a nice girl. It was just a coincidence she met up with some lousy man who got nasty. The girl wanted to have a clean life—but there are a lot of men who happen to be bums at heart." Anne, in turn, blamed the press for the disturbing new narrative, "making us all out [to be] a bunch of bums looking for trouble."

The tidal wave of cautionary tales allowed ordinary citizens comfort in a rapidly changing and dangerous world. The message was crystal clear: they would not fall prey to a monster if they led a virtuous, respectable life, unlike the reckless and sexually charged Elizabeth Short. On February 10, the narrative swung wildly again when forty-four-year-old former pilot and nurse Jeanne French was found brutally stomped to death in a barren patch of West LA real estate known as "the Moors." On her horribly bruised body a message was written in red lipstick: "Fuck you, B.D." Had the killer of the Black Dahlia struck again?

A series of shocking murders soon swept the city, each one bringing a new wave of terror. An already overstretched Homicide Department failed to find the culprits, leading to an all-out assault on the LAPD that culminated in two successive district attorney investigations and grand juries in 1949 and 1950. Ultimately, the LAPD was absolved of any corruption in the investigations: "The LAPD records and reports indicate some stupidity and carelessness on the part of some of the more inexperienced officers who were working on the case from time to time, but as of this report dated October 29, 1949, there has not been found any indication of payoff, misconduct or concealment of facts on the part of any officers."

LA City Councilman Lloyd Davies demanded five hundred additional officers be hired immediately. The first sex offender registry was proposed. But most impactful was the stunning 1950 election of William H. Parker to chief of police over shoe-in candidate and Chief of Detectives Thad Brown, brother of Finis. A reform candidate, Parker was unthinkable as chief of an entrenched, divided, and territorial police department. With an enraged public clamoring for change, Parker's moment arrived, and his sweeping transformation of the LAPD into a militarized, organized, and aggressive enforcement machine forever changed the city.

Chief Horrall and his successor, William Worton, were swept away, as were many of the old-guard officers who had supplemented their meagre incomes over the years with bribes and payoffs. Behind the scenes, a handful of detectives led by Finis Brown continued to work the Black Dahlia investigation, determined to break the case haunting the LAPD. Suspicious characters were reinterviewed, overlooked leads were chased down, evidence reexamined. Nevertheless, time was running out under Chief Parker's impatient gaze. By 1950, investigators had narrowed the suspect list to a handful of names who could not be cleared.

At the top of the list reemerged Carl Balsiger.

CHAPTER 15

HOLLYWOOD BABYLON

On February 1, 1950, Robert "Red" Manley was questioned by investigators one more time at his home. In hopes of jarring his memory, they read out a series of names Elizabeth Short may have mentioned in his presence. Only three names from the LAPD suspect list were asked of Manley: Mark Hansen, Chancellor Hotel manager Glenn Wolfe, and Carl Balsiger.

Anne Toth, too, was called back for further testimony and was asked for the first time if Elizabeth Short had ever been picked up by someone in an Oldsmobile, the make of car that Carl Balsiger drove. While hundreds of suspects had been crossed off the list over the three years since the Black Dahlia murder, Balsiger had proven to be a Gordian knot of lies, half-truths, and shifting narratives.

Finis Brown and Frank Jemison of the district attorney's office reignited the investigation into Balsiger with a new theory tying him to Short much earlier than his self-admitted first encounter on December 6, 1946. In the early days of the Black Dahlia murder investigation, detectives had traveled to Camp Cooke in Santa Barbara County, 170 miles north of Los Angeles, where Short had been employed and Balsiger stationed in early 1943. Multiple officers and acquaintances of Short claimed she had dated a violent soldier named "Sergeant Chuck," who was infamous for having pulled out fistfuls of hair from the head of a man he beat up in a bar.

The story was consistent among the multiple witnesses: in a violent rage, Sergeant Chuck had threatened Elizabeth's life, causing her to complain to his commanding officer. Chuck was court-martialed and quickly sent overseas, leaving behind many of his belongings, some of which Short took into her possession. The LAPD made multiple trips to Camp Cooke throughout 1947 and 1948 to take witness statements but was unable to locate any evidence of the court-martial proceedings or the name of the mystery sergeant. And yet the multiple witnesses stood firm in their memory of the abusive boyfriend's court-martial.

The unidentified "Sergeant Chuck" had been named in every suspect list since the beginning of the Black Dahlia investigation. By 1950, district attorney investigators and the LAPD began to suspect that two of their top suspects were actually one and the same man. The DA's grand jury report stated, "It was further suspected that this suspect Balsiger had known Short at Camp Cooke and had been court-martialed and sent overseas as a result of testimony of Short, who then had laid claim to the personal effects and property of this suspect."

Indeed, shortly after Elizabeth's exit from Camp Cooke in early March 1943, Carl Balsiger was shipped overseas to the Southwest Pacific Area of Operations under the command of General Douglas MacArthur. The DA also took note of Balsiger's sudden and suspicious departure from Los Angeles soon after Elizabeth Short's murder, moving from job to job in various states. By mid-1950, suspicions about the similarities between the murders of Elizabeth Short and Leila Welsh had grown so strong that authorities began investigating George Welsh, whom they believed had been living in LA in January 1947.

Welsh had moved to Los Angeles in the fall of 1941 but returned to Kansas City in 1942 upon his arrest and subsequent trial. By 1947, he was firmly settled in Houston, Texas. Once again, George Welsh was wrongly placed at a setting and time that neatly fit the needs of a murder investigation but didn't fit the facts. The LA district attorney's suspect description read, "Claude Welsh, in 1941 was acquitted by Supreme Court jury of the murder of his sister, Dorothy, age twenty-two, in the city of Kansas City. Her body was cut by a sharp knife, a piece of flesh was cut from the cheek of her buttock and left on the ground near an open window of the victim's bedroom where the suspect had apparently made his escape. This suspect's fingerprint was in the room, but standing alone was not sufficient evidence for conviction. There is now information that he was in Hollywood at the time of the murder of victim Short, however, so far it is not established that he knew the victim. Kansas City police have failed to send complete information on this suspect as they had agreed to do. The investigation of this suspect is still pending." The Claude/George Welsh inquiry would eventually sputter out with no further proof he was in Los Angeles or had any connection to Elizabeth Short.

Finis Brown could not shake his suspicions about Carl Balsiger. He tracked down and located Balsiger in St. Louis, Missouri, 250 miles east of his hometown, Kansas City. Brown flew out to administer a lie detector test and confront Balsiger with the contradictions in his earlier questioning. When faced with the timeline of Elizabeth Short's movements from December 6 through December 8, 1946, Balsiger admitted he had lied to the police and had been with her for the full three days. However, he convinced Brown he was not the sergeant who was court-martialed at Camp Cooke in 1943 and had not seen Elizabeth Short after December 8.

Despite the lie detector results, whatever Brown encountered in the lengthy questioning of Balsiger failed to resolve his suspicions.

Months later, in the February 1951 district attorney's report, Carl Balsiger remained listed as the number one suspect, followed by Claude/George Welsh, followed then by the still-unidentified Sergeant Chuck. Finis Brown would continue to investigate the case for years to come on his own time and own dime, spending vacations and weekends looking into the few remaining suspects and unresolved evidence. None of it ever brought the killer closer to justice.

With Chief William H. Parker at the helm, the newly militarized LAPD shed its noir-era past through aggressive policing, much of it aimed at the city's rapidly growing minority populations. However, the war had released many genies from their bottles. And there was no putting them back. Nowhere was that more vividly illustrated than in Los Angeles, the postwar poster child for American lifestyle, values, and culture.

To much of the country, LA was the city of the future. But the slew of unsolved murder cases kicked off by the Black Dahlia threatened the sun-kissed utopian image Los Angeles sold to the country. By the mid-1950s, the Black Dahlia case remained a distant but open wound that most wanted to forget. For the occasional newspaper article, a reporter would reinterview some of the original players who were willing to speak, always ending the story with the regrettable choices Elizabeth Short had made in her life, which had somehow placed her in the killer's grasp. The myth of Beth's partial culpability in her own murder became an intrinsic part of Black Dahlia lore.

Abandoned by the press, the public, and the police, the case went ice cold. In 1974, interest in true crime exploded when former LA County DA prosecutor Vincent Bugliosi released the bestselling book *Helter Skelter* about the Manson Family murders. A year later, filmmaker Kenneth Anger reignited the public's fascination with Hollywood scandal when his groundbreaking, banned book *Hollywood Babylon* was released in the United States. The follow-up,

Hollywood Babylon II, published the first publicly seen crime-scene photos of the bisected body, springing the story of Elizabeth Short back into the limelight. The splashy 1975 television movie *Who Is the Black Dahlia?* cemented the case in the public imagination. The publication of true crime author John Gilmore's 1994 exposé *Severed: The True Story of the Black Dahlia* helped launch the Black Dahlia into internet infamy, where it remains one of the most visible and debated cold cases in history. Repeated endlessly is the irony that Elizabeth Short found the fame she sought in life only in her death. Much less mentioned is the fact that Beth Short never sought fame.

Though a minor, Lynn Martin was granted a handful of interviews with the press following her 1947 detention by LAPD youth services. With a maturity beyond her years, she described the life of her Hollywood contemporaries with much greater sympathy and understanding than the press would ever offer. "You're always lonely in Hollywood, even when you're out with people. They don't belong to you—those people. None of them really care what happens to you. Lots of times you can hardly stand the man you're with, but you can forget about that after a few drinks. Lots of times the girls talk to each other about getting out of Hollywood and starting all over again. They're going back home, or they're going to get married to someone. Down in the heart of all of them is sort of a hazy dream about a husband and a house and a baby."

Lynn's own dream was anything but hazy. She was singularly focused on finding her biological siblings. "If I could find them I'd have somebody who really belongs to me." After weeks in juvenile detention, Lynn was returned to the unstable home of Fred and Marion Meyer, where she reclaimed her name Norma Lee. Days later, Norma walked out and never returned. One of the only major players in the Black Dahlia saga to completely escape its notoriety, she disappeared from public view.

Several months after the murder of Elizabeth Short, Anne Toth moved out of Mark Hansen's home and into her own apartment down the street. The notoriety of the case adversely affected her acting career. Anne eventually moved to Reno, Nevada, where she married, divorced, and remained out of the public spotlight. Weeks before her death in 1991, a young writer from Hollywood found her and interviewed her for the last time. The interview elicited a flood of emotion. Shedding tears so many decades later, Anne remained loyal to the memory of Elizabeth Short and her character.

Mark Hansen would successfully receive two investments in the Florentine Gardens from Las Vegas hotel owner Barney Vandersteen, but they would not be enough to save the floundering club. He barely averted death in 1949 when he was shot by a disgruntled former taxi dancer and model named Lola Titus. Upon recovery, Mark moved back in with his wife, Ida, at her nearby home on Canyon Drive in Hollywood. Soon, however, he returned to the house on Carlos Avenue, much diminished from his once-powerful position atop the social strata of Hollywood nightlife.

Avoiding any interviews with the press, Mark Hansen would slowly sell off his theaters and real estate properties. Hansen remained in the Carlos Avenue house alone until suffering a heart attack and dying in 1964. Soon after the Florentine Garden's closing in 1948, master of ceremonies Nils Thor Granlund would depart for upstart Las Vegas, where he introduced the glittering, high-kicking showgirl revue to casinos and resorts and once again revolutionized the American stage show. Though he died in poverty in 1957, Granlund's contribution to twentieth-century live entertainment is nearly unparalleled.

Robert "Red" Manley separated from wife, Harriet, months after he was released from police custody in January 1947. He would continue to live and work in Huntington Park. By the early fifties, Manley suffered a series of nervous breakdowns and was committed for treatment at Patton State Hospital. In 1954, Detective Harry Hansen was contacted by doctors at the Veterans Administration in Los Angeles, who relayed that Manley had been confessing to the murder of Elizabeth Short. Though doctors believed he was either lying or had misled himself, sodium pentothal truth serum was administered to Manley in Hansen's presence, followed by a thorough requestioning of his role in the Elizabeth Short affair.

Red kept to the original story he told investigators years earlier, but Harry Hansen's well-honed instincts sensed something from his testimony was missing. Hansen was convinced Manley had not killed Short but was keeping some important piece of information from the police and the guilt was eating away at him. His mental health teetering, Manley was eventually found living in a trailer by an investigator seeking information for the 1975 television movie *Who Is the Black Dahlia?* Manley chatted with him for a bit but became enraged when asked about Elizabeth Short, eventually chasing the inquisitor out of the trailer with an axe. Manley passed away in 1986.

The Short family was devastated by Elizabeth's murder. For years, they continued to send LAPD homicide detectives any scrap of relevant information, any of Beth's letters they found, any names of past acquaintances in hopes something would help identify the killer. The family buried Elizabeth at Mountain View Cemetery in Oakland, California, near the home of sister Virginia West, the location she had told so many people she was headed to next.

In 1951, the district attorney concluded that nearly every piece of evidence in the case had eventually been made public through the press, save for one fact that had never been released and was kept from the public. In 1971, lead investigator Harry Hansen was interviewed by the *LA Times*, and he revealed that the Key Question asked of suspects and false confessors related to "the condition, appearance or attitude of Elizabeth Short's body at the time it was discovered." Hansen stated that this secret clue was known only to himself, the killer, and a handful "of carefully screened officers." He further stated the clue would not be publicly revealed until the case was closed, no matter how many years it took.

Retired in Palm Springs, the much celebrated and lauded Hansen would continue to speak over the years about the Black Dahlia, demeaning Beth's character while at the same time expressing his despondence over the lack of justice brought in her murder. In 1982, Hansen shared his thoughts on "the one case that got away," which continued to haunt him and his contemporaries. "It was his [the killer's] first and last killing. He never killed before and he hasn't killed since. The very MO has never had anything to compare with it. If it had, the killer might have tripped up and left a trail."

Hansen did not realize that the killer had, in fact, left a trail. The mistake was in trying to find that trail following the murder of Elizabeth Short. His partner, Finis Brown, had wisely found that the trail had started six years earlier in Kansas City. Hampered by the Kansas City Police Department's years-long refusal to send along the case documents, Brown was never able to fully investigate Carl Balsiger or the Leila Welsh murder. Had he been able to, he would have known just how close he had come to solving America's most famous cold case.

PART III
CARL BALSIGER

St. Louis Globe-Democrat, February 2, 1947: "In Los Angeles murder is nothing. There were 116 murders in this city last year—highest in the country. But every so often a murderer shows a delicacy of imagination or a surpassing brutishness that marks his crime as out of the ordinary. Such a one was the person who murdered Elizabeth Short. He—or she—was so imbued with his paroxysms of hate that he achieved the distinction of being termed, in one of the city's more garish newspapers, a 'werewolf.' But werewolf or no, the murderer was a sure-handed, vicious butcher."

—James Murray,
special correspondent for the
St. Louis Globe-Democrat

CHAPTER 16

BLUE BABY

Kansas City was crowded, chaotic, and sweltering in the summer of 1927. Just twenty miles away lay rolling hills and thick forests dotted with small lakes fed by the Kansas River, making for ideal balmy getaways. There was Lake Quivera for the rich, and for the masses there was jam-packed Winnwood Beach, with its amusement rides and Monkey Island attraction. But the hidden gem was Lake of the Forest, an oasis of solitude and peace for middle-class families.

Herman Balsiger was rapidly ascending the business ladder of Kansas City, having helped build Schulze Baking Company into a national brand. As a statement of wealth more than status, Balsiger had proudly purchased a rustic yet comfortable Craftsman-style cabin on the choicest property fronting Lake of the Forest. With the cabin's direct view of the community's stately stone and wood-beam clubhouse and its sandy beach, his wife, Ada, and three children—Anna Marie, Carl, and Helen Elizabeth—could escape the oppressive city heat each summer for the cool winds, swaying cottonwood trees, and inviting waters of their lake retreat.

Herman was often away for days at a time, but there was much to occupy the family: swimming at the beach, daily events at the clubhouse, tennis courts, a modest golf course, and a community of families. While twelve-year-old son Carl spent his days hunting, fishing, and exploring the burial sites of Wyandotte Indian chiefs, his seven-year-old sister, Helen Elizabeth, took swimming lessons at the beach near the clubhouse. By July 7, she was an accomplished swimmer, having spent two full weeks in the lake. At 12:00 P.M., her group lesson ended and she readied to return home for lunch.

Several of the swimmers' mothers had been chatting in rocking chairs on the clubhouse's broad patio overlooking the beach. Watching Betty scramble to get home, one mother offered to drive her the very short four-hundred-foot distance back to 102 Lake Forest Drive. Betty politely refused the offer. She had her beloved bicycle with her and could ride home in minutes along the dirt road that skirted the lake.

At 2:00 P.M., Ada Balsiger was worried. Betty still hadn't returned home for lunch. She looked out the kitchen window again at the clubhouse across the lake and saw no sign of her daughter. She called several friends. Nobody had seen her. Now alarmed, Ada ran to the clubhouse, only to be told Betty had left for home two hours earlier. The lake community's handyman and laborer, Samuel Shannon, fanned out with several others along the southern bank of the lake between the clubhouse and the Balsiger home. Within minutes, he spotted Betty's bicycle sitting in the water by the lake's edge, approximately a hundred feet west of the clubhouse. Ada's heart sank.

Shannon waded into the lake and dove in. Ada prayed he would come up empty-handed. After an hour and a half of scouring the bottom of the lake, Shannon emerged with the seven-year-old girl's body, drowned. Ada screamed in horror. Shannon carried the body to shore as local police gathered on the scene. They surmised Betty's bicycle must have hit a rock on the country lane, sending the girl careening into the water's edge.

In their haste to explain the drowning, no officer seemed to question the circumstances in which a competent swimmer drowned in only twelve inches of water, her bicycle laying half submerged and half exposed above the water. A spillway at the southwestern corner of the lake provided a slight current in the lake but not enough to carry a sixty-pound body and certainly not in the opposite direction toward the center of the lake, where the body was discovered.

The dirt road was smooth, having been well traveled by cars daily, and photographs of the road taken in the 1920s display no large rocks that could have caused a bicycle to jerk violently toward the lake. The walled embankment next to the dirt road was only a foot above the waterline. Had the bicycle somehow jumped several feet away from the road and into the lake, the fall would not have sent a body flying any distance away from the bike.

If Betty's head had somehow hit a rock, her body would have lain in the shallow water next to the bicycle, not drifted five hundred feet in the opposite direction of a very-mild-to-nonexistent current. However, her head evidenced no trauma wound, making a headfirst fall into the rocks impossible. Newspaper reports as far away as Omaha and Texas hinted that the explanation given by the police was not entirely satisfactory.

Over the last 120 years, there has been only one other death in Lake of the Forest, an adult male who suffered a heart attack in the water. To this day, Helen Elizabeth Balsiger remains the only victim of death by drowning. The lake's deepest point is ten feet at its center, with a slight incline from its banks. The water is shallow, clear, and almost completely placid, making the lake naturally safe and drownings nearly impossible.

The Balsiger family gathered by the clubhouse to speak with the police as Helen Elizabeth's body was carted away. There was no need to disturb the traumatized mother with an investigation. The girl would be transported back to Kansas City and quickly buried, per the instructions of father Herman, who served as president of the Lake of the Forest Board of Directors. The death would be kept within the family and not even mentioned at a board meeting just three days later, which Herman would attend and preside over.

Carl Balsiger watched people gather on the banks to witness the tragedy that had befallen one of the lake's most prominent families. Amid the crowd, he spotted a boy his age whom he frequently saw at the clubhouse dances, swim meets, and hunting outings. His name was Richard Funk.

The day Carl Balsiger was born, a part of him died. On June 16, 1915, Herman Carl and twin sister Mary Helen were delivered to parents Ada and Herman Balsiger. Soon after birth, Mary's body alarmingly changed color. Deprived of oxygen from a congenital heart lesion, she passed away after seven hours, the death certificate recording her a "blue baby." For the remainder of his life, Carl would list his birth year as 1916 or 1917, forever distancing himself from the first death to traumatize his family.

The sudden loss of infant Mary was an ordeal, but the Balsigers' rugged Midwestern roots had prepared them for hardship. Carl's grandfather, Rudolph, had immigrated from Switzerland to Illinois in 1861 at fifteen years old. With the outbreak of the Civil War, he joined the 43rd Illinois Infantry, composed of German and Swiss immigrants who were prized for their intense European military discipline. Constant attention to strict regulation and avoidance of leisure was backed by the threat of severe punishment. When the devastating Battle of Shiloh commenced in April 1862 with a surprise attack by Confederate troops, the 43rd was the only Union regiment dressed, in order, and prepared for battle.

Rudolph survived the horrors of the Civil War, returning to his farm in Highland, Illinois, on the outskirts of St. Louis. With a religious devotion to hard work, self-discipline, and denial of pleasure, he found a kindred spirit in his former drill sergeant, Johann

Haeinne. Rudolph married Haeinne's daughter Anna, who birthed five children, all of whom helped tend to the farm.

Though he left school after the seventh grade, Herman embodied his father's values of discipline, hard work, and no play. By 1906, he and his brother Fred had saved enough money to open Balsiger Brothers Market in Kansas City. Just west of downtown lay the Kansas City Stockyards, a sprawling complex of slaughterhouses that brought in millions of hogs, sheep, and cattle each year via the sixteen railroad lines that converged in the city. The Kansas City Stockyards were second only to Chicago's Union Stockyards in size. Much of the nation's livestock passed through Kansas City's extensive meatpacking industry, which butchered, processed, and distributed slabs of pork, lamb, and beef.

The Balsiger Brothers Market did a brisk trade in canned goods and produce. But like all grocery markets in Kansas City, real success lay in its butcher shop, where employees disassembled large blocks of "primal cut" meat direct from the stockyards. Herman's three children were expected to continue the family's strong Swiss work ethic. Carl spent afternoons and weekends toiling in the Balsiger Brothers meat department, breaking down primal cuts into secondary cuts, separating bone and muscle with long-bladed butcher knives.

A natural leader, Herman was elected by his peers to the post of president of the Retail Grocer's Association, a co-operative organization representing the interests of Kansas City grocers. But once elected, his unforgiving authoritative nature revealed itself and was used to punish his own members as much as advocate for them. Grocers citywide were bound by a 9:00 P.M. closing time to avoid unfair competitive practices, a law that was often ignored. Balsiger put his fist down, sending decoys into stores that were open past the curfew, who would then report the transgressors.

Having established a close relationship with the Kansas City Police Department, Herman would ride with police officers to the offending grocery stores, where owners and managers were arrested on site at his direction. With Kansas City rapidly becoming a center of food and produce, the National Grocers Association moved its headquarters to the city, and Balsiger was elected secretary. He was invited to address major conventions, where his fiery speeches invoked an aggressive and uncompromising expansion of the grocery industry.

In one speech, he chastised the hundreds of grocers present, saying, "Grocery men do not take the pride in their business that they should. Their standing in the community should be just as high as the banker, lawyer, or a doctor. If it is not, it is their own fault." His emotional appeal reached a fever pitch with dire warnings of predatory immigrants who were threatening the existing network of grocers with stores of their own.

He rallied the crowds in demanding legislation barring those without full citizenship from owning a grocery, butcher shop, or market, never mentioning his own father and mother were immigrants themselves. In 1924, Herman brought his nativist diatribe to the National Association of Retail Grocers convention in Los Angeles, California. The entire Balsiger family joined him for the business trip and stayed at the fanciest hotel in the city—the newly opened Biltmore.

Known as the "Mother of Bakeries," Kansas City had birthed five of the nation's top six baking corporations. Local teen Roy Nafziger inherited his father's ailing bakery, turned it into a success, and then opened a second bakery in the basement of Christian Church, where he had been baptized as a baby. Within a few years, he had built a series of baking plants that would become Interstate Bakeries and eventually Hostess Brands. In 1927, the Schulze Baking

Company was the jewel in his burgeoning empire's crown, and he found an eminent general sales manager for the prized company in Herman Balsiger.

Nafziger's private airplane transported Balsiger and other top executives around the country to visit and refine his vast network of bakery plants from Los Angeles to Peoria, Illinois. Herman rubbed shoulders with the cream of Missouri society, becoming close friends with beer magnate August "Augie" Anheuser Busch Sr. When a city manager was killed in a drive-by shooting down the street from the Balsigers' home, Anheuser Busch sent armed guards to escort the Balsiger children to and from school.

With the Balsiger family's wealth and social status climbing, the city's top country clubs and most exclusive black-tie affairs were now within reach. But they were of little interest to Herman. Recreation, leisure, the spoils of a rich man's lifestyle were anathema to the son of austere Rudolph Balsiger. The summer months at Lake of the Forest were the only time of the year the children were allowed amusements and freedom, though disciplined pursuits such as hunting, swimming, and reading were heavily encouraged.

Back in Kansas City, Herman would avoid the dangerous comforts of wealth and ensure his children remained just as chaste and regimented. While his four siblings grew close and enjoyed hearty family gatherings, Herman kept his own family away. Thanksgiving and Christmas were not for celebration, but rather self-reflection. Three-piece suits with ties and formal dresses were worn every day, even by the children. Piano was practiced religiously, while laughter, frivolity, joking, even smiling were frowned upon, all under threat of corporal punishment.

Church was attended every Sunday at Second Presbyterian. Though the church had a thriving social scene, Herman attended strictly for his soul and not for the good graces of wealthy families like that of influential church elder James Welsh and his wife, Leila McKee Welsh, whose philanthropy had bought the best seats in the house.

Nonetheless, Herman would make a statement to the Welshes and other society families with the purchase of a corner lot at Wornall Road and 55th Street in the heart of the ritzy country club district. Bordering elegant Jacob Loose Park, the highly exclusive block was home to many of Kansas City's wealthiest residents, including the Welshes themselves, just two doors down.

Construction costs of a home worthy of the surrounding mansions proved too much, and the property was sold off. Herman bought a suitably stately home four blocks away at 5711 Main Street in the upper-middle-class Rockhill Heights district. Daughter Patricia was born to the Balsigers in 1930, but they remained haunted by the death of daughter Betty at Lake of the Forest. Ada had a three-foot-tall statue made of the little girl, which was prominently displayed in the home as a constant reminder of the loss.

Despite his father's relentless hectoring to succeed on his own merits, Carl Balsiger was growing into a thin, gangly youth with an awkward personality, no athletic skill, middling grades, and a deviated septum that produced a whistling sound every time he breathed in, a source of much humiliation at school. As Herman's status and influence grew, Carl seemed to falter in all his endeavors, taking small roles in school plays and being relegated to piccolo player in the school band. School elections won him the lowly position of Literary Club treasurer.

In 1932, Carl found his calling in the DeMolay organization, a boys' fraternity that had been founded by Freemason Frank Land in 1919. Named after a thirteenth-century grand master of the Knights Templar, DeMolay's mission was to instill in young men the values and work ethic they would need to become future leaders. Under the tutelage of Land, whom everyone called "Dad," the founding

Mother Chapter met frequently at Ivanhoe Masonic Temple, an imposing seven-story building of brick and stone that was fronted by forty-foot columns. In the ornate parquet wood and terra-cotta hall, the boys kept ritual and planned events to rival those of the Masons, whose large portraits hung on the walls. Carl took to the strict hierarchy and instant social circle provided by DeMolay and rose through the ranks with the hard-won approval of his father, a Freemason himself.

Two years into his DeMolay service, Carl was surprised by the arrival of new initiate named Richard Funk. The Funks were well known to the Balsigers at Lake of the Forest, where both families owned cabins. In the tightknit community, every family knew each other and the teenaged boys would spend afternoons together. Richard had joined Carl and the other boys on outings into the forests north of the lake to hunt white-tail deer with rifles. Carl was trained in preserving the meat immediately after death by "field dressing" the deer—gutting it with a knife and disposing of the internal organs.

The delicate procedure required a skilled hand able to separate tissue from bone without cutting the organs, which could leak fluids that would taint the meat. After gutting the animal, the carcass was drained of blood and then washed before being carried back to the clubhouse to be processed for dining. Richard wasn't much of a hunter. He was much more suited to the Saturday night dances at the clubhouse, which every teenager at the lake attended. There was much competition throughout the week to secure a date for the big night. Rivalries extended to the dance floor, where boys often cut in on each other.

Sweet-natured and good-looking, Funk was a popular fixture at the dances and never wanted for a date. Carl, on the other hand, rarely showed up with a date and would avoid dancing, preferring to stand on the periphery or leave early. Still, Carl wasn't lacking in confidence. His father sat on the Lake of the Forest Board of Directors, and the Balsigers were well respected and admired. Carl, himself, was on the fast track to becoming master councilor of the DeMolay Mother Chapter, the highest rank a boy could achieve, while Richard had just entered on the ground floor as a lowly preceptor and had years ahead of him before reaching Carl's status, if he ever did.

Just as Carl's high school senior year was coming to an end, the soon-to-be-opened University of Kansas City began taking applications for its first class of 250 students. Despite Carl's unremarkable grades, Herman would pull strings, guaranteeing his acceptance into the school. Carl bonded with other DeMolay members who had also enrolled in the KCU freshman class, and they soon formed the first fraternity on campus, called Kegon.

While other fraternities and sororities would pop up, Kegon was first on the block, and the eleven founding members would carry themselves with the superiority they believed they had earned. As new students arrived, Kegon swelled its ranks with probationary pledges who toiled for the brotherhood—washing cars, raking lawns, and bowing down before the founding members on their hands and knees. Twice-yearly Founder's Day Banquets would celebrate Balsiger and the other founding members, starting with a lavish meal at the Brookside Hotel and concluding at the famed jazz club Tooties.

With the student council firmly in the hands of Kegon and other Greek houses, an Enforcement Committee was set up by Balsiger and Student Council President John Chaney to ensure incoming classes respected and feared the first students enrolled on campus. To make their point widely known, Carl set up a demonstration in the quad at the heart of campus. With hundreds of students watching, Balsiger pulled freshman Fred Patt out of the crowd and ordered him to bend over, touching hands to ankles. Balsiger produced a large wooden paddle and raised it. Just before he swung it toward Patt's backside, Dean Orin Sanford muscled through the crowd and ordered the demonstration be ceased.

For any student who didn't get the message, the *UNews* school newspaper made it crystal clear in an interview with an aliased "mystery" student who sounded suspiciously like Carl: "George Paddlebutts, well-known upperclassman, was perhaps most enthusiastic of all in fervently approving the punishment side of the plan. 'Yeah man,' said Paddlebutts to a news reporter, 'it's great stuff. I'm gonna cut all my classes tomorrow and whittle me out a paddle. And just whittle I start whacking those Frosh. Wassail!'" The paddling continued into Kegon's Hell Week, during which pledges were submitted to brutal initiation rituals, including severe paddling of bare bottoms administered by Carl Balsiger.

Despite his domineering presence on campus, Carl never held an official position within Kegon or student government. His grades faltered and his electives suffered. Romances swirled on campus, many of the details bubbling up in the gossip column of the *UNews*. For all of Carl Balsiger's notoriety, no gossip about dates or potential love interests was ever mentioned about him. The only news he made were the questions surrounding the dirty, antiquated hat he always wore on campus and his five strikeouts at bat in the campus-wide baseball derby, earning him derision and the epithet of "dub," or clumsy loser. The *UNews* poked fun at his failed attempt at growing a moustache. Even his haircut was mocked in the paper with a made-up interaction between Carl and his father:

Mr. Balsiger: "Where in the world did you get that hair cut?"
Carl: "I cannot tell a lie, father. I did it with my own little hatchet."

The paper summed up Carl's reputation in one word: "clown." While his best friends Ken Spry, Charles Myers, and John Chaney held high ranks in student government with their good looks and easy-going charm, Carl Balsiger was an oddity, a bully, a charmless mystery. Herman Balsiger feared for his son's future and ordered him to work part-time at the company he had recently founded, the ABC Bread Company. Carl worked in "dealer service," was quickly shuffled to another department, and then left the company altogether to return to his active social life at KCU.

While Carl enjoyed an endless stream of themed events like Kegon's notorious Palm Beach party, Summer Fantasy party, swing band soirees featuring Thompson's Top Hatters and the Chuck Donn Orchestra, black-tie formals, and treasure hunts, Richard Funk walked back into his life on the arm of KCU's most captivating new arrival, Leila Adele Welsh.

CHAPTER 17

MY OWN LITTLE HATCHET

L eila Welsh captured attention the moment she stepped onto the University of Kansas City campus in September 1935. Unsophisticated yet elegant, naïve yet strong-willed, socially adept yet academic, she had arrived from a farm only thirty miles away from Kansas City. Her dark, luxurious hair and dimples framed her greatest feature—eyes that were "pools of expression, animation, youth." Everyone loved the fresh-faced arrival.

To Carl Balsiger, Leila was no newcomer. He had seen her throughout his youth at Second Presbyterian Church, where she often attended Sunday services with her venerable aunt and uncle. Carl lived only four blocks from the Welshes' home, which Leila frequently visited from her farm throughout her childhood, and his aunts and uncles had homes in the surrounding Rockhill neighborhood just blocks from Leila's extended family members' homes.

Richard Funk did not attend KCU but was soon accompanying Leila, not only to the myriad Greek social events on campus but also to the formals and dances held by the DeMolay organization. Carl had ascended to become a master councilor of DeMolay, a point of great pride, but Funk was rising rapidly and was tapped to succeed

Carl in the top position. Richard had won accolades as leader of Boy Scout Troop 128, where he ran the Christmas toy drive, volunteered for several service organizations, served on the Junior Chamber of Commerce, and captured headlines by winning the national Jimmy Allen model airplane races. A self-made success, Richard was dating Leila Welsh to the envy of much wealthier and better-connected campus fraternity members like Carl Balsiger who had been given, not earned, so much of their spoils.

While most social events were held on campus, at hotels, or at clubs, the small circle of elite Greek members at KCU frequently threw parties at their parents' homes, all within blocks of each other. Carl Balsiger lived eight blocks from Leila's close friend Ann Bichler, who lived nine blocks from Kegon member Ken Spry, who lived eight blocks from Leila's best friend and fellow Cho Chin sorority sister Phyllis Wetherill, who lived five blocks from Leila's sorority sister Mary Ann Peeler, who lived twelve blocks from Kegon President Charles Myers, who lived eleven blocks from Leila Welsh, who lived thirteen blocks from Carl Balsiger, whose home lay directly northeast of the Welshes.

In the summer of 1936, the triumphant four horsemen of Kegon who had dominated the campus—John Chaney, Ken Spry, Charles Myers, and Carl Balsiger—set out on an epic road trip to Oregon. Sleeping on blankets by the side of the road, they barely made it to Portland, where they sold their dilapidated car, got jobs, and saved money to buy bicycles for a trip down the California coast. After four days, they grew tired of the bicycles and hitchhiked down to Los Angeles, where Myers, Chaney, and Spry bought bus tickets back to Kansas City. Carl stayed behind with relatives in Los Angeles and returned to Kansas City at the end of the summer.

When the 1936–1937 school year began, everything had changed. Waves of new students were challenging the dominance of the senior class and the Greek system that had held the reins of power. When a new student political party, Vo-Camp, emerged to challenge the Greek Co-Op party, Kegon responded with intimidation tactics. During elections for Vo-Camp candidates in the school assembly hall, Co-Op party members John Chaney, Carl Balsiger, and two other burly members walked in, sat down, and eyed the proceedings meant only for Vo-Camp members. The tactics backfired as Student Council President Charles Myers was ousted by challengers Frank McKibben and Leila Welsh. The Enforcement Committee was abolished, and Balsiger found himself on the periphery of social life once again.

At the glittering Vice President's Ball, which every student was made to attend, Leila and the other members of the new student government stood at a receiving line alongside the school's dean and the members of the board of trustees to welcome the guests. In her form-fitting blue gown, Leila was the striking picture of elegance, beauty, and achievement, landing the scene a photo in the *Kansas City Star* newspaper.

Carl's tenure as master councilor of DeMolay ended abruptly as Richard Funk ascended to the top position and succeeded in helping to bring Walt Disney out from Los Angeles for the first DeMolay Founder's Conference. While Carl never returned to DeMolay, Richard Funk became a model leader and was upped even further to commander of the DeMolay Group, overseeing multiple chapters across Missouri. Carl's academics continued to flounder, and he was unable to graduate in his senior year, staying on for a fifth year at KCU and graduating in 1938, in the same class as Leila Welsh.

After graduation, most members of the intertwined KCU Greek system got engaged to each other, were married, and began their careers and families. Carl remained single and jobless with no prospects. Herman threw him a lifeline with a position at ABC Bread Company. Once again, Carl did not last in the job, and Herman's disappointment grew to crisis levels. He had tried to instill in his son every trait that had made him a success, but something was missing in Carl. No matter the threats and intimidation Herman used to try and mold him, Carl continued to live in his parents' home—aimless and without motivation.

In early 1939, Carl made a sudden and surprising move to study at the American Institute of Baking in Chicago. Herman also secured him a job as a salesman at the local Interstate Bakeries offices. Living on his own for the first time at twenty-four years old, Carl traveled a sales route that took him across Illinois, but most frequently to Peoria, where Interstate owned a large production plant that had been visited by Herman Balsiger on company founder Roy Nafziger's private plane many times. The Peoria plant was responsible for production of Interstate's top-selling Butternut Bread, which was distributed across the country.

Coincidentally, Peoria was also home to Princeville High School, where Leila Welsh's new love, Elery "Gabby" Boynton, taught physical education. Forty miles west was Knoxville, Illinois, the tiny town to which Leila Welsh had moved to teach kindergarten months earlier. Carl would remain in Illinois on his sales runs until he stopped working for Interstate Bakeries and returned to Kansas City to live with his parents in May of 1940, the exact month Leila Welsh returned to Kansas City. Once again, Carl Balsiger spontaneously appeared at the same place at the same time as Leila Welsh, his life a virtual mirror to hers.

The crossed paths would continue into the summer of 1940. When Leila returned to Kansas City, her relationship with Richard Funk reignited, and the couple spent weekends at his family's cabin at Lake of the Forest, twenty miles outside the city. Funk described their enchanted summer in testimony given to the George Welsh grand jury: "Last June my folks had a home at Lake of the Forest located in Wyandotte County, Kansas. Leila would come out there over Saturdays and Sundays, and on Sunday night

I would bring her back to town and sometimes I would have several dates with her."

Police Chief Lear Reed would offer further details. "Dick's parents had a place at Lake of the Forest in Wyandotte County, Kansas. The dates became more frequent. She was invited to the lake resort and she spent a number of weekends there, returning to the city Sunday nights with Dick. Those moonlight rides from Lake of the Forest back to town were not made in haste."

Leila and Richard were not alone at the lake. Just a quarter mile down the country lane from where his sister had drowned under mysterious circumstances thirteen years before, Carl Balsiger was holed up at his family's cabin, alone. His sister having moved away and his parents back in the city, Carl lingered at the lakeshore, facing an uncertain future. The girls he had grown up with at the lake were nearly all married or engaged, while he remained single and unemployed.

Each weekend, DeMolay Commander Richard Funk arrived at the Lake of the Forest clubhouse on the arm of Leila Welsh, the girl so many men at the University of Kansas City had pined for. They whirled on the clubhouse dance floor, feasted on frozen watermelon and crawdads at the lake's community dinners, and appeared to fall deeper in love with each passing day.

Lake of the Forest's corn roasts and canoe regattas were worlds away from the carnage ripping across Europe, which would soon transform Kansas City, with its interlacing railroad lines and vast warehouses, into an industrial war machine. President Roosevelt had assured anxious Americans that they would not be drawn into the unfolding war thousands of miles away. "The nation will remain a neutral nation. As long as it remains within my power to prevent, there will be no blackout of peace in the United States."

But behind the scenes, Roosevelt began preparations for the likely expansion of hostilities that the country could ill afford to ignore. On June 14, 1940, German Panzer tanks rolled down Paris's Champs Elysee. By July 1, the Nazis had conquered the Channel Islands, with Britain sure to be the next domino to fall. On July 10, the Battle of Britain began.

Congress quickly responded to the tidal wave of disasters that summer with the Vinson-Walsh Act, which funneled billions of dollars toward construction of navy ships and aircraft carriers, while fifty aging destroyers were lent to the United Kingdom. But the earthquake that would shake the United States out of its isolationist crouch arrived on September 16, 1940, with the passage of the Selective Service Act, the first peacetime draft in the country's history. No matter the public pronouncements of neutrality, the United States was officially preparing to enter "the War." Registration for the draft of all men between the ages of 21 and 45 would begin on October 16.

Herman Balsiger proudly announced in the *Kansas City Star* newspaper that his son Carl had volunteered for duty days before the draft registration rule took effect, proving his patriotism and commitment to his nation. But Carl—or his father—had lied, having actually enlisted on October 19, three days after the mandatory Selective Service registration started.

On November 10, 1940, Carl Balsiger stepped off a bus filled with draftees for intake at Fort Leavenworth, Kansas, a massive military base and war college thirty-five miles north of Kansas City. The 120-year-old institution had been at the center of the nation's military history and advancement across the continent throughout the nineteenth century. Its legendary U.S. Army Command and General Staff College had graduated the officers who would lead the United States in the ensuing war: Dwight D. Eisenhower, George Marshall, Douglas MacArthur, and George Patton. Nineteen thousand more officers would be trained and graduated from Fort Leavenworth before the end of World War II.

As the son of Kansas City baking royalty, Carl Balsiger was selected for officer training in a division beset with major technical problems and desperately in need of expertise. The Quartermaster Corps is one of the three major logistic branches of the U.S. Army, tasked as a supply force whose function is to provide food, clothing, and bath and laundry facilities to United States military forces across the world. During World War II, it was also tasked with the collection, identification, and burial of war dead in addition to providing for prisoners of war and displaced civilians.

In the Spring of 1945, the Quartermaster Corps fed, clothed, and provided necessities for more than seven and a half million people across Europe alone. Crucial to troop morale in World War II was the daily production and distribution of fresh baked bread, which was the only food product produced in the combat zone. With most rations proving unpalatable, fresh bread made meals tolerable and fueled millions of soldiers through years of hellish combat.

In 1940, the Bakery Division of the Quartermaster Corps had barely advanced from the primitive days of World War I, when dough was sluggishly kneaded by hand and baked in hastily constructed, wood-fired brick ovens that had been built into dirt dugouts and patched with asbestos tape. With war on the horizon, bread would be a critical secret weapon that could make the difference between a demoralized unit and a savage fighting force. Officers at Fort Leavenworth found an intriguing candidate in H. Carl Balsiger, who they believed had the experience to help modernize its all-important and nonexistent baking strategy, despite his proven inability to hold a job.

While most Selective Service draftees inducted at Fort Leavenworth were sent to military bases around the country for basic training, officer candidates remained at the famed Command and General Staff College. Throughout the fall of 1940 and winter of 1941, Carl Balsiger was immersed in the army's baking program, with frequent furloughs spent back at his parents' home in nearby Kansas City.

In the final week of February 1941, Carl received news he would be promoted to sergeant and soon shipped to McChord Airfield near Tacoma, Washington, where he would serve in Quartermaster Company No. 254. Before his relocation, however, Carl would receive two weeks' leave in Kansas City, where he stayed at his parents' home. Most of his Kegon fraternity brothers from the University of Kansas City had remained in the city after graduation. Close friend Charles Rouse had avoided the draft and subsequently secured a junior executive position at Skelly Oil.

On the night of March 8, Rouse was strolling down Wyandotte Street in downtown Kansas City with his wife when they ran into KCU Greek alum Leila Welsh, who was window shopping with her boyfriend, Richard Funk, who also worked at Skelly Oil. The two couples chatted for several minutes as Leila raved about the Police Circus she and Richard had just attended. The Rouses would be deeply shaken by the next day's news of Leila Welsh's savage murder. Word about the slaying rapidly spread across the city, reaching every family in every home. Neighborhoods within walking distance of 6109 Rockhill Road were especially abuzz with rumors and fears.

The Balsigers lived just blocks north and east of the Welsh home at 57th and Main Streets. Within days, Carl would disappear from the city for Tacoma, Washington, 1,500 miles away.

With the United States' entry into World War II following the attack on Pearl Harbor, Carl Balsiger was shuffled to a series of West Coast airbases, including Pendleton in Oregon, Fort Warren in Wyoming, and Van Nuys Air Base near Los Angeles, California. Herman Balsiger would gleefully announce his son's promotions and frequent visits home in the *Kansas City Star* newspaper.

By mid-1942, Carl served in a bakery platoon stationed in Pasadena, California, twelve miles outside of Los Angeles, where he oversaw the daily production of four thousand pounds of bread shipped to military bases across Southern California. His education was accelerated at the American Institute of Baking. Next came enrollment in the Cooks' and Bakers' School at Camp Cooke in Santa Barbara County in early 1943, where he was assigned to the massive United States Sixth Army, code-named "Alamo Force." The balmy climate of Camp Cooke, with its swaying palm trees and Saturday night movie shows, would prove a deceptive calm before the hellish storm into which the Sixth Army was about to sail.

In mid-1943, the entire South Pacific Theater of the war had not a single field bakery in operation. With combat raging on far-flung islands infested with disease, tropical rot, and malaria-bearing mosquitos, troops were fed canned bread, canned vegetables, and canned meats that often arrived moldy and tasteless. Bitter complaints of the poor, rotted rations overwhelmed officers. The production of fresh bread became an urgent necessity for morale. Balsiger and the field bakery units he commanded in the Alamo Force would be needed in one of the most inhospitable war zones in the world, the island of New Guinea.

In early 1942, the Empire of Japan invaded and conquered the critically strategic Australian colony, which U.S. General Douglas MacArthur was determined to wrest back and use as a forward base for the eventual reconquest of the Philippines. Halfway across the world, Quartermaster Corps field bakeries sent into the European Theater arrived at large docks, where specially fitted trucks transported their extensive baking equipment to dedicated warehouses and makeshift buildings.

In the Pacific, no such luxuries existed. The Sixth Army's field bakery teams would assemble their ovens under canvas tents in the searing heat of dense jungles, as close to the front lines as the combat units they would be feeding. Newly designed electro-diesel dough mixers and state-of-the-art mobile ovens had improved production, but upon landing, the baking companies were faced with a supply crisis. Flour, butter, salt, and sugar were all in short or no supply on the island beaches precariously held by U.S. and Australian forces. Over-active yeast quickly spoiled in the humidity.

Field bakery units were forced to scavenge in the jungle for local replacement ingredients under enemy machine gun fire and bombing raids. Despite taking casualties, the units scrounged for coconuts, which, when fermented, replaced yeast. Wheat cereal replaced flour. Sea water was boiled to extract salt. Old clothes were used to cover and proof bread, wells were dug for fresh water, and fifty-five-gallon drums were retrofitted for use as additional ovens.

Teams even located decades-old abandoned Dutch ovens in the jungle and fired them up for twenty-four-hour nonstop bread baking. Balsiger personally devised an ingenious use of jeep motors to power multiple dough mixers when diesel gasoline ran out and the mixers ground to a halt. For the first time in his life, Carl Balsiger became a respected leader, finally living up to the hopes of his demanding and exacting father.

In September 1944, Balsiger's remarkable success in New Guinea earned him elevation to commander of Baking Operations for the Sixth Army, which had driven Japan back from much of the island and was preparing for the long-awaited amphibious assault on the Philippines. On October 20, General Douglas MacArthur arrived at Leyte Island in the heart of the Philippine archipelago and famously declared, "I have returned." While Japan and the United States faced off at Leyte Gulf in what would become the greatest naval battle in world history, the U.S. Sixth Army landed and established a beachhead on the island of Leyte.

Field bakery units led by Captain Balsiger accompanied the assault teams in a finely choreographed advance. Nonetheless, enormous logistical problems surfaced. Much of the baking equipment from New Guinea was shipped to the wrong islands, forcing units to improvise with World War I–era wood burning ovens. Starving Japanese soldiers attempted to overrun and raid bakery positions. Pillboxes and fifty-caliber machine gun nests were set up and manned by dough makers, bakers, and cooks to fend off the attacks. Despite suffering sixty-three casualties, the baking units succeeded in churning out tens of thousands of two-pound loaves a week. Within three months, all of Leyte was taken by Allied forces.

On February 3, 1946, six months after the end of World War II, Carl Balsiger was discharged from the army. Instead of returning to Kansas City a war hero and grabbing the spoils of an executive position at one of the city's many baking corporations, he moved to Los Angeles with no such prospects. Having commanded an enormous force in the Pacific Theater's most intense and critical war zones, Carl returned to form as a salesman for a wholesale baking company, a nearly unfathomable demotion for such a high-ranking officer.

He rented a room on the second floor of a storefront building at Sunset Boulevard and Gardner Street. Sandwiched between Hollywood Boulevard and the Sunset Strip, the busy intersection was bisected by a Pacific Electric Trolley line, its sidewalks crowded with commuters and clubgoers coming to and from the popular nightspot Club Tabu, just three blocks away. But Carl was soon offered a plush upgrade from the cramped, loud confines of his rented room.

J. W. Costello was to Los Angeles baking history what Herman Balsiger was to Kansas City. Called "the dean of Southern California bakerymen," Costello had served as president of Western Bakeries Corporation in Van Nuys and Weber Bakeries in Burbank, and vice president of Interstate Bakeries when the corporation bought out Los Angeles's top baking companies. In 1940, Costello retired from the bakery business and moved his family to helm a beverage company in a dusty desert town called Las Vegas on the hunch folks might be attracted to its casinos.

Despite the relocation, the Costellos maintained ownership over their two Los Angeles residences, a large ranch home in the San Fernando Valley, and a retreat in the forested canyons above Beverly Hills. Carl Balsiger had been introduced to the Costellos years earlier through his father and the family of Interstate Bakery executives. Soon after arriving in Los Angeles, Carl was offered the unoccupied canyon home as a temporary residence, which would provide space and quiet. It would also offer near total isolation, the kind of place where no one could hear a scream.

CHAPTER 18

DESTINY IN THE DIRT

Benedict Canyon is one of a series of mountain passes that stretch over the Santa Monica Mountains, separating the Los Angeles basin from the sprawling, suburban San Fernando Valley beyond. The coiled north-south road rises out of Beverly Hills's most exclusive neighborhoods, past cramped, bungalow-style, wood-framed homes and celebrity estates, and terminating abruptly at the crestline.

The fog-shrouded ravine, with its bony-limbed sycamore trees, has an eerie mystique, its snug, steep slopes blocking much of the famed Southern California sun. It has an equally unnerving history, having played host to some of Los Angeles's most shocking murders, among them the mysterious 1959 suicide—or was it?—of Superman star George Reeves, Robert Durst's 2000 execution of writer Susan Berman, the 1954 bludgeoning of film talent scout David Johnson, the 2023 triple homicide carried out by Chicago gang members, the 1932 suicide—or was it?—of Jean Harlow's husband Paul Bern, and most notorious of all, the 1969 slaughter of Sharon Tate and her three houseguests at the hands of the Manson Family.

Before real estate frenzies built up its every available hillside lot, Benedict Canyon in 1946 had a split personality. At its base alongside the celebrity-studded Beverly Hills Hotel were the grand estates of Mary Pickford, Charlie Chaplin, and studio mogul Jack Warner. A half mile up the hill, the red-carpeted road transformed into a craggy rural lane dotted with a smattering of houses amid long, empty stretches of wilderness.

The Costello home at 1957 Benedict Canyon was just a six-minute drive from the heart of chic Beverly Hills but felt like a rural outpost. The 1,900-square-foot Spanish Revival structure, with its compact yard, backed up to the canyon's sheer hillside. A twenty-by-twenty-foot garage with a concrete pad and thick stucco walls had been recently converted for residential use. Thick clusters of oak trees hid much of the property from view. Though set in a remote stretch of Benedict Canyon, the house still came with a much-coveted Beverly Hills "Crestview" telephone prefix, which always got attention.

As World War II rationing eased, sugar, milk, flour, and other staples became more available, and the baking industry rose to the moment. Though Carl was busy with wholesale bakery sales runs in the black 1940 Oldsmobile he had purchased, he picked up extra work selling cheese, evaporated and condensed milk, whole milk powder, butter, and syrup for Marwyn Dairy Products, a company headquartered in Chicago that had recently expanded to Los Angeles. The daily sales drives crisscrossing Southern California were a drain on gasoline, finances, and spirit. But a chance encounter would open a huge opportunity for Carl, one that his father could have turned into an empire.

Though Ventura County lies directly north of Los Angeles County, they are geographic, cultural, and economic worlds apart. While Los Angeles and its vast concrete environs have served as an international urban hub of entertainment, military defense, aerospace, and Pan-Pacific trade, Ventura County has remained a bucolic bastion of vast farms, elegant Spanish-influenced towns, blissful wineries, and picture-perfect cultivated slopes of citrus trees glistening in the early morning mist. The pastoral mirage easily shrouds a megaindustry that has provided much of the world's beans, avocados, and strawberries for over 120 years.

Within this agricultural jewel, the prominent Thacher family looms large, having first arrived in the 1880s and serving as founders and namesake of the county's—and the nation's—top private high school, the Thacher School. Despite his proud lineage, Walt Thacher had tried to escape his ancestral destiny and moved to Chicago in the 1920s. Fate and financial opportunity brought him back in 1940 with his wife and fourteen-year-old son, Walt Thacher Jr., to the family avocado ranch in Camarillo, California, at the base of the precipitous Conejo Grade Road that linked Ventura to Los Angeles. With Walt Sr.'s experience in avocado farming, Thacher Ranch thrived over the ensuing years, making the family comfortable if not wealthy.

Walter Patterson Thacher Jr., spent his teenaged years toiling in the dirt of his family ranch, but he was infused with an entrepreneurial energy and yearned for a life outside of farming. In 1942, he met and married Dorothy Jean Cleveland, a glamorous, blond seventeen-year-old from Beverly Hills who had already landed roles dancing in short films and advertisements that ran in movie houses before the feature film. Jean had just graduated from Beverly Hills High School, where she had known future actor Betty White and was friends with Samuel Goldwyn Jr., son of the famous movie mogul. Jean had been a frequent guest at the Goldwyns' palatial estate, where she attended dazzling parties.

It was a stark contrast to life on a rugged avocado farm. Nonetheless, Jean fell in love with Thacher Ranch and its slow-paced, pastoral beauty. She found lifelong friends on nearby farms and was soon pregnant when, suddenly, Walt Jr. was drafted into the military in 1943. Frontline battles in Europe earned him a Purple Heart, a Bronze Star, and war wounds, which sent him back to Camarillo in early 1945. While recuperating at a local hospital, Walt dreamed of building a new business, something that would keep him close to his ancestral ranch but wouldn't require working in the dirt. In mid-1946, he met Marwyn dairy salesman Carl Balsiger, who had a grand idea for him—open a bakery in Camarillo that would offer all of Ventura County a taste of premium breads and pastries, not the ubiquitous "wartime loaf" and stale cookies that were the staple options. Carl had the experience and Walt had the money. But Jean had suspicions.

Walt had just the place in mind. Since 1939, the Pleasant Valley Café had served the town of Camarillo and its surrounding farms with its chicken, rabbit, and steak dinners. Its location on Ventura Boulevard in the heart of the village made it a popular gathering place for church groups and various clubs. Owner and manager Joe Lillie was eager to sell. Walt made an offer for the business that was heartily accepted. On November 9, 1946, Walt and Carl took possession of the Pleasant Valley Café.

While Lillie continued to manage the restaurant for them, a portion of the building was converted into a top-of-the-line bakery, kitchen, and pastry shop, the four thousand dollars in costs paid for by Walt. But the real triumph wasn't the brand-new industrial dough mixers and freezers. It was Bernhard Sobanja. A master baker who had apprenticed in his native Zechin, Germany, from the age of eleven, Sobanja had been trained in a wide array of candies, chocolates, fancy cakes, ornamental bakery goods, and sugar sculptures. An astounding artisan, Sobanja had served as a top baker in Chicago for twenty years when Thacher and Balsiger offered a position as their head baker in beautiful, balmy Ventura County.

Tiring of Chicago's cold winters, Sobanja bit. With a baking genius at the helm of their state-of-the-art kitchen, Balsiger and Thacher opened Homecraft Bakery on November 30 to a public that had never tasted German Black Forest cake, crème chantilly éclairs, rum balls, linzer cookies, and fresh pumpernickel bread. Homecraft was an immediate success, drawing patrons from all over the county and beyond. Lines went out the door as ranchers and farmers waited for a fresh batch of jelly-filled "Camarillo rolls" or Berlin rye bread to exit the oven. It was a culinary revolution in one kitchen. Finally, Carl Balsiger had struck gold.

On December 6, 1946, one week after Homecraft's opening, when all hands were needed to ensure a smooth launch, Carl turned up in Camarillo with a girl he had picked up in Los Angeles. Her name was Elizabeth Short. They spent the night at Camarillo's Candle-Lite Motel, the only place to rent a room in the rural town and conveniently located two blocks from Homecraft Bakery. The next day, they drove back to Los Angeles in Carl's Oldsmobile, with Walt hitching a ride. Carl dropped his business partner off in Reseda in the San Fernando Valley, then continued on with Elizabeth into Los Angeles.

For the next day and a half, Balsiger and Short were together. With an impressive canyon retreat at his disposal, it is highly likely Elizabeth Short spent the night of December 7 at the Benedict Canyon home. Twenty-four hours later, Elizabeth deserted Carl and hopped a bus for San Diego. Balsiger remained in Southern California through the holidays while Homecraft Bakery continued to build a loyal following and enviable word-of-mouth. In January, Walt took out large-format advertisements in the *Camarillo Star* newspaper thanking the community for the wild success of his and Carl's new bakery. But trouble was brewing for Walt Thacher and Homecraft.

In the third week of January 1947, the horrific slaying of Elizabeth Short—the very girl Carl Balsiger had brought to Camarillo in early December—was all over the radio and newspapers. Just north of Ventura, Santa Barbara County was crawling with LAPD

detectives and newspaper reporters looking into her past at Camp
Cooke and environs in 1943. With every date, boyfriend, friend,
and enemy of hers being pursued, surely LA's hard-bitten investigators would turn up in Camarillo any day. And yet Walt never
stepped forward with the crucial information of Elizabeth's presence in Camarillo the previous month.

At the tail end of January 1947, the Los Angeles Police Department discovered Walt's business partner's name in the victim's
address book. Carl Balsiger became a suspect in the murder of Elizabeth Short. Questioned at length by police officers, Carl wove a
tapestry of outright lies, claiming he had only been with Short for
a day and a half when he had actually been with her for three. He
claimed to have taken her to at a motel on Yucca Street in the heart
of Hollywood and signed his name in the register when no such
record existed at any hotel in the area.

LAPD identified those lies, but Carl's sworn statements contained other grave fabrications that police and the subsequent district attorney investigators would never discern. Balsiger claimed
he had gone to Camarillo with Elizabeth to make a sale of baking
supplies to a local baker. He failed to divulge his ownership stake in
the newly opened Homecraft Bakery, the real reason for his travels to Camarillo. The police believed they had identified his residence at Sunset Boulevard and Gardner Street, the one room rental.
He failed to tell them of his real residence, the house in Benedict
Canyon.

During his interrogation, Carl let slip that Walt Thacher had
ridden with him and Elizabeth in the car ride back from Camarillo
on December 7. Thacher was subsequently questioned by the LAPD
and corroborated Balsiger's lies. No mention of Homecraft Bakery
or the house in Benedict was ever made to the police.

Balsiger and Thacher had kept something else from the LAPD, a
crucial piece of information that could have undone Balsiger's entire

story. In the fall of 1946, as they prepared to start their new business venture, Walt and his wife, Jean Thacher, dined with Carl Balsiger at a nightclub in Beverly Hills, Jean's hometown. Carl brought a date with him to that dinner—Elizabeth Short. Jean would long remember that haunting evening and periodically mentioned it to her children over the ensuing decades.

Carl Balsiger had not met Beth Short at a real estate office on the morning of December 6, 1946, as he had told the police and asserted during his lie detector test in 1950. He had met Beth well before that date. Just how far before is unknown. A devoted Presbyterian, Balsiger may have attended the enormous First Presbyterian Church of Hollywood on Carlos Avenue, a one-minute walk from Mark Hansen's home on the same small street. First Presbyterian was the largest and most dominant Presbyterian church in the city and attracted congregants from all over Southern California.

Balsiger could also have met Elizabeth during her outings to Club Tabu, which was only two blocks from the apartment Carl kept on Sunset Boulevard. Or he may have met her at Camp Cooke in 1943, when both of them were stationed there. Regardless, when Beth arrived in Camarillo on December 6, Walt Thacher was already familiar with her. Both Carl and Walt steadfastly held back this critical information from the LAPD.

By mid-February 1947, the police had thoroughly questioned Carl Balsiger and Walt Thacher, but they would have done well to interview Jean Thacher as well. Her suspicions about Carl were raised after Beth Short's murder, but they rose to an alarming level when Walt divulged to her a secret piece of information the LAPD had dropped on him during his questioning. This single clue may be the reason the LAPD continued to suspect Carl Balsiger until the last days of the Black Dahlia investigation.

When the bisected body of Elizabeth Short was autopsied, cocoa fibers from a stiff brush were found clinging to her skin, specifically concentrated in exposed wounds. Investigators surmised the killer had used a brush to wash her body thoroughly after the bisection and exsanguination. The presence of the brush bristles had been well documented in the press, all except for one detail, which had been uncovered in the crime lab. Detectives confronted Walt Thacher with this hidden detail. The cocoa fiber bristles, they believed, came from a pastry kitchen scrub brush used to clean surfaces of dough.

With the LAPD's understanding that Carl Balsiger was a salesman of bakery supplies and had gone with Elizabeth Short in December 1946 to Camarillo, "where he made a sale of supplies to a baker," the presence of pastry brush bristles on the murder victim's body was damning evidence. Clearly alarmed by the information, Walt had confided in his wife. Jean recalled that Carl had once taken their three-year-old son on a day-long outing in his car. Horrified, she demanded that Balsiger never be allowed near the family again.

Walt Thacher had much to protect in keeping his business partner out of the LAPD's crosshairs. Walt's family had deep ties in Ventura County, and his parents and siblings were members of various civic and charity groups in the area. If Camarillo had anything resembling "socialite families," the Thachers would have been honorary members. Had word gotten out in the tightknit farming community that Walt's business partner was a top suspect in the notorious Black Dahlia murder investigation, it could have harmed his family's reputation and destroyed the Pleasant Valley Café and Homecraft Bakery.

But if Walt believed his wildly successful bakery could blithely sail through the rough waters Carl Balsiger had churned, Bernhard Sobanja had other ideas. Homecraft had become every bit the success Sobanja had hoped for, and he toiled each night after closing time, experimenting with never-before-seen pastry marvels for the bakery's showcase the next morning. His wife had served as cashier since opening day nearly three months earlier. Without notice,

Sobanja showed up to work on February 24, 1947, and informed Walt Thacher he was done and would be moving to Santa Monica. Completely blindsided, Walt pleaded with him to stay. Sobanja would not reconsider his decision and promptly disappeared.

Despite Homecraft's outward success, the events surrounding Carl Balsiger and questions of his culpability in the murder of Elizabeth Short had caused a sudden and irreparable disruption behind the scenes that scuttled the entire business. Two days after Sobanja quit, Walt Thacher shut down Homecraft Bakery, a three-months-old pastry and bread-baking miracle in the unlikeliest of small towns. Carl Balsiger would never step foot in the Thachers' lives again.

Walt continued to operate the Pleasant Valley Café, remodeling and adding expensive new steak broilers, but business never returned to the levels brought in by the bakery. The restaurant went through several incarnations and was renamed Thacher's Pantry, but it continued to struggle until Walt was forced to sell his cherished business in late 1947. He next started up an agricultural irrigation company, returning to his destiny in the dirt. Though her husband had tried to keep the truth about Balsiger and Elizabeth Short quiet, Jean Thacher would not let the secret die.

Carl Balsiger, commander of all baking operations for the U.S. Sixth Army in the tide-turning Philippines campaign, would never work in the bakery business again. Days after Homecraft shut down, with the police breathing down his neck, he left for Kansas City, where he stayed with his parents. Back in Los Angeles weeks later, Carl was drinking heavily. In May 1947, he was pulled over and arrested for drunk driving. As part of his court-ordered sentence, a scarlet-letter sticker was forcibly placed on his windshield for thirty days, publicly labeling him a DUI driver. Carl had his fun at the police, outsmarting them with a replacement windshield, sans the shameful sticker. The ploy backfired. Carl was pulled over for another violation. When officers discovered his traded-out wind-shield, he was arrested again, this time spending twenty days in the LA County jail.

Soon after his release, Carl disappeared, slipping out of the LAPD's sights. He popped up in Delaware in 1948, then South Bend, Indiana, and the next year in St. Louis, Missouri, where his father, Herman, helped him secure a public relations position in Anheuser Busch's yeast products division, owing to a close relationship with the now-deceased August Anheuser Busch.

Also new in his life was Jane Moyer, a highly accomplished lawyer who had worked in her father's law firm before rising to assistant attorney general of Nebraska. She had attended the University of Nebraska, received her law degree from the University of Iowa, and in 1948 worked for the Department of Justice in Washington, DC, followed by the Department of Justice in Los Angeles as a special assistant to the U.S. District Attorney. Jane was eight years younger than Carl and shared a Freemason lineage with him, her father having been a thirty-second-degree Mason. Jane was smart, disciplined, and focused. She also came from money. Carl attached himself to her, securing a girlfriend for the first time in his thirty-four years. Weeks later, the two were engaged and then married in a small ceremony at Jane's parents' home in Nebraska. The groom's only guests were his parents.

With a new bride, a good job, and a posh apartment in St. Louis, Carl Balsiger had reinvented himself. And yet, in his closet remained a skeleton he had managed to keep private from everyone. Having lost track of Balsiger's whereabouts, the LAPD had gone silent and seemed to be in his rearview mirror. Then, the skeleton awoke.

On June 2, 1949, Los Angeles Police Chief Clemence Horrall sent a letter to the U.S. Army's Adjutant General's Office in St. Louis, Missouri, requesting Carl Balsiger's military files. What the LAPD received back would prove to be even more important: Balsiger's current location in St. Louis. Finis Brown set up a direct line of communication with the St. Louis Police Department. It was time to make his move.

Brown demanded further questioning of Balsiger under administration of a lie detector test. Three years after the Black Dahlia murder, Carl now learned he was still on the suspect list. He had little choice but to comply. Brown flew out to St. Louis and confronted Carl on his earlier sworn statements. Strapped to a lie detector, Balsiger admitted he had lied to the police about the length of time he spent with Elizabeth Short: he had spent three days with Short, not one and a half. But he also maintained and convinced Sergeant Brown that he was not the violent Sergeant Chuck who had known Elizabeth Short at Camp Cooke, nor had he seen Elizabeth Short after December 8, 1946. Despite his cool nerves on the polygraph test, Carl remained under investigation, rising to the number one spot on the district attorney's March 2, 1950, suspect list.

Soon after the lie detector interrogation, Jane and Carl were separated. She left St. Louis, returning to her native Madison, Nebraska, where she served as city attorney. While driving home in Carl's car on Highway 30 just outside Rising City, Nebraska, on the night of January 20, 1952, she inexplicably drifted across the median and into oncoming traffic. The car hit the stock rack of a truck, was "plowed underneath" and sent flipping repeatedly, shearing away the top and tearing off fenders and doors with such force they were compressed into balls.

Jane was thrown from the car, her arm severed, her body and head crushed. The first patrolman to arrive said it was the worst accident he had ever seen. While debris littered the road for over a hundred feet, the truck driver was completely unharmed. Shortly after Jane's horrific death, Carl returned to Kansas City and moved back in with his parents. Herman Balsiger's star had faded in recent years with the shuttering of his ABC Bread Company. He picked up work at Interstate Bakeries again, but with his health failing he was forced to sell the beloved waterfront home at Lake of the Forest as well as the myriad bread delivery routes that had been an important source of income for the family. In 1953, Herman died, leaving Carl alone with his mother, Ada, in the family home.

A string of jobs followed that never seemed to last long: work control clerk for TWA airlines, public relations director for the Berkshire Hotel, campaign manager for a local politician. Money became increasingly tight; the home on Main Street fell into disrepair. In 1955, Ada passed away, giving Carl full possession of the home. He drew the window shades as the house grew cluttered and disheveled. But in 1956, a ray of light entered his life.

CHAPTER 19

UNUSUAL MANNERS
AT UNUSUAL HOURS

O ver the decades, friends, family, and even strangers compared Tabitha Teall to Rosalind Russell's famous stage and film alter-ego, Auntie Mame. Bigger-than-life, beautiful, vivacious, a sculptor, a jazz singer, a social butterfly with a bottomless Rolodex, and full of stories from a life spent spinning around the globe, Tabitha became the center of every room she entered.

Portly, awkward, and off-putting, Carl Balsiger was not anywhere close to her league. But when a chance encounter brought them together in 1956, Tabitha was instantly drawn to the mystery man who had grown up only six blocks away from her in Kansas City. She had also grown up only two blocks from Leila McKee Welsh's home. It is highly likely Tabitha's prominent family members were familiar with and knew the Welshes and were as shaken by the murder of Leila Adele Welsh as the rest of the neighborhood.

Carl and Tabitha spent the evening gleefully sharing the scores of friends and acquaintances they knew in common, and soon she was smitten. For all her fabulous charm and wit, Tabitha had one weakness: she fell in love easily and married often, and always to the wrong man. Still, she never stuck around long enough to let a bad marriage slow her down. When things got boring, Tabitha would exit a marriage just as quickly as she entered. And she had the means to do so.

Her father, known as Daddy Doc, was a prominent Kansas City doctor and had amassed a fortune that Tabitha inherited, allowing her the exhilarating independence her personality commanded. With his finances in turmoil, Carl was attracted to her deep pockets. As for Tabitha's attraction, she would claim she didn't marry Carl for money or sex. She married for nostalgia.

On December 8, 1956, Tabitha Teall wed for the fifth time to Carl Balsiger at Second Presbyterian Church in Kansas City. The couple would reside at the Balsiger home, but changes had to be made before she and her twelve-year-old daughter Tibbie would move in. The filthy, dark home was filled with closed-off rooms and a strange staircase that ascended to the second floor and then plummeted back down to the opposite side of the first floor. With her interior decorating skills in hand, Tabitha spent lavishly of her own money, fixing the home up, turning a sunporch by the master bedroom into an expansive closet for her sumptuous wardrobe and shoe collection, and remodeling the moldy kitchen.

Once settled in, Tabitha found Carl was not nearly as charming as he had been the first night they met. Seemingly unable to care for himself in the most basic ways, he asked her to supply his every creature comfort, such as toilet paper, socks, food, money. He claimed not to know how to buy groceries and clothes, relying on her to shop and pay for everything. Pleading poverty, Carl claimed he could not make his mortgage payments and begged Tabitha to shoulder them. In exchange, he offered to add her name to the deed and brought home paperwork for her to sign, ensuring she would share in the proceeds of the eventual sale of his house.

Looking to secure much-needed cash for himself, Carl took out a promissory note of nine thousand dollars from the Plaza

Bank of Commerce, using Tabitha, with her significant assets, as a cosigner. With Carl draining his wife financially and emotionally, the sexless marriage soon ran aground. Tabitha filed for divorce, her petition stating, "The plaintiff at all times during said marriage has demeaned herself faithfully and treated her said husband with love, kindness and affection, and has contributed to the expenses of the household and her upkeep, but that defendant has treated her coldly, has failed and refused to perform the proper function of a husband, has failed to provide for and maintain plaintiff, causing her to suffer great humiliation and embarrassment, and has offered these and other such indignities to plaintiff as to render her condition intolerable."

As the divorce unfolded, Tabitha was shocked to discover Carl had never added her to the deed of his home. The papers she had signed were fraudulent, and she was now on the hook for the nine-thousand-dollar loan he had taken out. A lawsuit ensued, which resulted in the sale of the Balsiger home and compensation to Tabitha for the mortgage payments she had made. Tabitha Teall put the sordid Balsiger chapter behind her, returning to the globe-spanning parties and adventures that charmed so many high-society friends and strangers. Her legend continued to grow. When Liza Minnelli and Joel Grey arrived in Kansas City for a performance of *Cabaret*, they socialized with local star Tabitha Teall.

After the divorce, Carl's life unraveled. He moved into a one-bedroom apartment at 301 West Armour Boulevard, just south of downtown Kansas City, a residential tower managed by the Fifth & Main Corporation. With multiple properties under their supervision, the employees of the management company dealt with all manner of tenants. But none would cause them as much distress as Carl Balsiger.

In July 1961, Balsiger was asked to vacate as his lease was up and his unit was to be rented by a new party. Carl refused to comply and stopped paying the $37.50 rent. Warnings not to enter the building went unheeded, bringing a lawsuit against him for "forced entry and detainer." Rather than comply or fight in court, Carl raised the stakes in a way no one saw coming. Beginning in mid-July, management company officials, agents, employees, and even their legal counsel awoke in the middle of the night to strange sounds outside their bedroom windows. A stalker was watching them, prowling their homes in the dark.

Peering through peepholes, knocking on doors, rummaging through trash cans, and making threatening phone calls, Carl obsessively harassed the helpless management company. A restraining order was filed by Fifth & Main Corporation against Carl Balsiger, charging "the plaintiff, its agents, servants, employees and counsel are being disturbed in unusual manners and at unusual hours." Balsiger lost the eviction case and was ordered to pay two hundred dollars back rent. At risk of losing far more in legal fees, he refused to give up, appealing the case with relentless court filings filled with irregularities and spelling errors.

On appeal, Balsiger had to submit a bond. He used his friend William C. Lucas Jr. and his assets as "surety," or collateral, to ensure he could pay for the damages should he lose as well as the costs to the court of the appeal. The court, however, discovered that the Lucas properties were worth only ten dollars, making the surety inadequate and the appeal all but done for. Carl vacated the unit and paid the two hundred dollars in back rent, his reign of terror over.

Carl moved into a bland apartment building near the city's downtown West Bottoms district, paid for with a new position as director of personnel for Guaranty Insurance Exchange. Facing significant legal action in several states, the company was founded and managed by Kansas City insurance executive Smith F. Brandom, who had run a slew of fraudulent and ultimately bankrupt insurance companies. An FBI investigation into his high-risk scams brought mail fraud convictions in Texas, Illinois, and Wisconsin. Though Guaranty Insurance soon became insolvent and Carl's paychecks ceased, the company had introduced him to an ethically compromised set of insurance company investors who had eyes on a new prize.

On March 24, 1966, a consortium of insurance companies and personal investors bought Minnesota's North Central Fire & Casualty Company which specialized in high-risk automobile policies. Among the investors was Carl Balsiger, who was appointed vice president and secretary of the newly managed company. Within twenty-four hours after his employment officially began, Balsiger removed $750,000 from the company's Minnesota-based bank accounts, which he then transferred into a Las Vegas bank before finally sending the money on to a shell company account in the Bahamas.

On May 2, Balsiger attempted to remove another $125,000 from the Minnesota bank accounts but discovered they had been frozen. The Minnesota insurance commissioner had been investigating the mysterious removal of assets out of the state and wanted answers. The stolen funds from North Central Fire & Casualty Company would not be the only insurance fraud to which Balsiger would be tied. His former employer, Smith F. Brandom, was indicted in 1970 for mail fraud in the collapse of Midwest Mutual Casualty Company back in 1965. Balsiger was named a coconspirator, though not a defendant, in that case.

With efforts ongoing across several states to locate and return the North Central Fire & Casualty funds, indictments for conspiracy to defraud were filed against Carl Balsiger and a slew of coconspirators. For five years, the tangled case continued through motions, court dates, audits, and testimonies. Finally, in 1971, the charges against him were dismissed. But by 1967, Carl had slipped

out of the United States for the Bahamas, the final location of the
hidden offshore bank accounts in which the North Central insurance money had ended up.

His island hideout came to an end, however, when the Baha-
mian government ordered him to leave after he "got into trouble,"
the details never disclosed to family or friends. Back in Kansas City,
Balsiger took his white Rambler station wagon out of storage and
hit the road for four years, traveling the Midwest. At night, Carl
would pull over by the side of the road and sleep in the car.

One night, he searched for a rest area, found a well-lit parking
lot and fell asleep. The next morning, he awoke to tapping on his
windshield. An angry prison guard stared into the car and began
shouting. Confused, Carl looked around and realized he had parked
on the grounds of the sprawling, gothic Mansfield Reformatory
Prison, where *The Shawshank Redemption* would be filmed twenty
years later.

Infrequent trips to sister Patricia's house in Ohio brought him
into contact with his niece and nephew, whom he would drive to
swim practice. They competed for space in the back of his Rambler
with milk gallons filled with motor oil used to keep his car running throughout his extensive travels. Back on the road, Balsiger
would use Highway 30 as his main artery, the same road on which
first wife, Jane Moyer, was decapitated in the horrific 1952 crash in
Carl's car.

Carl reappeared back in Kansas City in 1974, living in a series
of increasingly miserable apartment blocks. The Presbyterian
Church, which had always been a part of his life and stood by him
through thick and thin, suspended him. With his sisters, aunts, and
uncles having long moved away, he spent the remaining years of
his life in a small, dark apartment. The end arrived on February 2,
1977, at Shawnee Mission Medical Center in Overland Park, just
over the county line from Kansas City in Johnson County, Kansas.

Sixty-one-year-old Carl Balsiger's official cause of death was heart attack. But rumors abounded among those who had known him that it was suicide.

Funeral services were held at Stine McClure Funeral Home, where thirty-five years and ten months earlier Leila Welsh's funeral was held. Even in death, Carl shadowed Leila. But in contrast to the thousand-plus attendees at Leila Welsh's funeral service, only a handful of people showed up to pay their respects to Carl Balsiger.

Herman Balsiger always expected just a little too much—from himself, from his employees at Schulze Baking and then ABC Bread Company, from the grocers whom he represented in the National Grocer's Association, from his daughters, whom he sent to expensive schools back East, and most of all from his only son.

Carl Balsiger could never live up those expectations, nor any others that Herman could have assumed for him. Having grown up in a joyless home in which children wore formal suits and free time was spent translating German newspapers to English, Carl became a socially awkward, oddly attired adult unable to maintain a job, a home, a romantic partner, a family, even basic self-care. In his first taste of freedom at the University of Kansas City, Carl never took a position on any student government or Greek council, even though all his friends held top ranks. He was mocked in the school newspaper for his lack of athletic skill, his strange hat, his haircut, even his attempt to grow a moustache. His grades were poor, and he graduated as a fifth-year Senior.

His father handed him plum career opportunities at his own ABC Bread Company and the national conglomerate Interstate Bakeries, from which Carl was either fired or simply quit. The war found him achieving astonishing success, but afterward failure again dogged his every step. His one attempt at entrepreneurship, the highly successful Homecraft Bakery in Camarillo, was aborted after three months. Balsiger would never return to the baking industry that he had mastered at the best cooks' and bakers' schools around the country and on searing South Pacific beaches. The Thachers and Sobanjas would sever all ties with him, and he had no real friendships over the years or business colleagues. Two loveless marriages came and went, as did a string of odd jobs in odd businesses that always ended abruptly. Carl never fulfilled even the lowest of his father's expectations.

And with that came a deep wound of inadequacy. In a family where hard work, success, and a house on the choicest lot at 55th Street and Wornall Road were all that mattered, Carl was an utter failure. Compensation for his profound self-doubt and powerlessness was expressed in a lifetime of lies. Carl lied about his birth year in every official document he ever filed, lied to his father about his Selective Service enrollment in the military, lied to his father about his business success in California, and presented himself as an entirely different person upon meeting his first wife, Jane Moyer, and then second wife, Tabitha Teall.

Carl Balsiger's fabrications extended beyond personal relationships into dangerous illegality. He lied to the LAPD about his occupation, his residence, the date he first met Elizabeth Short, his reason for going to Camarillo with her, the length of time he spent with her, where she slept the nights she was with him, and he denied ever knowing Leila Welsh. He was arrested for drunk driving in May 1947 and forced to place a drunk driver's sticker on his windshield, which he then replaced, landing him in jail for twenty days. He offered his second wife, Tabitha Teall, fraudulent documents that stated he was adding her name to his home's lease, presented a fraudulent securer to back his appeals in court, stole $750,000 from an insurance company less than twenty-four hours after he joined as vice president, and lied to a federal court about the routing of the stolen funds.

Extending beyond perjury, fraud, and embezzlement, his deep-seated feelings of insecurity and powerlessness exploded in violent behavior. His seven-year-old sister drowned under mysterious circumstances at his family's lake house when he was twelve years old. He led the paddling of new students at the University of Kansas City, in which men and women were bent over and painfully swatted multiple times. He led the brutal paddlings of Kegon fraternity pledges in the basements of members' homes. He beat up at least two women he took on dates in Los Angeles. He refused to vacate an apartment he was no longer paying rent for, and when sued, he stalked the homes of the management company's employees in the middle of the night, making violent threats and forcing a court to issue a restraining order.

Against a backdrop of lies, fraud, theft, stalking, and violence lies the unsolved mystery of two women, both known to Balsiger personally, who were murdered in eerily similar ways.

CHAPTER 20

ARID SOIL

"Romantic obsession is like a cataclysm breaking up the
empty landscape. Like a strange exotic plant, it grows in
arid soil."

—ROSEMARY SULLIVAN

D ogged by deep feelings of inadequacy, Carl Balsiger grew
up watching Leila Welsh become an unattainable jewel
of beauty, grace, wealth, intelligence, and popularity.
She was always crossing his path and always just out of reach.
Carl first laid eyes on the storied heiress at Second Presbyterian
Church, which she frequently attended from childhood with her
aunt, Leila McKee Welsh. Seated several pews behind them, the
Balsigers would have envied the wealth and stature that made the
Welshes such admired figures in the church.

Herman Balsiger bought a lot just two houses from Leila McKee
but was unable to afford the construction of a luxury home, settling
instead four blocks away on Main Street. Leila was in the neighborhood often and made friends easily with other children whose
families lived on streets adjoining the Balsiger home. At the University of Kansas City, Leila was in the same elite social circle as Carl,
knew all the same people, attended all the same parties, banquets,

and dances, and visited their homes, which were within blocks of each other.

Her sorority was known for its defiance of his fraternity's drinking, carousing, and sexual advances, and she spurned a paddling attempt by Carl Balsiger's Enforcement Committee. Leila helped unseat the political party led by Balsiger's best friends, who had kept a firm grip on student government. She helped found the Women's Pan-Hellenic Council, which challenged male students' domination of Greek life. She was present at dances and other social functions thrown by the Order of DeMolay, of which Carl was master councilor. She and Carl were in the same KCU graduating class.

He moved to Chicago, Illinois, at the same time she moved to Knoxville, Illinois, just two hundred miles away, and returned to Kansas City the same month she returned. They both spent the summer of 1940 at the remote Lake of the Forest, their residences separated by just a quarter mile. Two weeks before her murder, Leila traveled with her family to Scott Field in Illinois, just twenty miles from Highland, Illinois, where Rudolph Balsiger had owned a farm and where Herman Balsiger grew up and frequently visited.

Though their lives were spent in near-constant intersection, Carl and Leila were polar opposites. While he stumbled and failed at nearly every turn, her confidence and self-reliance took her from achievement to achievement. When Kansas City Police detectives read through Leila's diaries and fifty letters she had saved, they could find no evidence of any animosities, any rivalries, any secret boyfriends or crushes, any anger or resentment toward or from another individual. They were baffled how someone so universally loved could be the target of such a vicious slaying. What they did not consider was that may have been the very reason she was targeted.

The seemingly perfect Leila Welsh was someone Carl could never live up to nor ever hope to be with. For someone with a deep well of insecurity and inadequacy, obsession over an exquisite and unattainable love interest could become a source of frustration, hate, and eventually rage. Carl Balsiger demonstrated his capacity to turn rage into violence when he brutally beat two of his dates in Los Angeles and when he stalked and threatened a management company's terrified employees and lawyers over the issue of vacating an apartment. He would certainly have been capable of the same for an obsessive love interest.

When the KCPD consulted abnormal psychology experts in 1941 for a profile of the Leila Welsh killer, their response fit Carl Balsiger to a tee: "It may be someone who saw the young lady and who was jealous of her achievements in school or in the social circles in which she moved. He could be any age but the circumstances would lead one to believe him to be about her age. Obviously, the crime was committed by someone who knew her personally but whom she would not have considered an acquaintance. It probably was someone who thought her too good for him and he resented it."

The slaying itself was an act of rage and destruction upon Leila, but there may have also been another target. Richard Funk, too, had been in Carl Balsiger's periphery for over a decade and was imbued with the same self-confidence and self-reliance as Leila. With his determination and an aura of leadership, Richard's accomplishments were legion. He had taken a job as a messenger boy in high school, had won a national model airplane contest that made news in all fifty states, had ascended to the top of the Order of DeMolay into a commander's post that was created just for him, and had begun a successful career at Skelly Oil Company. He had known Carl Balsiger as a boy at Lake of the Forest, where both families owned cabins, came up at DeMolay at the same time as Carl, was present at University of Kansas City dances and events that Carl attended, and was present at Lake of the Forest at the same time as Carl in the summer of 1940, months before Leila's murder. While Carl struggled to find work and any measure of success professionally or personally, Funk was a constant reminder of what could be accomplished and what Carl never would accomplish. Tearing apart the love of Richard's life would be the ultimate act of settling the score and evening the playing field.

How could a clumsy twenty-five-year-old amateur like Carl Balsiger commit such a complex and daring murder within proximity of so many people, both inside and outside the Welsh home? The bewildering slaying overwhelmed the police as well as the public. The killer was a seeming phantom capable of inexplicable stealth, shocking bloodlust, and malevolent genius in leaving a trail of evidence. But what appears to be almost supernatural prowess turns out to be a combination of luck and inexperience. Incredible and unnecessary risks were taken by the killer before ever entering Leila's room.

Two houses down from the Welsh home, just before midnight, Marguerite Garner sipped coffee nervously, sensing something was wrong outside. Her sixth sense may have been more than intuition. The next day, she found muddy footprints all over her porch, which had been washed just the day before. With nobody having yet stepped foot on her property that morning, the prints almost certainly had been left by the killer wiping off muddy shoes. Had Garner opened her kitchen window shades and peered onto her porch at the right moment, she would have spotted the killer and called the police.

Before Leila arrived home, the killer had attempted to enter her bedroom. Leila had always opened her north window at night, the east window having lost its screen months before. Having likely stalked and watched her nightly routine on previous evenings, the killer knew to try and open the north window, as it might be unlocked. After prying the screen open, the killer discovered the window was locked, foiling his plans. Leaving the screen hanging awkwardly from its upper hooks, the killer had unwittingly caused the north window to be jammed from opening more than several inches. Unable to pull the window up because of the blockage, Leila would open the east window instead, handing the killer an unexpected, easier passage through an open window with no screen to block his way. It was the critical lucky break that would save him from waking Leila Welsh.

Another stroke of luck for the killer was the foiling of his plan to enter the room before Leila arrived home. Had he successfully entered the room, he would have been faced with virtually no place to hide, the closet used by Leila before she went to bed being too small and the underside of the bed too visible a spot in which to hide. Chief Lear Reed could find no other places where the killer could have hidden.

Though having planned and assembled his murder kit days before, the killer's inexperience was reflected in the mismatched tools he chose for the task, including a nearly five-pound hammer, far greater a weight than would be needed to incapacitate Leila Welsh. The work of a twelve-inch butcher's knife could have been accomplished with a pocketknife. The killer wore gloves that proved much too small. He also came unprepared, realizing only too late a critical component was missing—a rag or cloth to block blood spray.

Smashing a glass panel in the next-door neighbor's garage, which could easily have alerted the resident or any number of neighbors, the killer fumbled his way inside and grabbed a box of clothing, which he then rummaged through in the backyard in full sight of other homes. The killer's entry into the garage alerted owner John Blackman's dogs, who went into a frenzy. Blackman peered into the Welsh backyard but just missed seeing the killer, yet another lucky break. The killer recklessly stood and waited for at least two hours in the open yard next to a chicken-wire fence in view of the neighbors, an undeniable risk that should have led to a panicked sighting. The police counted thirty-six windows in neighbors' homes overlooking the Welsh yard toward Leila's room. Only luck saved the killer from being spotted by the many pairs of eyes behind those three dozen windows.

Blind luck would again save the killer as he slipped through the east window with the heavy murder kit cradled in his left arm, his foot slipping on the exterior wall and leaving a marking of mud. Having just taken a sedative for her menstrual discomfort, Leila was in a deep sleep and more resistant than usual to waking up. However, the high presence of adrenaline in her system later identified by the KCPD crime lab proves she did awake just before the hammer struck her. Had she not taken the sedative or had she awoken just one second earlier, she likely would have had time to scream, alerting Marie and George to the attack.

The killer took an unfathomable risk in raining down two hammer blows with Leila's mother and brother mere feet away. Indeed, the strikes to the skull were loud enough to awaken Marie, who could have easily opened the door to check on Leila and interrupted the murder in progress. When Marie walked into the living room instead, the killer impulsively placed a chair against the bedroom door to bar her from entering. However, the top of the chair was already broken off and its small size could in no way stop the door from being swung open. The ill-conceived barring attempt was made with haste and inexperience.

When the killer exited through the east window, he accidentally held on to the window curtains and clumsily tore them off the wall along with its support rod, nearly waking up George and Marie. He then ran past multiple homes, crossed a street, and even stopped to wash blood off in melting ice water, all while carrying a piece of human flesh in his hands. From his first arrival in the backyards behind Rockhill Road to his escape from the murder scene, the killer was saved only by a fortuitous series of lucky accidents, his own ineptitude nearly ensuring his capture. Chief Reed had correctly identified the killer as an "awkward but fiendish amateur."

Certainly, in planning the crime, the killer was aware of the extreme risk he was taking. With countless opportunities to be seen, heard, or walked in on, it was mission impossible. Yet he persisted in the commission of the crime. Only someone utterly obsessed with Leila Welsh, who had long fantasized about committing atrocities upon her helpless form, would be willing to take a chance so fraught with near-certain discovery. This was the one and only opportunity to be alone with her undetected, and he would not let it slip away, however great the risk and physical discomfort as he waited for hours in frigid thirty-two-degree weather.

Leila had opened Marie's window when she arrived home at 1:30 P.M., and the back door to the house was often left unlocked. Yet neither of those entrances was touched by the killer. His eyes were firmly planted solely and obsessively on Leila's bedroom. Once inside, he was in no rush to butcher his victim and make his escape. Instead, he would take his time, savoring the moment he had long awaited. The *Kansas City Star* gathered, "It was a planned crime, carefully and deliberately executed by one not pressed for time."

The killer would patiently wait for Leila's skull to bleed out before tearing open her neck. He took precious minutes attempting to separate her head from her body. Up to thirty more minutes would pass with blood draining out of her neck before he would cut the flesh from her thigh. He took the time to place the pound of flesh on the windowsill before he ceremonially inscribed a bloody letter S or G on her calf and pulled the bedspread over her head, hiding the carnage from view. After accidently tearing the curtains from the wall, he placed it atop the windowsill and carefully folded it in "an artistic manner as a person would arrange a plated corner decoration." These were not the actions of wanton murder for its own sake. They were obsessive, ritualistic steps in a killing sequence long imagined and lusted after.

In the backyard of the Welsh home, investigators found discarded newspaper pages that had been used to wrap the hammer. Concealing the murder tool in newspaper and thus shielding it from public view was a shrewd choice made by the killer because he likely walked to the crime scene rather than drove. The first stop the killer made once in the alley behind Rockhill Road was Marguerite Garner's porch, where he wiped his shoes off, suggesting he had trudged some distance and picked up layers of mud.

Throughout the murder, the killer had taken significant pains not to allow blood to touch his clothes, placing the T-shirt rag over the knife blade to suppress blood spray and even stepping carefully on and off the bedside rug to avoid treading in the gathering pool of blood on the floor. Once finished, he discarded the hammer, the bloody rag, and the butcher knife: critical pieces of evidence that could aid the police in his capture. Nevertheless, the need to discard those items was greater than the risk they posed to him. Desperate to remain unencumbered of any suspicious items and clean of any telltale blood marks, the killer planned for a safe exit through the streets on foot. There could be no visible evidence on him as he made his way home out in the open. He even took the time to wash traces of blood off in the snow, not the action of someone rushing to get back to the safety of a getaway car.

Having made the fateful journey to the Welsh home on foot, the killer almost certainly lived within the surrounding area. Many of his actions demonstrated a familiarity with and comfort in the Rockhill neighborhood, such as his use of the backyard alleys rather than the sidewalks, his readiness to break into, enter, and rummage through a strange garage, his confidence in hiding just twenty feet away from neighbor Lois Malsness's car while she listened to a radio program. Someone unfamiliar with the neighborhood would have felt too vulnerable, exposed in a backyard surrounded by houses with thirty-six windows peering in.

The killer had no such fears and seemed to already know what Police Chief Lear Reed would later find out when he tested the neighborhood's alertness. Making odd sounds, stepping into and out of Leila Welsh's bedroom window, and walking up and down the backyard alley late at night, Chief Reed was shocked that none of the neighbors noticed his presence just outside their homes. With houses built close to each other and no fences separating backyards, neighbors simply tuned out foreign sounds, something only a resident of the Rockhill neighborhoods would know.

One of those residents was Carl Balsiger, whose house at 5711 Main Street in the Rockhill Heights district lay just thirteen blocks from Leila Welsh's home. At a jog and cutting diagonally through backyard alleys the distance could be traversed in less than ten minutes. The Balsiger home is directly northeast of the Welsh home, the same direction the killer was traveling when he made his exit. Balsiger was intimately familiar with the neighborhood, having grown up there along with all his extended family members. He knew the residents, the alleyways, the garages, the height of the windows, the layouts of backyards. He knew traveling by foot would cause much less commotion than the noisy engine of a car either leaving a home or returning to it.

The killer of Leila Welsh was an inexperienced, nervous, clumsy, vicious amateur willing to take startling risks to fulfill an obsessive fantasy of murdering, slashing, and beheading a beautiful, wealthy heiress with whom he could never otherwise be intimate. He had planned the crime and assembled his murder kit for days or weeks, and yet he still arrived without all the items he would need and botched his initial plan of sneaking into her room before she came home. Only a series of lucky accidents saved him from identification and arrest. But one aspect of the murder impressed investigators with its skill and experience. Though the hammer was used to incapacitate Welsh, the knife had been used to kill her, drain her of blood, and nearly sever her head. It was not just any knife. It was neither a chef's knife, a kitchen knife, a hunting knife, nor a utility knife, all commonly found in the home. Indeed, over 90 percent of all stabbing murders are committed with a kitchen knife.

Instead, this killer brought a butcher knife, a very specific tool for a specific profession. The butcher knife is not easy to wield. Built to slash through a thick carcass and separate bones in a meat market, it is heavier, wider, longer, curved, and requires a different grip and cutting motion than knives commonly found in a home or professional kitchen. With the intention of slicing through Leila Welsh's neck and separating her head from her body, the killer discovered the butcher knife was unable to split the thick discs of the cervical spine found in the human neck. Knife-mark notches were found lodged in Leila's cervical bones, evidence the killer had used extreme force to try and pry open the spine, with no success.

This was not the work of a mad slayer ripping at flesh in uncontrolled rage. It was the work of someone experienced with a butcher knife who knew their way around flesh and bone, intent on severing the body. Investigators further identified marks on the T-shirt rag as evidence the killer had experience as a butcher: "Straight, sharp smears in the folds of the bloody shirt revealed clearly that he had drawn his dripping blade through them as a butcher, after slashing the throat of a steer, would wipe his knife."

Reflecting on the sequence of events in the murder, Police Chief Reed offered a competing theory—the killer displayed the experience of a hunter. "He had prepared himself as if about to butcher a steer—a blow to the head, cut the throat, retain the side."

Reed zeroed in on the cutting of the jugular vein in the neck, which would allow the greatest draining of blood from the body. The *Kansas City Star* reported, "Reed stressed the killer showed a knowledge of anatomy in his use of the shirt to keep blood from spurting on him from the neck wound. Perhaps the slayer was experienced in killing chickens and hogs, the Chief added."

In a city where slaughterhouses reigned supreme and an industrial conveyer belt of beef, pork, chicken, and lamb carcasses exited daily in the tens of thousands, the telltale signs of deft knifework and meat processing became an all too recognizable and sickening skill set used in the butchering of a human victim. Carl Balsiger had spent his youth working in his father's grocery store, cutting and processing large sections of meat direct from the slaughterhouses. He had stalked, killed, and field dressed deer in the vast wilderness around Lake of the Forest, and he remained an avid hunter throughout his life.

The skills Chief Reed and police investigators recognized at play in the Welsh murder were all familiar to Carl Balsiger, despite his cosmopolitan, plain demeanor. The psychologists who built the killer's profile for the KCPD concluded: "That side of the slayer's personality responsible for this crime would not under ordinary circumstances appear on the surface. . . . He probably keeps it well guarded. It would be impossible to classify him. In ordinary life, he may and probably does appear to be a most harmless looking person. He may be an intelligent individual. The type of personality pictured here never is feeble minded."

Ultimately, Chief Reed and his team of detectives could never establish a motive behind the murder, stating, "When I opened the door of the victim's bedroom there were many more reasons to stand still and look—not only to see but to attempt to understand the scene that lay before me. . . . The cases that baffle are those in which no motive previously established appears to fit; those in which a motive, of any reason for a logical motive, is beyond conception." What Reed did not understand was that the motive was right in front of him: the total destruction and desecration of the perfect woman.

CHAPTER 21

CRESTVIEW 1-4666

Nearly six years after the murder of Leila Welsh became a national sensation and traumatized Kansas City, Elizabeth Short's murder grabbed national headlines and traumatized Los Angeles. Just as with Welsh, Short's murder was shocking in its brutality, with the victim carved up and left in a disfigured horror pose that haunted even the most experienced detectives. And just as with Welsh, the killer remained infuriatingly elusive, with no arrest ever made in either case.

What separated the two cases was the killer's communication in the weeks following the discovery of Short's body. Of the letters confirmed as authentic to Short's killer, the most important and telling message he conveyed to the police and the public was "Dahlia killing was justified." This was not the statement of a maniac intent on threatening and terrifying the city with a prolonged reign of terror. It meant the killing was personal, just like the Welsh murder. Only this time, it was for very different reasons.

On the morning of December 6, 1946, Elizabeth Short was in a bind, unable to get her all-important luggage back from Chancellor Hotel manager Elsie Ringo until she paid her third week's rent of five dollars. She zipped out early, returned with the five dollars, and packed up, telling roommate Linda Rohr, "I've got to hurry he's waiting for me." Soon, she was on the road with Carl Balsiger for the long trip to Camarillo. Clearly, she had gotten the five dollars from Balsiger, who was waiting for her as she packed up.

Balsiger's claim to have met Elizabeth Short that morning at a real estate office makes no sense, especially in light of Elizabeth's history. She had spent her five months in Southern California living off the largesse of friends—sleeping on their couches, sharing their beds, anywhere she could stay for free. Her only true rental arrangement was the five dollars she owed weekly at the Chancellor Hotel for the privilege of sharing one room with six other women, and even that was cause for financial stress. She had spent three weeks at the Chancellor, the first of which was paid for by Anne Toth, the second week paid for by frequent date Michael Otero, and the third week paid for by "the stranger" from whom she took five dollars on the morning of December 6.

Flat broke and desperate to leave Los Angeles, Short would hardly be perusing a real estate office that morning, looking to buy or rent a home or apartment on her own. Nonetheless, the LAPD seemed to buy Balsiger's story as well as his reasons for taking her to Camarillo. Despite Balsiger's claims, Jean Thacher established that Carl Balsiger had known Elizabeth Short well before December 6.

Anne Toth recalled Beth phoning a strange number in Beverly Hills with a Crestview phone prefix. Carl Balsiger is the only known acquaintance of Short's who lived in Beverly Hills. His number was Crestview 1-4666. And now, in an hour of need, Elizabeth would call Carl for money and he would come through for her. With his road trip to Ventura County that day, she saw an opportunity to get out of Los Angeles and avoid the crosshairs of a police investigation into her roommates' marijuana possession. It would not be the last time she got money from him.

The five dollars Elizabeth gave Chancellor manager Elsie Ringo was the only money she had, leaving her flat broke again. But on the night of December 8, 1946, she left Balsiger and went to the

Greyhound bus station on Cahuenga Boulevard in Hollywood, where she bought a ticket to San Diego, followed by the purchase of a movie ticket at the Aztec Theater the next morning. Since she had spent three days solely with Balsiger, he was the only person who could have given her the money for the bus ticket.

That would have been the second time he gave her money. After disappearing for a month to a city that she had never been to before nor knew anyone in, Elizabeth Short decided on January 7, 1947, that she would leave California for Chicago, where she had work opportunities awaiting her, and where she hoped to be reunited with former boyfriend Gordon Fickling. With the Chicago-bound bus leaving from Los Angeles, Red Manley would provide the transportation from San Diego to the Greyhound bus terminal in LA, where she would buy a ticket to Chicago for $36.85, more than $500 today. The problem she faced was where she would get the money for the bus ticket.

On January 7, she called Mark Hansen to ask for money, but he only offered a bed at his home. Beth did not need a place to stay— she would be in Los Angeles only long enough to get the money for the bus ticket. On January 8, Red Manley picked Beth up from the French home in San Diego. Once in the car, Beth asked to be taken back to Los Angeles that day. Red explained he could not drive back until the next day, January 9. She then asked if he could drop her off at the Greyhound station in San Diego later that night so she could grab the first bus back to Los Angeles, to which Red agreed.

The pair returned to the French home, packed her belongings, and then stopped for dinner at Patrick's Café, where she made calls at a phone booth while Red remained out of hearing range at their table. The *LA Examiner* stated that the police had established the calls she made at the pay phone were to a number in the Los Angeles area, but were never able to identify the specific phone number. After the phone call, she informed Red she had changed her mind and would return with him to Los Angeles the next day. Whoever she called at 7:30 P.M. from Patrick's Café at 2768 Balboa Avenue changed her plans. With one thing on her mind—the substantial amount of money she needed for a bus ticket to Chicago—Beth was clearly angling to meet this stranger for financial reasons.

She could only go to one person for money. Spanish teacher Michael Otero had given Elizabeth a few dollars here and there but could ill afford a nearly forty dollar request. Gordon Fickling had already rejected a request to send money and was pushing Beth away. Broadcast voice artist Maurice Clement had bought Beth dinner several times in November and early December but did not lend her money. Mother Phoebe Short could not be expected to wire money in time and likely did not have the funds for such a request. Anne Toth was in Richmond, California, and was not contacted by Beth.

With all other bridges burned, abandoned, or out of touch, Carl Balsiger remained the one person whom Beth had successfully extracted money from on at least two occasions and who could afford the forty dollars she needed. She would now go to him in her hour of need. However, the circumstances under which they had parted were murky. Beth had never before left a city under cover of night with no word to friends and family about where she was headed, as she did when she left Los Angeles for San Diego on the night of December 8. She had explained her bizarre San Diego detour to Mark Hansen as an escape from a "screwball" who had scared her. Because Carl Balsiger was the last person she was with in Los Angeles, it is certain she was referring to him. However desperate for money she was, though, why would she reach out to a screwball who had scared her enough to hide out in a strange city?

Anne Toth's boyfriend, Leo Hymes, had a front row seat to many of Beth's interactions at Mark Hansen's house. A frequent visitor who lazed about for hours at a time, he watched girls come and go from the home but was particularly struck by Elizabeth Short, who baffled him. When questioned during the district attorney's investigation, Hymes offered an unusually blunt and illuminating insight into the character of Elizabeth Short:

Q: Would you say that she was on the make for you; that she was trying?

A: No, I don't think the gal even considered me, but she—there, was something always—I know was wrong with that girl. I don't know what it was. The few times I saw her there Mark would be talking to her. Naturally I would hear—you couldn't help but hear the conversation that went on, and she was peculiar. I mean I never did bother to really figure out—I wouldn't want to ask Ann [sic] about it; she might think I was interested in her. The girl lacked something; I don't know what it was.

Q: Well, would you say she lacked experience?

A: Definitely.

Q: With men?

A: I don't think she knew anything about men, I really—I think she thought she did, but she didn't seem to.

Anne Toth, too, felt that Elizabeth's instincts about people were off and that her naïvety and good nature had left her ill-prepared for the sordid city and the real motives of questionable men. "She seemed to have confidence in a lot of people," Anne recalled with disapproval. She went further, identifying a paradox in Beth's choice of boyfriends: "[Beth] was skeptical of people but despite this she often stumbled into trash."

Elizabeth Short returned to Los Angeles on January 9 desperate for money. The only choice was Carl Balsiger. If she could get him to meet her in public in busy downtown Los Angeles, she could control any violent or threatening behavior from him. There would be no return to his canyon home, no checking in to a hotel. She would simply spend time with him at a café or bar and get the money she needed one last time. But Elizabeth did not really know anything about men and what certain men are capable of when a woman steps into their car.

Carl Balsiger had given Elizabeth Short money at least twice, had taken her out to dinner in Beverly Hills, and had given her a place to stay for several nights, and yet she disappeared from his life as easily as she entered it. She had suddenly abandoned him at a bus station on December 8 and lied about her destination. He had no idea how long she would be gone or where she was going. And then she reappeared a month later, but this time her agenda was front and center. She needed money right away and couldn't spend more than an hour with him because the last bus to Chicago was leaving at 11:00 P.M. Carl had recently beaten up dates with no provocation. He just snapped and pounded the hell out of them. Now Elizabeth Short was going to try and chisel him for forty dollars and disappear once again. In his mind, whatever happened next would be justified.

Beth Short had lived the last five months on the run. She knew she would leave Los Angeles. The weather was good for her asthma, but the people were not her kind. By choice, there were no auditions, no meetings with directors, no casting couches for her. She had no aspiration to make it in Hollywood because she had no aspiration to stay in Hollywood. And so, every encounter, every friend, roommate, boyfriend, or date was just a distraction until the inevitable exit. Many women were offended by her lack of emotional connection. Many men were angered by her disinterest in romance.

But Beth had no reason to establish anything deeper than superficial attachments because soon she would be gone.

On the night of January 9, 1947, Elizabeth disappeared and was held in an unknown location for five and a half days until her body was discovered in the weeds of Norton Avenue the morning of January 15. While many sightings of Elizabeth Short during "the missing week" were later reported, the LAPD could not verify a single one of them. There was good reason to establish that Short had been held captive somewhere and had not been out on the town, as was so widely speculated. Short's luggage contained her most important and prized possessions—her clothes and makeup, which she was never away from for more than a handful of hours. She did not wear others' clothing or share her own. Her makeup bag was sacred to her and always at the ready. She had stored her luggage at the Greyhound bus station, to which she intended to return later in the night. There is no possibility she would have left her luggage in storage for five days while she stayed with a friend.

LAPD searched in vain for a remote location where a woman could be imprisoned for nearly six days without eliciting any suspicion from neighbors. Carl Balsiger lived in a remote house deep in a country canyon with few other homes in sight. The property featured an attached garage with a concrete pad, thick walls of stucco, and only two tiny windows for ventilation. Dark and shut off from view, the garage was an ideal chamber in which to bind, torture, kill, and exsanguinate a victim. A drain in the center of the room would swallow the river of blood, easily hosed down in the aftermath.

The Benedict Canyon home would offer two key advantages Leila Welsh's bedroom lacked: isolation and time. Upon first examining the bisected body of Elizabeth Short, autopsy surgeons were amazed by the delicate, surgical-like bisection of the body. The person who did this avoided puncturing any organs and expertly sliced through the lumbar discs of the spine. Investigators assumed the work had been performed by a surgeon: "These cuts were made by some expert who must have had an education in surgery."

With homicide detectives certain a doctor was behind the murder, Captain Donohoe revealed a surprising discovery. The murder weapons used were not surgical knives, the logical tools of a surgeon. Instead, the crime lab team had microscopically analyzed the cuts to the body and concluded the murder tool was a butcher knife. The *Herald-Express* reported, "Minute examination of the victim's body revealed the tools used in the murder were a sharp butcher knife and a straight razor used to torment the victim." Donohoe stated, "We believe that a very sharp knife of the long bladed butcher or carving type was used to sever the body. It is also possible that the killer may have inflicted torture and mutilation with a straight razor." Why would a surgeon wield a butcher knife to bisect the body, a completely foreign and clumsy blade that could easily be replaced with surgical knives that would be far more comfortable and familiar?

While the LAPD expended enormous time and resources in an expansive search for suspicious doctors with questionable practices, a parallel investigation was run into every slaughterhouse and butcher across the city. And just like the investigation into medical professionals, the search for suspicious butchers turned up no suspects. The police missed the fact that the killer possessed the skills of a butcher but was not an active butcher in the city. Nevertheless, the work of a butcher was evident in the manner with which organs were carefully preserved despite the complete severing of the victim through the midsection. The LA *Daily News* shrewdly observed, "The cutting indicated a meticulous desire to avoid damaging any vital organs."

One of the important tasks carried out by butchers is the careful preservation of internal organs, each of which is a commercially sold entity, such as the stomach, which is used for tripe, and the liver, the kidneys, and the lungs. But the most prized organ is the intestines, which is used for sausage making. Butchers have to be extremely agile in preserving this slippery, fragile organ, as any errant cut can potentially rip it open and spill fecal matter into the animal carcass. The most delicate cut is the severing of the duodenum, which connects the intestines to the stomach. Similar in both pigs and humans, the duodenum lies buried within the coils of the small intestines, and it requires an experienced and careful reach to successfully pull it out and sever it.

Elizabeth Short's body was perfectly bisected through the duodenum, a difficult operation with which very few surgeons would have been experienced in the 1940s. Chief Autopsy Surgeon Dr. Frederick Newbarr was amazed the killer was able to bisect the body in the limited time between the death of the victim and the disposal of the body on Norton Avenue. A butcher, who is used to rapidly cutting through and separating bone, flesh, and organs in a matter of minutes, would have had no problem completing the task. So successful was the severing of the duodenum that fecal matter within Elizabeth Short's intestines was undisturbed and remained encased in the coils, the mark not of a skilled surgeon but of a skilled butcher.

Despite the oft-repeated claims that the bisection was a perfect surgical procedure with the organs completely undisturbed, the autopsy noted, "There are lacerations of the intestines and into both kidneys." The killer had not avoided making unwanted cuts and was not as perfect in the bisection as is widely accepted.

Further evidence of a butcher or hunter's work is found in the layered cuts of the victim's midsection. Rather than one consistent incision through the body, the killer performed a sequence of layered cuts, starting with skin, then tissue, fascia, and muscle, and finally through the organs, just as a hunter or butcher carefully cuts each layer of a kill so as not to accidently slice the organs and cause fecal matter or internal stomach bacteria to invade the meat. The cut through the skin layer was smooth and consistent, one long draw. But the cut just below it into tissue, fascia, and then muscle was completely different—a scalloped, segment-by-segment series of slices. This was not the work of a surgeon cautiously taking their time in a smooth, clean arc. It was the work of someone quickly disassembling a carcass but extremely sensitive to organ disturbance.

On January 24, 1947, the killer sent the *LA Examiner* Elizabeth Short's address book, among many other personal effects that she had on her person when she disappeared. Seventy-five to one hundred names and numbers were written in the book, in no particular order. While the address book was originally composed of 400 pages, sections had been torn out. Some were only two or three pages, torn out by hand, likely by Short herself. Other sections, including a 125-page-chunk, were cut with a straight razor, likely the work of the killer.

Elizabeth Short made a habit of inscribing the name and phone number of every person she met in her address book. But Carl Balsiger's name was not written in the address book. It was written on a loose piece of paper inserted into the address book. Of all the people Short met and wrote into her book, only four were written on loose pieces of paper. The first was written on "letter paper" and bore the name of Wayne Gregg, the bandleader of the Hacienda Club, where Red Manley and Elizabeth Short had danced on January 8. In the midst of a whirlwind night on a dance floor, Gregg slipped her his number on a piece of paper, which she kept. His information was written in ink.

The other three names, including that of Carl Balsiger, were written on notebook paper torn from the address book itself and were all written in pencil. Why would Short have torn out a piece of paper from the address book and written down Balsiger's phone number, which she would then insert, loose, into the address book? Further, the phone number on the piece of paper was not Crestview 1-4666, the number at his primary residence in Benedict Canyon. It was Hempstead 4377, the Hollywood number for his rented room on Sunset Blvd. Balsiger kept his real residence in Benedict Canyon hidden from the police. The loose piece of paper suspiciously supports that deception—perhaps by design. Having sliced out the page containing his name and Benedict Canyon phone number, and likely multiple pages on either side in order to avoid leaving any imprints of his information on other pages, Balsiger slipped the Sunset Boulevard number into the address book.

But why would Carl Balsiger send the address book containing his own name to newspapers and thus to the police when he wasn't even on the LAPD's radar yet? In early December, Carl had traveled to his bakery in Camarillo, which had opened just a week earlier. Very likely, he brought Short with him to the bakery, where Bernie Sobanja, his wife, and the Thachers, who had already dined with Short, would have interacted with her.

By January 24, 1947, the Black Dahlia murder had become a huge national news story. The police were imploring the public for any shred of information about Short. Anyone with whom Elizabeth Short interacted in Camarillo would have been distressed by her presence at Homecraft Bakery just over a month before her murder and would have pressed Balsiger to divulge whether he had informed the police.

Jean Thacher was the most alarmed by Balsiger and demanded her husband cut off all contact with him. Undoubtedly, she was a liability for Carl. But so were the other Homecraft employees who had seen Elizabeth Short in Camarillo, any of whom could have tipped off the LAPD and sent suspicions soaring over the mysterious "boyfriend" who held back crucial information from the police. Sending the address book to the press could allow him cover in which he would appear to be just another acquaintance out of many. Interviewed by the police, he could lie about the circumstances of his association with Elizabeth Short and defuse any potential informant from sending a panicky message to the police. Which is, of course, exactly what happened. When interviewed by the LAPD within days of sending the address book, Balsiger wove a tapestry of lies, most of which were never detected. Though he was a target of the Black Dahlia investigation until the bitter end, the ruse actually worked.

In 1950, LAPD Sergeant Finis Brown located Carl Balsiger in St. Louis after a long search and flew out to confront the suspect on his many lies. Strapped to a lie detector, Carl finally came clean on the length of time he spent with Elisabeth Short, admitting he had spent three days with her and not the day and a half he had previously admitted to. However, he held fast to his assertion that he did not see Elizabeth Short after December 8, 1946, which "convinced Brown," according to the files of the district attorney investigations of 1949 and 1950.

Though the wording of the entry does not specifically state that Balsiger passed the lie detector test, it suggests he did. And if he did pass with no other lies detected, then he succeeded in tricking the machine. Admitting only to that which he absolutely had to, Balsiger repeated numerous fabrications that were not detected, such as the real date he met Elizabeth Short, much earlier than the December date which he claimed. Carl held fast that he was in Camarillo only to sell bakery equipment and never divulged his ownership of Homecraft Bakery.

He never revealed the Benedict Canyon home. He never admitted to knowing Leila Welsh. And yet he seemingly passed the lie detector test. It is evident that Balsiger lied about these crucial matters because a year after the polygraph test, the police and DA records maintain these fictions. Brown never learned the truth. If he had, the record would not be filled with significant inaccuracies. Balsiger succeeded in keeping his deceptions intact in the minds of the LAPD.

With so many fabrications undetected, the accuracy of the polygraph test comes into question, either by operator error, technical error, or Balsiger's ability to remain calm and thus "beat the machine." The lie detectors of the 1940s were notoriously erratic, and capable operators were not in abundance. Brown administered the test in St. Louis with an operator whom he would not have known on equipment with which he would not have been familiar.

Even modern lie detector results are not admissible in court because of their scientific unreliability. In the best of circumstances, there is still a long history of murderers coolly deceiving polygraphs to the dismay of investigators. Responsible for forty-nine murders, the infamous "Green River Killer," Gary Ridgway, passed a lie detector test in 1984 and went on to kill many more times until his arrest in 2001. Responsible for as many as forty victims, "Angel of Death" Charles Cullen passed a polygraph test in 1993 and went on to murder for another ten years. Lee Anthony Evans killed five New Jersey teenagers in 1978, was arrested, passed a polygraph test, and was set free, with the case remaining cold for another thirty-two years.

Despite convincing Sergeant Brown that he had not seen Elizabeth Short after December 8, which should have eliminated him as a suspect, Carl Balsiger remained at the top of the suspect list a year later. Finis Brown clearly was not convinced.

While Carl Balsiger may have hated Leila Welsh for her unattainable perfection, his hatred for Elizabeth Short may have been rooted in all her imperfections. Like a mirror, Carl Balsiger shared those very same qualities which he would have hated about himself. Both Carl and Beth lied frequently, both sought money from others in questionable ways, both mismanaged money, neither could hold a job, both had odd personalities, neither had enduring friendships or romantic relationships, both were drifting and unsettled in their future plans, and both lied to their parents about their achievements. Most notably, Beth did not enjoy sex and avoided it, while Carl struggled to maintain intimacy and later avoided sex with his wives. The things Carl hated most within himself, he may have seen in Beth. And that could have been the spark that started an inferno.

Over and over, Carl Balsiger got lucky. Not tied to any of the groups with which Elizabeth Short ran—the Carpenter Drive-In crowd, the Hawthorne Hotel group, the boys at the Guardian Arms apartment, Mark Hansen's circle, the women of the Chancellor Hotel—he remained unknown by anyone in Short's network of acquaintances, who all were relentlessly grilled by the police for information. Walt and Jean Thacher cut off all communication with him soon after the Black Dahlia made front page news, while Bernhard Sobanja and his wife suddenly quit Homecraft Bakery. Yet none of them relayed their suspicions to the police.

Finis Brown spent years tracking Balsiger but never unraveled the crucial lies that could have led to an arrest. Just like the Welsh murder, a witch's brew of sheer audacity, deception, inexperience, extreme risk-taking, viciousness, and luck combined to aid the killer, to his extraordinary benefit.

CHAPTER 22

HOW THEY
WERE BOUND

Upon departing his post as police chief of Kansas City, Lear Reed offered the public a prediction . . . and a warning. "If the slayer of Leila Welsh has killed before, or if he kills again, with the exception of sudden slaying in combat, certain methods of his operation will stand out, be comparable, no matter how carefully he plans his crime."

Six years later, Los Angeles detectives looked into the past of suspect Carl Balsiger and noted, "A young twenty-two-year-old woman by the name of Dorothy [sic] Welsh with whom he had attended a school in Kansas City was murdered in that city in 1941 in a similar manner as victim Short." LAPD detectives never found out just how right they were. Both in the killer's method of operation and signature, the Welsh and Short murders bear a list of striking similarities so comprehensive they can only be described as beyond coincidence.

The telltale signs of a common killer begin with the initial assaults. Both victims were first incapacitated with multiple blows to the head, though not enough to shatter or crush the skull in either case. The hammer that struck Leila Welsh twice on her right temple was not used "in a full blow," though it did fracture the skull and formed a three-inch depression, causing blood to pour out of her ear. Likewise, Elizabeth Short's autopsy referred to a "blunt instrument that struck the victim's right temple three times, fracturing the skull and causing massive internal bleeding, a subarachnoid hemorrhage or stroke of the brain."

In both instances, a heavy object was used to strike the victims' heads, but neither was pummeled mercilessly and bashed into submission. The killer showed the same vicious but controlled restraint in both instances, hitting the head in the same location and causing similar injuries. With the killer holding back the full force of the heavy weapons he wielded, neither victim died from the strikes to their heads.

Next, Leila Welsh's neck was sliced open to the spinal column, forming a massive opening and nearly separating her head from her body. With an incision line that spread from the top of the neck to a midpoint farther down and then back up to the other side of the neck, the opening spread from ear to ear in what Coroner Leitch described as a V shape. Chief Reed noted, "Her throat had been gashed to the vertebrae. It gaped wide open as though a V had been cut out." Though incapacitated, Leila Welsh was still alive when her neck was cut open. Elizabeth Short's face was cut open from the edges of either side of her mouth toward her ears.

Interviewed by the *Desert Sun* newspaper in 1975, lead detective Harry Hansen stated, "She had two V-shaped cuts on either side of her mouth, probably made while she was still alive." Both acts of ripping open the victims' neck and face were the causes of death. While Welsh died from "an acute hemorrhage due to an incised wound to the neck," causing massive loss of blood, Elizabeth Short died from "hemorrhage due to shock and loss of blood" from the incised wounds to her face.

After cutting Leila Welsh's throat, the killer patiently waited thirty minutes for the body to bleed out. Elizabeth Short drowned in her own blood, which poured out of her facial lacerations and into her lungs. The killer then bisected her body, draining nearly all of the blood from both her torso and lower half. While total exsanguination of a murder victim is extremely rare, what happened next to both victims in the same killing sequence is even more rare.

Once the bodies were drained of blood, the killer used a sharp razor to slice a bloodless, horseshoe-shaped piece of flesh an inch thick from both victims. At the junction of Leila Welsh's right thigh and buttock, a five-inch diameter, one-inch-thick chunk of skin and "subcutaneous soft tissue and muscle" was sliced, pulled, and ripped out, leaving a cavity free of any blood or dirt. From Elizabeth Short's left thigh, a four-inch-diameter, one-inch-thick chunk of skin and subcutaneous soft tissue and muscle was sliced, pulled, and ripped out, leaving a cavity free of any blood or dirt.

The Short autopsy report stated, "There is an irregular opening in the skin on the anterior surface of the left side [of the thigh] with tissue loss. The opening measures 3½ inches transversely at the base and 4 inches from the base longitudinally to the upper extremity. The laceration extends into the subcutaneous soft tissue and muscle. No Ecchymosis seen."

Both excised pieces of flesh weighed approximately one pound. Both were bell- or horseshoe-shaped, a flat bottom topped with a flared, circular curve. Both horseshoe-shaped incisions were noted by the respective police departments as having been made in one smooth motion, with no hesitation or secondary cuts made along the blade's path. Coroner Leitch noted of Leila Welsh's missing flesh, "I will say it was a very purposeful act with definitely dexterous handling of the knife." Chief Autopsy Surgeon Dr. Frederick Newbarr noted that the incision into Elizabeth Short's thigh was also made with one arc of the knife blade, with no secondary cuts. The walls of flesh within the incisions into both victims' thighs were absolutely clean of any dirt, foreign matter, or blood. Chief Reed marveled at the precision and cleanliness of the knife work and was left with dismay at the killer's "strange, inhuman passion."

Reed observed of the Leila Welsh murder, "A circular or horseshoe-shaped incision clear through the fatty part of the buttocks has been made by the slayers blade. The pattern had been pulled back and then hacked off at the base. . . . The head had been bashed, the throat cut, blood drained from the body and still the killer was not satisfied." Had the word "buttocks" been replaced with the word "thigh" and the word "throat" replaced with the word "face," the passage could serve as a precise description of the Black Dahlia murder.

The piece of flesh torn out of Elizabeth Short's thigh was thrust into her vaginal canal by the killer. When it was discovered in the autopsy, Dr. Newbarr observed a series of "criss-crossing lacerations" cut into the skin. A matching series of "criss-crossing lacerations," described as a tic-tac-toe pattern, were also discovered cut into Short's hip at the junction of her right thigh and buttock, the exact anatomical location where the pound of flesh had been sliced out of Leila Welsh. Like a map key, the killer marked a tic-tac-toe symbol on Short in the same place where he had sliced a bloodless, horseshoe-shaped pound of flesh out of Leila Welsh. And within Elizabeth Short's vagina was found hidden a bloodless, horseshoe-shaped pound of flesh bearing the matching tic-tac-toe pattern.

Elizabeth Short had been bisected into two pieces. Nearly the same had been attempted with Leila Welsh at the neck. The notches found in the cervical spinal column within her neck revealed the killer's aborted attempt to sever her head from her body. Unable to separate the thick column of bones, he abandoned the severing attempt. Nonetheless, his intention was to disassemble Welsh's body into two pieces, just as Short was disassembled into two pieces.

Both murders displayed a professional deftness with a knife that led investigators to speculate whether the killer was a surgeon or butcher. The blades used by the killer were virtually the same, a murder kit composed of a large butcher knife used to cut the bodies in two and a sharp, exacting straight razor used to cut the pieces of flesh. Quoting LAPD captain Jack Donohoe, the *Herald-Express* reported, "Minute examination of the brutally slashed body has revealed that the mad slayer's weapons were an extremely sharp butcher or carving knife used to bisect the torso, and possibly a straight-edged razor employed in tormenting the victim while she was still alive. All local cutlery establishments, wholesale and retail surgical instrument shops and barbers' supply houses are being carefully checked for recent sales to suspicious appearing men or women, according to Capt. Jack Donohoe of central homicide."

Likewise, the Kansas City police believed the butcher knife left behind by the killer was used to rip open Leila Welsh's neck, but the flesh was cut out using a much sharper and smaller straight razor, "The knife and the [flesh] pattern did not agree. The line of the incision was smooth, unbroken, not jagged. . . . It appeared to have been made with a short, stiff and sharp blade. The butcher knife blade was long, flexible, with a dull end."

While both victims' bodies were cut open and drained of blood, the killer displayed a surprising sensitivity to blood avoidance. While the act of cutting flesh was his prize, blood appears to have been a hindrance for the killer to avert, empty from the body, and wash away. In the Welsh murder, the killer went to great lengths to avoid coming into contact with blood, using the white T-shirt to suppress spray from the jugular vein, stepping carefully around the pool of blood on the floor, avoiding any blood stains on his white gloves, carefully wiping the butcher blade of blood, and washing blood off in dripping ice water. In the Elizabeth Short murder, not only was blood drained out in the bisection, but the body parts were also washed of blood in a bathtub or basin followed by a thorough cleansing with a stiff coconut-fiber brush.

Similarly, the killer displayed an acute sensitivity to leaving fingerprints, going to extreme lengths to ensure not even partial prints or smudges were left on the bodies. In the Welsh murder, the killer wore gloves throughout the entire process. No prints were found on the hammer or butcher knife left behind, suggesting he had been careful to clean them prior to the murder or had never touched them without gloves. In the Short murder, the fiber brush bristles used to clean the body were found primarily clumped in the open-mutilation wounds, where the killer's fingers had likely been touching. Later, the killer would douse the envelope of evidence sent to LA newspapers with gasoline to dissolve any potential latent fingerprints left behind.

Both victims displayed strange markings on their bodies, baffling investigators. Leila Welsh's left calf was left "boldly exposed" from beneath her blue bedspread, a strange symbol similar to a letter S or G written in blood on the skin. But there was more. The KCPD searched the Welsh property and surrounding neighborhood for a two-tined carving fork that was never found. While the reason for the search was never publicly revealed, the only possibility is the presence of stab marks left on the body matching the shape, depth, and space between two carving fork tines. Elizabeth Short bore tic-tac-toe symbols carved into both her right thigh and the flesh cut from her left thigh. A patchwork of lacerations were carved into the suprapubic region above her genitals. The letters *E* and *D* were detected in the knife blade marks, though never verified.

The killer of Leila Welsh and Elizabeth Short did not act in a frenzy, tearing apart his victims in a blind rage like Jack the Ripper. Instead, he acted patiently, methodically, and controlled—like a hunter. An adage says, "The hunter's surest weapon is patience." The capacity to tolerate hours or even days in uncomfortable, monotonous conditions awaiting prey often means the difference between success and failure in a hunt. Leila Welsh's killer waited for hours in freezing conditions until she arrived home at 1:30 A.M. He then waited at least another ninety minutes before entering her room. As a deer hunter does with his kill, he then bled out his victim for up to thirty minutes before performing more mutilations. Elizabeth Short's killer patiently kept her prisoner for five days of torment before initiating her torture, mutilation, and murder. Like a hunter, the killer's work of draining blood and cutting pieces of flesh was slowly performed in quiet solitude, much of it executed after the victims' deaths.

Surprisingly, neither victim was sexually assaulted. No evidence of rape was detected nor spermatozoa found. Nonetheless, sexual satisfaction may have been achieved in other ways, through the act of killing and maiming. Both murders displayed the characteristics of erotophonophilia, or lust murder, in which an offender achieves sexual climax through the death of another person, not through sexual intercourse. Elizabeth Short's breasts, genitals, lips, legs, and anus were beaten, cut, penetrated, and mutilated, while Leila Welsh's thigh and buttock was sliced and torn open, all of which fit the criteria for a lust murder.

Vernon Geberth, author of the seminal police investigative manual "Practical Homicide Investigation," states, "Lust murders are homicides in which the offender stabs, cuts, pierces, or mutilates the sexual regions or organs of the victim's body. The sexual mutilation of the victim may include evisceration, piquerism, displacement of the genitalia in both males and females, and the removal of the breasts in a female victim (defeminization). It also includes activities such as 'posing' and 'propping' of the body, the insertion of objects into the body cavities." With attention paid to the stomach, neck, face, and sexual regions, the killer did not touch either of the victims' fingers, toes, hands, feet, lower legs, or arms.

At the center of both murders was the act of cutting, ripping, and slicing. Lacerations of Elizabeth Short's flesh were found in multiple locations on her body. A diamond-shaped piece of flesh was cut open below her stomach. A square-shaped piece of flesh was cut from Short's right breast. A diamond-shaped piece of skin was ripped from the side of her left breast. The pound of flesh was cut out of her left thigh, while Leila Welsh suffered the same fate in her right thigh and died when her neck was sliced through. In both murders, the killer drained the bodies in order to cut flesh cleanly with no blood spray or flow in the wounds.

The act of cutting or penetrating skin as a source of sexual pleasure is called picquerism. Stab wounds and cuts to erogenous zones, genitalia, the face, or the neck all replace sexual intercourse and combine with the subjugation of the victim to satisfy intense sadistic urges. Most of the mutilations in picquerism are performed postmortem, the perpetrator ejaculating uncontrollably while in the act of cutting. In a twisted reverse image of sexual intercourse, destruction becomes pleasure.

The similarities between the Welsh and Short cases are found not only in the slayings themselves but also in specific personality and behavioral characteristics of the killer. Both murders evidence a perpetrator with a tolerance for extreme risk. Welsh's killer was plainly visible in her backyard for hours and then slipped through an open window while his victim slept just five feet away with two family members present in the house. A trail of evidence was then left by the killer out in public view.

Elizabeth Short's killer incapacitated and abducted her in pedestrian-crowded downtown Los Angeles and then deposited her body six days later on a heavily trafficked public street visible from nearby houses. The oil fields and vast empty swaths of the nearby Baldwin Hills area were just a five-minute drive farther and would have provided far more isolation. The killer openly carried Short's purse and shoe through an alley to the back of a restaurant, fully in view of passersby. Despite the extreme and reckless risks the killer took, he nonetheless was highly organized, intelligent, methodical, and cautious not to leave fingerprints or personal identifiers, and he extensively planned and prepared for his crimes.

And yet, he made glaring and sloppy mistakes. The envelope filled with Elizabeth Short's personal items sent to the *LA Examiner* opened up at one end while in postal transit, the gasoline having dissolved the glue that held it closed. Any of the items could have spilled out and been lost while in the mail, rendering the envelope and its message ineffective. Another crucial correspondence from the killer to the police was mailed without a stamp, which could have led to its disposal by postal workers. Latent fingerprint smudges were found within one of the messages sent into the police, though without enough detail to identify the sender. Similarly, the Leila Welsh murder was a series of mistakes and blunders, any of which could have caused the killer to be identified and captured.

The killer's ego in both cases demanded a statement of authorship. The S or G mark written in blood on Leila Welsh's calf was his last act upon the body, not unlike the signature of a painter upon a finished canvas. The only trace of blood on the white gloves was the right index finger, which had been used to paint the bloody symbol. After haplessly tearing down the east window curtains and their hanging rod, the killer left them precariously balanced over the windowsill with the curtains folded in pleats like a formal dinner napkin. It was no accident.

Testing whether the curtains and rod could have landed in their position by falling, Chief Reed experimented with "dropping" the items from their upright hanging position dozens of times. In none of the tests did they land in the position they were found. He concluded the curtains had been deliberately arranged on the windowsill after the killer stepped through the window. There was no need to leave such an elegant presentation, and yet the killer felt compelled to do so while standing outside the window in full public view. It was no doubt a statement of mockery and fun.

Elizabeth Short's killer left the piece of thigh flesh buried within her vagina and stuffed her shorn pubic hair into her anus for the police to later find, leaving his personal stamp within the body. Ten days after the murder became front page news, the killer sent in her personal effects followed by several messages to LA area newspapers and the LAPD, mocking investigators with the message "HAD My FUN AT POLiCE." In both cases, the murderer left his mark, claiming personal authorship over the domination and destruction of these two women he hated.

Once each of the slayings was finished, the killer displayed a subtle yet telling clue to his mindset. When Marie Welsh first walked into her daughter's room at 9:15 A.M. on March 9, 1941, she noticed nothing unusual. Her first thought was the chill in the room and moved to close the open east window. She next noticed a pool of blood on the floor and asked Leila if she had a nosebleed. Marie did not see any of the horror that lay on the bed five feet from her because the bedspread covered the entire scene—the fractured head, the gaping neck, the blood-soaked mattress, the gaping cavity in her daughter's thigh. Before leaving the room, the killer's final act upon the body of Leila Welsh was to pull the bedspread over her body and head, hiding the scene from view. It was a slight yet very revealing action: this was his work and he wanted it shrouded from anyone else's eyes.

On January 15, 1947, the two halves of Elizabeth Short were deposited in a lonely, weed strewn lot two blocks in length. Contrary to every account made that morning or since, the body was not posed for public view on the sidewalk as a shocking display of the killer's maniacal genius. The body was discarded in thick clumps of tall weeds twelve feet into the lot, hidden from view of every passerby until Betty Bersinger stopped to take a closer look. The killer did not expose his victim to public view on Norton Avenue—he hid his victim from public view on Norton Avenue. Both murders were personal. Both murders were his. And the bodies of both horribly mutilated women were consciously or subconsciously shielded from the prying eyes of others, despite the fact that they would invariably be discovered.

Among all the behavioral patterns common to the killer in both crimes, one stands out as the most exceptional and astounding. Within half an hour of the arrival of the first set of police officers to the Welsh home at 6109 Rockhill Road on March 9, 1941, officers fanned out in search of clues among neighboring backyards. At 11:00 A.M., Officer Alvin Hymer arrived at 6042 Harrison Street, the home of Mabel Murphy. The house was just four houses up from the Welsh home, and the officer asked to look into Murphy's backyard. The two stepped out onto her porch and stared down into the well-maintained, compact yard. No precipitation had fallen the night before, nor was there any dusting of snow on the ground. Every inch of the yard was scanned and nothing was seen. An hour later, Murphy received a phone call from a neighbor informing her that groups of men were scouring her yard. At 1:50 P.M., Officer Lawrence Ober combed through her property and found nothing. And yet, at 2:30 P.M., Murphy finished lunch and stepped onto her smooth, tidy lawn, where she immediately spotted the missing piece of flesh the police had been searching for over the previous four hours.

At nearly the same time, Officer Ober returned to the backyard of the Dunham family home at 6032 Harrison Street, two houses farther north of the Murphy home, and discovered the missing gloves. The same teams of officers who had searched the Murphy property that morning had also searched the Dunham property. Alvin Hymer had visited the Dunham property. Even Lawrence

Ober had previously searched the Dunham property. No gloves had been found.

At George Welsh's trial, defense attorney Roy Rucker grilled Officer Ober about his failure to find the gloves earlier in the day despite having extensively walked the property. Rucker asked him sarcastically, "How long have you been nearsighted?" to the uproarious laughter of the courtroom. But Lawrence Ober was neither nearsighted nor sloppy. Nor was Alvin Hymer, nor the teams of officers who had searched the neighborhood that morning.

The only explanation as to the mysterious sudden appearance at 2:30 P.M. of the flesh in the backyard of 6042 Harrison Street and the gloves in the backyard and driveway of 6032 Harrison Street is that the killer returned, hidden among the crowds lining the streets, and dropped the items in the yards. No perimeters had been set up yet in the neighborhood. Police officers visited the properties but were not stationed there to keep out the public. Even the Welsh backyard was crawling with random strangers observing the action.

Anyone from among the crowds walking through the neighborhood could have stepped into the Murphy and Dunham yards. The killer returned to observe the aftermath of his work and deposited three crucial pieces of evidence that he knew would set the case on fire. And it would happen again six years later when the Black Dahlia killer sent to the *LA Examiner* the personal effects of Elizabeth Short.

"HERE! is 'Dahlia's' BeLONGingS," read the envelope. Within were the address book, a trove of photos, her birth certificate, and other items she had carried in her purse the night she was taken. Once again, the killer deposited important clues and evidence into the hands of the police, seemingly helping the investigation but actually making it more convoluted, more baffling, and more futile. Among all the incredibly rare circumstances common to both murders—draining a body completely of blood, cutting and ripping out a horseshoe-shaped piece of flesh, severing a body in two—the killer's delivery of evidence to the police well after the murders stands out as virtually unprecedented.

These are not coincidental behavior patterns. Carl Balsiger knew, had access to, and had the motive to kill both Leila Welsh and Elizabeth Short, leaving an extensive catalogue of evidence that the same hand was behind both murders.

CHAPTER 23

WEREWOLF

The exceptional brutality of the Welsh and Short murders had similarly devastating effects on Kansas City and Los Angeles. Both cities experienced a panic that forever changed them.

Unprecedented resources were marshalled in both investigations, newspapers blared every major and minor development in multiple daily editions, lines of "Confessing Sams" ambled into KCPD and LAPD police precincts claiming responsibility for the murders, six hundred people were questioned in the Welsh murder and even more in the Short investigation. Both police departments received scores of crank letters with false clues and book-length "murder solution treatises." House-to-house searches spread for miles, and people at hundreds of businesses were questioned in both cities. For weeks, lines of cars crawled along Rockhill Road for a peek at the notorious Welsh home; Norton Avenue in Los Angeles became a spectacle and eventually a must-see tourist destination. In the wake of the investigations' failures, police chiefs in both cities resigned and political earthquakes followed.

At the time of the murders, both cities were experiencing fearsome crime waves. Kansas City was still inundated with the second-story men, mobsters, hustlers, holdup men, con artists, burglars, and crooks who found such a fertile home under Pendergast rule. On March 9, 1941, the FBI's most wanted man in New York State, Emanuel Weiss of Murder, Inc., was on the lam and sitting pretty in Kansas City, a mile from the Welsh home. Blocks away, seventeen-year-old Velma Holcross awoke in her bed to find a strange man kissing her. A few streets away, Amy Smith was accosted in her home on Cherry Street by twenty-five-year-old drifter James Coddell, who had been seen lurking in the neighborhood. Just six blocks from the Welsh home, the police shot multiple times at a stolen car. Assaults, rapes, robberies, and gruesome murders were a regular occurrence.

Things were no better in Los Angeles, where the district attorney investigation detailed "extensive trafficking networks of dope peddlers, abortionists, bookmakers, gamblers." On March 15, 1947, in just one twenty-four-hour period, the city suffered forty-one burglaries, seven assaults with a deadly weapon, one murder, and twelve robberies. On the same day, West Covina police chief John Thomas Brown was shot by two men who had the bound body of a woman in their car, and noted conductor Otto Klemperer was robbed and beaten. Seventeen people were killed in the first seventeen days of March 1947.

And yet, with both cities numb to their daily horrors, the Welsh and Short murders still caused a wave of terror.

Why had the cases struck such a nerve? With Leila Welsh, it could have been the spectacle of a young heiress with all the money in the world helpless against her fate. Elizabeth Short exposed the underbelly of Hollywood, where glamour and fame protected only a few while armies of new arrivals faced the harsh realities of Tinseltown. But other murders of heiresses and Hollywood ingenues never gained traction with the public. Was it the puzzle of Leila Welsh's love life or Elizabeth Short's mysterious nightlife that attracted so much attention? Other cases provided far more romantic intrigue.

What ultimately made the two cases so distressing to the public was the macabre carving and bloodletting of two beautiful, young women who were sliced, dissected, and disassembled by a malevolent force acting with control, restraint, and intelligence, not the mad rage of a lunatic. Neither killing was the work of a deformed monster lurking in the shadows, as represented by the hugely popular Frankenstein and Dracula movies of the 1930s. It was the work of a friend, a neighbor, a coworker, a business partner—someone who wore the mask of civility to hide a face of horror. A werewolf. At the dawn of the Age of the Serial Killer, before BTK, Ted Bundy, John Wayne Gacy, Ed Gein, and Jeffrey Dahmer, the United States was just beginning to discover the monster was us.

Awkward, clumsy, plain-looking, gangly, and portly, with a flat Midwestern accent, Carl Balsiger never stood out to anyone. But behind the slight smile and unassuming nature was a violent sociopath who embezzled, stole, stalked, assaulted, defrauded, misrepresented himself, and lied to the police with impunity, oblivious or attracted to the enormous risks he constantly courted. His unassuming demeanor would aid in his slipping through the many suspicions that surrounded him. Above all, he personally knew two women who were murdered in strikingly similar ways, many of which were extremely rare, and some unprecedented. The murder of Elizabeth Short was the first and only instance of a perfectly bisected and purposely exsanguinated murder victim in U.S. history. Leila Welsh had come close to being the first, six years earlier.

Though the murders caused immeasurable loss of security for millions of residents, tremendous loss of city resources, and loss of faith in law enforcement, the greatest losses were the lives of Leila Welsh and Elizabeth Short. As a devoted volunteer for the Red Cross and many other charities and nonprofit organizations, Leila undoubtedly would have used her wealth for great social benefit had she not died. Clyde Evans at the University of Kansas City's

Education Department noted her exceptional teaching skills, especially with small children. Surely, Leila would have left an indelible mark on hundreds of youngsters who would always remember such a special teacher.

Elizabeth Short, too, was lauded by the residents of Medford, Massachusetts for her warmth and care for small children in the community. She was remembered by many more throughout her life not for the way she walked, or her fashion, or the way her hair stood like a black dahlia. They remembered her smile, her curiosity, her naïve sweetness and good nature, her light. With so many captivated by her, Elizabeth Short proved how truly special she was. Surely, she would have found her own happiness . . . somewhere, somehow.

At the heart of the Welsh and Short saga is the mystery of obsession and its bottomless pit of desire. The thin, fragile line between passion and obsession is easily jumped, and almost always without self-awareness of that one dangerous step. Elizabeth Short was an object of passion and arguably obsession for many—Mark Hansen, Gordon Fickling, Jack Egger, the tens of men who wrote her telegrams and letters begging for a hint of her affection. Even Matt Gordon, in his own way, was infatuated with the girl whom he had asked to marry after only one date. The obsession continued past Elizabeth's death, when the press reported every detail about her they could find, when one thousand police officers searched for any clue to her movements and associations. And the obsession continued well after with innumerable films, television shows, books, podcasts, and internet sites forever conjecturing about what befell the Black Dahlia.

Leila Welsh was an object of passion for Richard Funk and Elery Boynton. She was pursued by innumerable men at the University of Kansas City and was courted aggressively by others in her own neighborhood. Nonetheless, Leila swore off marriage and avoided serious commitment, despite the era's expectation that young women seek and receive engagement rings by their mid-twenties. In death, her every move, her every association was scrutinized and reported to an obsessively hungry public. It is human nature to want what we cannot have. In life, Elizabeth Short was captivating one moment and gone the next, creating a desperate desire to chase her, which continues to this day. Likewise, Leila Welsh was always just out of reach for anyone hoping to possess her.

The fire that rages within an obsessive mind eventually has to face its own futility and be doused. But some rare flames refuse to be extinguished. Unchecked, desire can become passion, can become obsession, can become pathological rage, and, finally, total destruction. The murders of Leila Welsh and Elizabeth Short are a faint but spellbinding window into the darkest recess of the human mind, where obsession's two-sided flame of love and hate burns eternal.

ACKNOWLEDGMENTS

It was January 6, 2021, when I finally got the chance every aspiring author dreams of—five minutes to pitch my heart out to Mel Berger, one of the publishing world's most respected and successful literary agents. Perplexed and distressed by the images pouring out of the Capitol Building in Washington, DC, that day, Mel was an especially distracted audience. I should have rescheduled. "Whaddya got?" he asked. It was "go time." My voice was a torrent of saleable buzzwords: Black Dahlia, unpublished details, epic story, eccentric characters, the real noir Hollywood, yadda, yadda, yadda.

Silence.

Finally, he spoke: "What's the story?"

I stammered and grasped for an arc, only to be interrupted by his second gut punch.

"Who's the killer?"

I stumbled and sputtered again.

Then came his dream-killing response: "Boy, I can hear the passes now."

The book was dead in the womb. My voice dripped with disappointment. "I guess I should stick to my day job."

But Mel said two words that turned my world around: "Keep going."

I was shocked. "Keep going?"

The volume of CNN's live broadcast began to rise in the background, and he was gone.

Mel's two words fueled an obsessive research project that consumed my life for the next three years. Not sure he would even remember my name, I called his office to report I had finished a book proposal. His assistant took my number, and I prayed he would call me back. Within five minutes, I was on the phone with Mel.

"Of course I'll read it," he said.

Two days later, on a Sunday morning, Mel sent me a four-word email: "Very strong and fascinating."

It was go time.

Monday morning, Mel presented a battle plan for selling the book project that was akin to a World War II general poring over terrain maps. "But there's one specific editor I want for this. Keep your fingers crossed."

Michaela Hamilton and Mel Berger go way back. Like, 1970s back. They helped build the publishing business for over four decades and remained steady friends throughout. But there was no guarantee that "Mike," as Mel called her, would respond positively. Thankfully, she did, and she became an inspiring and steady hand, guiding the project to fruition.

Getting a book published is a pipe dream. But when Mel Berger steps into your corner, dreams become possible. And when Michaela Hamilton steps in, the possible becomes real. I cannot express enough gratitude to both Mel and Mike for believing in me, believing in this book, and—most importantly—believing in Elizabeth Short and Leila Welsh. I also thank the entire amazing team at

Kensington Books, who have withstood market pressures to remain independent in their business and in their literary gifts to the world.

The trail into the mist-shrouded world of the Black Dahlia is a rocky one, where the half-truths and exaggerations of countless witnesses to Beth Short's life wove a tail too unbelievable to take at face value. It is also a well-traveled trail, with countless authors, web sleuths, and couch detectives having scoured every corner of the mysterious case, each and every detail picked through and torn apart, leaving little yet to discover. It took many months of laborious research through a hodgepodge of leftover files and dusty archives to arrive at a rare dark corner of the case that had never seen the light of day. In the darkness, I discovered a tunnel to another murder that hadn't been traveled at all—save for one person.

In the journey to uncover the truth about unsolved murder cases, there is no greater discovery than another wanderer passionately dedicated to the same dark task. A cold call to the University of Missouri—Kansas City led me to the school's archivist and resident historian, Christopher Wolff, who had been captivated years earlier by the 1941 murder of Leila Welsh. The word *genius* may be overused in our hyperbolic modern era, but Chris Wolff is the real deal. His knowledge of practically everything under the sun is spectacularly impressive, and when his heart is in it—as it was throughout our long trek to uncover every detail of the Welsh case—he breathes life into that which is long dead. I may have collected many of the details, but Chris provided the critical missing pieces and, more importantly, the roadmap to the soul of the story. Stumbling upon Chris Wolff was more than a coincidence. Fate brought us together, and for that I am humbly in awe and grateful to him.

My eternal appreciation goes to Leila Beeby, niece of Leila Adele Welsh, who opened my eyes to the rich tapestry of the Welsh family and the burden her father, George Welsh, continued to carry to his last days as a result of his beloved sister's murder and the subsequent trial that almost broke him. Leila's deep introspection took me back in time to relive through her eyes the consequences of the great injustice foisted upon George and his mother, Marie, and how their bond saved them. Standing with Chris Wolff and Leila by the grave of Leila Adele Welsh, I could feel the weight of history. Many thanks also go to Leila's amazing husband, Craig Beeby, who richly detailed to me his youth on an Oklahoma ranch and the horrors of the outhouse that was only serviced once a year by a putrid truck colloquially called "the Honeywagon."

Through thick and very thin, there has been one person who never wavered in his absolute and complete support of my dedication to the book project—my brother, Etan Frankel. As the true writer of the family with an insight and skill I could never possess, he inspired me to not stop at any cost. He taught me that it doesn't need to be great. It doesn't even need to be good. It just needs to be. No matter what has come my way, my brother has made me the luckiest man in the world. I owe my life to him.

Speaking of lucky, I have been blessed with three extraordinary children. Late at night, they each would wander to the couch and ask what I was writing about in my book. Needless to say, I lied extensively about the story to shield them from the subject matter. Each of them would knowingly raise a suspicious eyebrow and accuse me of lying. I now know what a police interrogation feels like. Their intelligence, perception, and boundless curiosity to understand things well beyond their age is owed to an extraordinary woman who taught me how to become the best version of myself. My wife, Karen, was never a big fan of my true crime obsession. Especially the Black Dahlia.

Within forty-eight hours of our marriage, she "asked" that I remove all the creepy murder books from our bedroom and throw them in the basement. But when life got tough, and the bank account lean, and I told her I wanted to pursue the book project, she demanded I follow my dream . . . as long as the dream didn't reappear on our bedroom shelves. Karen was there every step of the way, looking at evidence, discussing my theories, and challenging me. She is the life partner every good person deserves.

My life has been blessed beyond measure with the two greatest parents a person could ask for. Danny and Gusti Frankel are a miracle. They have saved me countless times, from when I nearly electrocuted myself to death at three years old to the current day, in ways too numerous to mention. Their selflessness, boundless love and admiration for a son who doesn't deserve it inspire me to try and be the best parent I can be. But there is no possibility of living up to the extraordinary model they serve. I am in awe of them. That alone is the greatest gift of all they have given me.

Many thanks go to Karen Tennant of Lake of the Forest, who spent afternoons walking the lake with me, showing me every inch of the clubhouse and spending hours poring through the archival materials she had collected over the years. I'm inspired by the love she feels for her very special lake community, where every Fourth of July, there are frog-jumping competitions, just as there were in the days of Mark Twain.

Karl Kanehl spent hours going through dusty boxes of Balsiger family photos without asking for anything in return. His generosity of spirit toward a complete stranger contributed so much to this book, and I thank him for his rich stories of the Balsiger family. Ralph "Bud" Ells also spent hours on the phone with me, recalling the Balsiger family history and bringing to life Kansas City so many ages ago. Bud's insight into his childhood and a world many decades old was both gripping and crucial to the story.

Dorothy Parris and I became fast friends on our first phone call together as she detailed the life of her mother, Jean Cleveland Thacher, and her father, Walt Thacher Jr. She gave of her time, energy, and spirit to help me string together the very heart of the story. And above all, she honored the legacy and memory of her amazing mother, whose greatest priority was protecting her children.

My heart is touched by the generosity of Anne Bersinger, who facilitated the all-important communication with her mother, Betty, in her final months of life. I owe Anne a great debt of gratitude. Tabitha "Tibbie" Pearson Ford and Laurie Smith regaled me with the unforgettable stories of their mother, Tabitha Teall. Their love and admiration for her stand the test of time, just as she has. Kurt Sobanja's enthusiasm in sharing his family's story brought to life his grandfather, Bernhard Sobanja, for me. Kurt possesses that rare energy that sparks the imagination. How fortunate I was to share time with him.

Many thanks are also owed to Jamie Costello, who proudly recounted to me the extraordinary narrative of his family.

Special thanks go to Joubin Mortazavi, Ramin Mortazavi, Patricio Fuentes, and Tom McGah, who always keep me laughing and thinking. For their abundant encouragement and inspiration, I thank Cynthia Kendall, Michelle Guzman, and Jay Diola. Josh Pyatt has remained a loyal and dedicated agent who combines hard work with that rarest of traits in the hard knocks world of talent representation—heart. I'm proud to also call him a close friend.

Very special thanks go to Joy Wiesenfeld Markman, whose decades of experience in criminal law provided a wealth of knowledge. To Leila Jarrahi goes more gratitude than I can express. Since sixth grade, she has proven to be a model human and an inspiration to always do better. To Elizabeth Davies, David Shaye, Ryan Holcomb, and Bobby Corbi, I am so very grateful. We went through war, and I am honored to have shared our many years together.

Brilliant author Jeff Guinn took my calls and offered inspiring advice that gave me the confidence to continue when I most needed it. Joy and Bill Todd of the Pleasant Valley Historical Society welcomed me into their home and into the history of their beloved town of Camarillo. They also introduced me to Camarillo native Joe Ortiz, who went on the hunt to uncover the long-buried past. Amber Hayes joined the mission to resuscitate the memory of her war hero great-uncle, Richard Funk. Ted Funk generously searched through boxes of documents and provided a treasure trove of Funk family history and photographs. Surprisingly, he also provided a trove of items relating to Leila Welsh, which the Funk family had kept all these decades. Ted's insights into his uncle Richard were deeply moving.

Daniel Winters, MD, spent hours analyzing the unsettling autopsy notes and photographs of Elizabeth Short in death. I thank him for his rich acumen, enviable energy, and years of medical experience.

It truly was a group effort. Go, team.

SOURCE NOTES

INTRODUCTION: THE KEY QUESTION

As Betty explained, "It was about the time kids were going off to school": Kyle J. Wood, interview with Betty Bersinger, 1996, YouTube video, audio, 1:13.

"I glanced to my right and saw this very dead, white body. My goodness": Larry Harnisch, "A Slaying Cloaked in Mystery and Myths," *Los Angeles Times*, January 6, 1997, 1.

"Within this group of questions was one that was relevant yet so bizarre": Tod Faulkner, "Farewell, My Black Dahlia," *Los Angeles Times*, March 28, 1971, 12.

At 11:09 A.M., Officers Fitzgerald and Perkins arrived and were alone at the crime scene: Frank Jemison, 1949/1950 Los Angeles district attorney files, "Summary of the Elizabeth (Beth) Short Murder Investigation," 6.

In one last interview, conducted with the author, she provided details: Author interviews with Anne and Betty Bersinger, 2021.

"The first thing we thought was that it was a mannequin.": Larry Harnisch, "A Crime Steeped In Mystery, Myth," *Los Angeles Times*, January 6, 1997, 13.

"She said that she [was] walking to the store": Sgts. Hansen and Brown, LAPD follow-up report, February 5, 1947

Even famed FBI profiler John Douglas assessed that the killer: Larry Harnisch, "A Slaying Cloaked in Mystery and Myths," *Los Angeles Times*, January 6, 1997, 14.

CHAPTER 1: HEIRESS OF THE PRAIRIE

Cole Younger, who had ridden with Jesse James, robbing banks and trains across the Midwest: "Cole Younger Is Dead," *Kansas City Times*, March 22, 1916.

Marie Fleming, had grown up in rural Kentucky: "Into Tragic Day," *Kansas City Star*, April 15, 1943.

From the moment Leila was born: "Into Tragic Day," *Kansas City Star*, April 15, 1943.

Leila's social graces and warmth helped cover his many social anxieties.: Author interview with Leila Beeby, daughter of George Welsh, 2024.

The Welsh family home was modestly furnished, their clothes simple: Lear Reed, "Chief Reed's Own Story of the Welsh Case," *Kansas City Star*, December 28, 1941.

universally praised as a pioneer in women's education: McKee–Welsh wedding announcement, *Danville (KY) Times*, June 24, 1904.

Having attended Western College for Women in Oxford, Ohio: "Mrs. Leila Welsh Dies," *Kansas City Star*, January 5, 1938.

Her greatest joy was her namesake and grandniece, Leila Adele Welsh.: "Fiend Slays Girl," *Kansas City Star*, March 10, 1941.

The stately family home at 233 W. 56th Street: James Welsh probate records/last will and testament, 1936.

Her great-uncle, James McKee, had served as an officer and pastor: Presbyterian Church Roll of Pastors, Roll of Elders, 1920–1929.

Aunt Leila had contributed handsomely, making the Welshes the church's most prominent family.: James Welsh last will and testament, 1926.

teaching her daughter Leila humility, simplicity, modesty, and a deep appreciation: Author interview with Leila Beeby, daughter of George Welsh, 2024.

So exclusive was the KCU Greek community: "Not Ready For National Frats," *UKC UNews*, May 8, 1935.

"Everyone seemed present. Webb, Swanson & Swanson, Balsiger": "Peter Pan—Hellenic," *UKC UNews*, November 15, 1935.

The most anticipated event of the spring season was Hobo Day: "Hobo Day A Bang," *UKC UNews*, May 27, 1936.

"juicy libel" was printed for all to read: "Peter Pan—Hellenic," *UKC UNews*, November 15, 1935.

"Tops Miller, that gorgeous Cho Chin, calmly breaks a date": *UKC UNews*, March 24, 1937.

Scurrilous rumors were printed about her in the school newspaper: *UKC UNews*, February 11, 1938.

The KCU yearbook had not spared its judgment of the raucous crew's sexual conquests: University of Kansas City *Crataegus* yearbook, 1937.

The *UNews* reported, "The Kegons were out in full color": *UNews*, December 12, 1937.

"Kegon—you will probably be dead (literally) when you get home": *UNews*, November 1, 1935.

Kegon member John Chaney headed the . . . Co-Op Party: "Election in Offing," *UKC UNews*, October 9, 1936.

His breezy two-word response was "See Balsiger.": *UNews*, May 20, 1936.

In the platform was a decree that all first-year students: "Council to Work," *UNews*, September 26, 1936.

Her simple response was printed in the newspaper: "Why Not? Frosh Answer," *UNews*, October 9, 1936.

Chaney and the powerful Co-Op Party effective control over every student election.: "Co-Op Party Sweeps Election," *UNews*, May 13, 1935.

An editorial in the *UNews* sharply criticized the rigged system: *UNews*, November 15, 1935.

her sorority sister Marjorie Bybee had invited a neighborhood friend from Independence: Testimony of Richard Funk at Welsh preliminary hearing, May 18, 1942.

CHAPTER 2: LOVE TRIANGLE

Richard followed his father's example to the letter of the law: "Scouts Renew Old Toys," *Kansas City Star*, November 17, 1932.

So, when the Jimmy Allen Air Races were announced in July of 1934: "A Record Making Flight Thrills A Big Crowd," *Kansas City Times*, July 2, 1934.

He and Balsiger had also served together as officials in the Order of DeMolay: "New DeMolay Officers In," *Kansas City Star*, July 9, 1934.

Richard's family owned a summer cottage at Lake of the Forest: Richard Funk statement to J. T. Byars, chief of detectives, Kansas City Police Department, March 9, 1941.

Their dates steadily increased over the months, a slow, traditional courtship rather than the slapdash affairs: "His Love Untold," *Kansas City Star*, May 18, 1942.

Richard was never quite sure whether she was seeing other men: Testimony of Richard Funk at Welsh preliminary hearing, May 18, 1942. See also: "His Love Untold," *Kansas City Star*, May 18, 1942.

Elery had been a star athlete in high school and college: Tom Wilson, "Gabby And Pistol Pete Were Very Good Sports," *Register-Mail* (Galesburg, IL), May 8, 2007.

He had declared his love for her three weeks after they first met: "Diary Into Welsh Case," *Manhattan Mercury*, May 22, 1942.

Weekends were spent at his family's summer home at Lake of the Forest: Wyandotte County Historical Society documents and newspaper clippings, 1921–1945.

One ended with the directive to "Please destroy this.": Walt Bodine, "The Murder of Leila Welsh", *Kansas City Town Squire*, November 1969.

Richard Funk had been kept in the dark about the trip: Testimony of Richard Funk at Welsh preliminary hearing, May 18, 1942. See also: "His Love Untold," *Kansas City Star*, May 18, 1942.

Leila told him everything.: Testimony of Richard Funk at Welsh preliminary hearing, May 18, 1942. See also: "His Love Untold," *Kansas City Star*, May 18, 1942.

He had planned to propose to her, himself, but everything was thrown off now.: Testimony of Richard Funk at Welsh preliminary hearing, May 18, 1942. See also: "His Love Untold," *Kansas City Star*, May 18, 1942.

George frequently cast off the family shadow: "Welsh Checks For Debts," *Kansas City Times*, January 30, 1942.

Leila felt pangs of menstrual discomfort: Audio recording, Walt Bodine interview with Judge Eugene Brouse, former defense counsel for George Welsh, 1969.

It was he who had broken the back of the Pendergast machine: Lear Reed, *Human Wolves* (Brown-White-Lowell Press, 1941).

but it was the danger acts that brought the crowds in, and Hamid-Morton always delivered.: "A Real Circus," *Kansas City Times*, March 8, 1941.

Among the throngs whizzing by him were Leila and Richard.: Lear Reed, "Chief Reed's Own Story of the Welsh Case," *Kansas City Star*, December 28, 1941.

The pair window-shopped up crowded Wyandotte Street, when Leila bumped: Testimony of Richard Funk at Welsh preliminary hearing, May 18, 1942. See also: "His Love Untold," *Kansas City Star*, May 18, 1942.

Two houses away, Marguerite Garner felt something was not right.: "From Lips Of A Child," *Kansas City Star*, March 12, 1941.

Reed found himself distracted by the event's risqué modern dancing: Lear Reed, "Chief Reed's Own Story of the Welsh Case," *Kansas City Star*, December 28, 1941.

CHAPTER 3: PROWLER

By the time Richard's car pulled up: Testimony of Richard Funk at Welsh preliminary hearing, May 18, 1942. See also: "His Love Untold," *Kansas City Star*, May 18, 1942.

Two houses northeast of the Welsh home, Lois Malsness and her husband: "Sold Welsh the Knife," *Kansas City Times*, May 21, 1942.

Marie paused to consider the sound that had awoken her.: "Into Tragic Day"/ Testimony of Marie Welsh at George Welsh trial, *Kansas City Star*, April 15, 1943.

Confused, Marie called out, "What's the matter, honey, have you had the nosebleed?": "Into Tragic Day"/Testimony of Marie Welsh at George Welsh trial, *Kansas City Star*, April 15, 1943.

She ran to the Welsh home to find Ruth Kennedy: "From Lips Of A Child," *Kansas City Star*, March 12, 1941.

"Hello, Chief—we've got a dead girl over here on Rockhill Road.": Lear Reed, "Chief Reed's Own Story of the Welsh Case," *Kansas City Star*, December 28, 1941.

"Come in, Chief," an officer invited. "Right back here." A detective motioned: Lear Reed, "Chief Reed's Own Story of the Welsh Case," *Kansas City Star*, December 28, 1941.

"Never have I viewed a scene of this type that impressed me": Lear Reed, "Chief Reed's Own Story of the Welsh Case," *Kansas City Star*, December 28, 1941.

There, at the junction with her hip, was a horseshoe-shaped cavity in her flesh: Lear Reed, "Chief Reed's Own Story of the Welsh Case," *Kansas City Star*, December 28, 1941.

Coroner Leitch saw an opportunity to break the silence and offered a blunt observation: "His Love Untold," *Kansas City Star*, May 18, 1942.

Reed would find one last piece just steps away in a small snowbank: Lear Reed, "Chief Reed Continues His Story of the Welsh Case," *Kansas City Star*, January 4, 1942.

He quietly directed Captain Anderson to search for a two-tined carving fork: "Crime A Puzzle", *Kansas City Times*, March 12, 1941.

Helen held George back on the front steps.: "Quiz on Hammer," *Kansas City Star*, April 16, 1943.

George felt the life drain out of him: Author interview with Leila Beeby, daughter of George Welsh, 2024.

a lowly patrolman like Officer Lawrence Ober faced nothing: "Sirens Scare Off the Stork," *Kansas City Times*, October 20, 1941.

He and five other officers had been unexpectedly called up and ordered to the corner of: "Wanted To Tell It All," *Kansas City Star*, May 21, 1942.

Two doors south, at 6042 Harrison Street, Mabel Murphy was barricaded in her home: "Wanted To Tell It All," *Kansas City Star*, May 21, 1942.

CHAPTER 4: AN AWKWARD
BUT FIENDISH AMATEUR

For half a century, "Boss Tom" Pendergast and his brother before him united German, Italian: "Harbinger of the New Deal Coalition," The Pendergast Years, https://pendergastkc.org.

When it was time to place bets on the horses: William M. Reddig, *Tom's Town: Kansas City and the Pendergast Legend* (J. P. Lippincott Company, 1947), 299.

As the political and criminal tendrils of the Pendergast network grew across the state: "Boss in Rough Era," *Kansas City Star*, April 7, 1939.

In 1934, former haberdasher Harry S. Truman would be selected by the machine: John Barker, *Missouri Lawyer* (Dorrance, 1949), 375, 376. See also: Jack Williams, "G.O.P Fuse In Scandal", *Kansas City Star*, October 9, 1949.

By 1938, all-out war was declared between Stark and Pendergast: "Ex-Governor Lloyd C. Stark Dies," *Kansas City Times*, September 18, 1972.

But tension gripped them the moment Jack Gibbs: "A Vicious Slayer," *Kansas City Star*, March 10, 1941.

Several days after the Welsh murder, a young couple, Jeanne Harvey and boyfriend James Persons: "A Clash on Witnesses," *Kansas City Star*, March 21, 1941.

Officers stepped toward the enraged deputy but froze: *Kansas City Kansan*, March 21, 1941.

Kansas City had gone into a panic since the murder: "Brutal Slaying of Leila Welsh Has Given Kansas City Murder Jitters," *Manhattan Mercury*, March 22, 1941.

He would test the Welsh neighborhood further, making noises in the room: Lear Reed, "Chief Reed Continues His Story of the Welsh Case," *Kansas City Star*, January 11, 1942.

Her autopsy revealed a significant amount of adrenaline: Lear Reed, "Did We Overlook Any Clue?," *Kansas City Star*, January 18, 1942.

The first hammer blow struck her right forehead: Testimony of Coroner Cecil George Leitch, MD, at preliminary hearing of George Welsh, May 19, 1942.

Having nearly decapitated her: "Fiendish Murder in Kansas City, Missouri," *FBI Law Enforcement Bulletin*, vol. 10, September 1941.

Carving a horseshoe-shaped trail in one smooth: "George Welsh II Is Accused In Brutal Murder Of Sister," *Sedalia Democrat*, January 28, 1942.

The official cause of death was "acute hemorrhage due to an incised wound of the neck": Leila Welsh certificate of death.

Commenting on the flesh wound, Reed conjectured, "It was a perfect curve, as though made by a surgeon.": Lear Reed, "Chief Reed Continues His Story of the Welsh Case," *Kansas City Star*, January 4, 1942.

"an awkward but fiendish amateur,": "Baffling Welsh Murder Case Finally To Court Action," *Sedalia Democrat*, January 29, 1942.

Each day that passed seemed to bring greater anxiety in Kansas City: "Door Locks Are Sold Out After Leila Welsh Murder," *Kansas City Times*, March 14, 1941.

CHAPTER 5: REVENGE OF THE MACHINE

Stewart lifted a well-worn photograph of the hammer: "Sold Welsh the Knife," *Kansas City Times*, May 21, 1942.

While George and his uncle Edgar Fleming waited in the hallway, Alport walked slowly past: "Sold Welsh the Knife," *Kansas City Times*, May 21, 1942.

Taken to a private room, Alport emphatically denied George was the man: "Blast At Welsh Clue," *Kansas City Star*, May 27, 1942.

Blocks from KCPD headquarters, Alport was ordered to lie down in the back of the car: "Quiz on Hammer," *Kansas City Times*, April 16, 1943.

with Leila gone, George stood to gain financially by having to split his family's inheritance: Audio recording, Walt Bodine interview with Judge Eugene Brouse, former defense counsel for George Welsh, 1969.

Missouri Governor Forrest Donnell had been inundated with allegations of police brutality against Kansas City's Black community: "They Forced the Chief Out," Dowdal H. Davis, *The Crisis*, October 1941, 314–16.

Dragged to the edge of the raging river: Walt Bodine, "The Murder of Leila Adele Welsh," *Kansas City Town Squire*, November 1969.

The knife had traces of cotton and rayon fibers that matched Leila's pajamas: "Knife Data Is In," *Kansas City Star*, April 14, 1943.

"a certain dime novel detective who said two days afterward": "Two Grand Jury Jobs," *Kansas City Star*, December 9, 1941.

"The time has ceased to be when we can boast of a fine Police Department": "Baffling Welsh Murder Case Finally To Court Action," *Sedalia Democrat*, January 29, 1942.

Leaving nothing to chance, the twelve-man jury had been stacked with nine Pendergast precinct captains: "Two Grand Jury Jobs," *Kansas City Star*, December 9, 1941.

Higgins and Brock were sent to Los Angeles to dig up dirt on George and keep tabs on him.: "Bullied By Jury," *Kansas City Times*, April 11, 1942.

One session that began at 2:00 P.M.: John Barker, *Missouri Lawyer* (Dorrance, 1949), 341–43.

He was accused of carrying on an indecent relationship with Leila: Audio recording, Walt Bodine interview with Judge Eugene Brouse, former defense counsel for George Welsh, 1969.

the grand jury convened each day over bottles of whiskey that were carried out in crates.: Audio recording, Walt Bodine interview with Judge Eugene Brouse, former defense counsel for George Welsh, 1969. See also: "Kills Welsh Jury Bill," *Kansas City Star*, May 4, 1942.

Chief Deputy Sheriff Jacques Purdome and Deputy Jack Brice walked to the house: "George Welsh Jr. Indicted As Killer of Sister, Leila," *Kansas City Journal*, January 28, 1942.

CHAPTER 6: FRONTIER JUSTICE

Waltner halted the proceedings to ask Ferrell, "Does the Jury have anything to report?": "George Welsh Jr. Indicted As Killer of Sister, Leila," *Kansas City Journal*, January 28, 1942.

He had run against Richart in the 1940 sheriff's race on the reform ticket: Kenneth P. Middleton, "Campaign Comment," *Kansas City Journal*, October 31, 1940.

Sheriff Richart denied Marie a visit with George, telling her, "He will be treated like any other prisoner.": "Reed Has No Comment," *Kansas City Times*, January 30, 1942.

Having beaten the powerful railroad and oil monopolies in the U.S. Supreme Court: John Barker, *Missouri Lawyer* (Dorrance, 1949), 115–22.

Assailing the grand jury's actions as "utterly shocking": "Kills Welsh Jury Bill," *Kansas City Star*, May 4, 1942.

"This family thought they had suffered the limit of grief from Leila's death": "Build Welsh Case," *Kansas City Times*, January 29, 1942.

Four of the huskiest sheriff's deputies covered him, one in front, one behind: "State's Case In," *Kansas City Star*, May 25, 1942.

Former KCPD fingerprint expert Gorman Raney stunned the courtroom: "The First Link," *Kansas City Star*, May 20, 1942.

Defense counsel Barker leapt into his cross examination of Smith with an experiment. "Sold Welsh The Knife," *Kansas City Times*, May 21, 1942.

He filed an aggressive writ of prohibition: John Barker, *Missouri Lawyer* (Dorrance, 1949), 346–47.

On June 4, George was released from his jail cell after four months: Kansas City Court of Appeals, Ex Parte Welsh, June 3, 1942.

George spent afternoons on walks: Walt Bodine, "The Murder of Leila Adele Welsh," *Kansas City Town Squire*, November 1969.

Gorman Raney again testified that a set of George's fingerprints: John Barker, *Missouri Lawyer* (Dorrance, 1949), 349.

With Gorman Raney's credibility in ashes: John Barker, *Missouri Lawyer* (Dorrance, 1949), 348.

"Now, let me refresh your memory. Didn't I buy an oven thermometer?": "A Link in Prints," *Kansas City Times*, April 13, 1943.

Attorney General McKittrick handed the knife to Alport: "A Link To Welsh," *Kansas City Star*, April 12, 1943.

Lead defense counsel John Barker had one more ace up his sleeve, an old friend of Alport's named Ralph Bullock.: "Welsh in Denial," *Kansas City Star*, April 16, 1943.

Nearly every single member of the courtroom audience was a mother or a daughter: "Into Tragic Day," *Kansas City Star*, April 15, 1943.

"It was about the closest brother and sister you ever knew" "Mother Takes Stand in Welsh Murder Trial," *Sedalia Weekly Democrat*, April 16, 1943.

CHAPTER 7: TO HELL AND BACK

He suffered dramatic nightmares in his sleep, a result of the trauma he had endured: Author interview with Leila Beeby, daughter of George Welsh, 2024.

narcolepsy, the neurological disorder that disrupts sleep and wake cycles: National Institutes of Health: National Institute of Neurological Disorders and Stroke, Narcolepsy, https://www.ninds.nih.gov/health-information/disorders/narcolepsy.

Awarded the Purple Heart, Funk was buried in Cambridge: Author interview with Amber Hayes, Funk family member, 2024.

Elery "Gabby" Boynton married his high school sweetheart, Muriel Leyshon: Tom Wilson, "Gabby and Pistol Pete Were Very Good Sports," *Register-Mail* (Galesburg, IL), May 8, 2007.

Uncovered by the Kefauver Committee was mafia crime boss Charles Binaggio's partnership with Purdome: "A Puny Law Fist," *Kansas City Star*, July 20, 1952. See also: John M. McCormick memo, RG46, U.S. Senate Special Committee to Investigate Organized Crime in Interstate/The Pendergast Years, https://pendergastkc.org/collection/national-archives-washington-dc/naradc-rg46-29-0016-0001/memorandum-re-j-purdome.

"In seventeen years of law enforcement work, I had the duty of investigating and helping to investigate crimes": Lear Reed, "Chief Reed's Own Story of the Welsh Case," *Kansas City Star*, December 28, 1942.

When the trial of George Welsh ended, so too did the investigation: Walt Bodine, "The Murder of Leila Adele Welsh," *Kansas City Town Squire*, November 1969.

CHAPTER 8: THE MYSTIC RIVER

Reporters slipped onto the flight and showered her with questions: "Cook Held in Murder; Missing Father Found," *Boston Traveler*, January 18, 1947.

She was desperate to keep her composure, and her voice trembled only when asked about her daughter's slayer, saying, "If I ever get my hands on him, I believe I will kill him myself.": "Trail New Suspect in Torture Slaying," *Los Angeles Examiner*, January 18, 1947.

Asked what was ahead for her, she replied with a washed-out smile. "I have suffered deeply, but the worst is yet to come.": "Mother of Slain Girl Arrives Here," *Los Angeles Herald-Express*, January 18, 1947.

"She was of the manic-depressive type . . . . She was ambitious and beautiful and full of life, but she had her moments of despondency.": "Mother of Slain Girl Arrives Here," *Los Angeles Herald-Express*, January 18, 1947.

In her book *Childhood Shadows: The Hidden Story of the Black Dahlia Murder*, Mary Pacios interviewed Joe Sabia, who, like Mary, grew up in Medford with Beth Short.: Mary Pacios, *Childhood Shadows: The Hidden Story of the Black Dahlia Murder* (AuthorHouse, 2007).

Seeking freedom outside the packed house, Beth explored the city of Vallejo and met a man with a criminal record.: Los Angeles County district attorney grand jury files, Lt. Frank Jemison, "Summary of the Elizabeth (Beth) Short Murder Investigation," 10.

An opportunity to restart came when the Yankes left Vallejo for Los Angeles, with Cleo and Beth in tow.: Los Angeles County district attorney grand jury files, "Movements of Elizabeth Short," 1.

"I was won over all at once by her almost childlike charm and beauty. She was one of the loveliest girls I had ever seen—and the most shy.": "Childlike Charm of Girl Got Her Job At Army Camp," *Los Angeles Examiner*, January 17, 1947.

Unkefer found an ideal guest in Beth, whose unflaggingly pleasant demeanor and compulsive neatness with clothes and hygiene surprised her.: "Mother Verifies Scars on Slain Girl's Body," *Los Angeles Examiner*, January 17, 1947.

"My sweetheart: I love you, I love you, I love . . .": "Elizabeth Short's Letters Told Hero Feelings About Love and Marriage," *Los Angeles Examiner*, January 19, 1947.

"Yes, I have dated since I have seen you last.": "Elizabeth Short's Letters Told Hero Feelings About Love and Marriage," *Los Angeles Examiner*, January 19, 1947.

CHAPTER 9: VIVID WOMEN

Fickling bristled at the thought of her seeing other men.: Mary Morris, "Black Dahlia's Life Shows She Was Mixed Up Emotionally," *Des Moines Sunday Register*, March 23, 1947.

But he cautioned her to come west for the right reasons. "You say in your letter you want us to be good friends.": "Boy Friend's Love Letters to 'Black Dahlia' Bared," *Los Angeles Herald-Express*, January 18, 1947.

She even told her date Freddie Woods she was a reporter from Massachusetts covering the case.: "Self-Admitted Dahlia Slayer Changes Mind," *Los Angeles Examiner*, January 30, 1947.

Beth spent the next two nights at Marjorie's hotel apartment.: Los Angeles County district attorney grand jury files, Lt. Frank Jemison, "Summary of the Elizabeth (Beth) Short Murder Investigation," 11.

When her sister was taken to a mental institution, Norma was taken to a train station.: Chuck Cheatham, "Society Blamed For Girl's Tragic Life," *Long Beach Independent*, February 3, 1947.

Neighbors called the police in alarm at the sounds they heard coming from the Meyer home: Chuck Cheatham, "Society Blamed For Girl's Tragic Life," *Long Beach Independent*, February 3, 1947.

Lynn later explained the rules in Hollywood. "Girls pick each other up in a store or a bar and start rooming together": Caroline Walker, "Tells Hollywood Pitfalls," *Los Angeles Herald-Express*, January 29, 1947.

From the moment Lynn met Elizabeth Short, she didn't like her.: "Vivid Women," *Daily News* (Los Angeles, CA), January 21, 1947.

Lynn Martin was a constant presence, as was Chuck Finkelstein, who attended City College: Los Angeles County district attorney grand jury files, "Statement of John F. Egger," March 1, 1950, 5, 9.

Alex Constance, a forty-four-year-old hairdresser who gave Beth henna rinses to highlight her black hair: Los Angeles County district attorney grand jury files, Lt. Frank Jemison, "Summary of the Elizabeth (Beth) Short Murder Investigation," 7.

When Marjorie and Lynn were invited up to Carpenter Drive-In regular Bob Granas's house: Los Angeles County district attorney grand jury files, "Statement of George Bacos," February 21, 1950, 2.

Days later, his response arrived at the Hawthorne Hotel: "Loving you the way I do would make me do practically anything I guess.": "Love Letters to Slain Girl Revealed," *Daily News* (Los Angeles, CA), January 18, 1947.

Howard "Dutch" Darrin was a legend in automotive design circles, having built super-luxury cars worth the price of a Hollywood mansion: Sam Gordon, "Car Designer 'Tailors' Supers For Hollywood," *Hollywood Citizen-News*, April 25, 1946.

He lured Lynn to the remote mountain house with vague enticements. As soon as she entered, he came on to her.: Los Angeles County district attorney grand jury files, Lt. Frank Jemison, "Summary of the Elizabeth (Beth) Short Murder Investigation," 7.

Zaid called out to a short man in a well-worn brown suit, who spun around and eyed the girls with the precision of a professional:. Los Angeles County district attorney grand jury files, Lt. Frank Jemison, "Summary of the Elizabeth (Beth) Short Murder Investigation," 11.

CHAPTER 10: THE CLIMATE WAS WARM. IT WAS THE PEOPLE WHO WERE COLD.

By 1920, Hansen was the proprietor of his very own movie theater in Williston, North Dakota: Los Angeles County district attorney grand jury files, "Statement of Mark Hansen," December 16, 1949, February 1, 1950, 1, 2.

In 1945, Ida and their daughters moved out of the Carlos Avenue bungalow after an argument with Mark related to, "his actions towards his daughters' friends": Los Angeles County district attorney grand jury files, "Frank Jemison Memorandum to Deputy DA Veitch," November 17, 1949.

Popular Florentine bandleader Muzzy Marcelino had fixed up the sixteen-year-old Stull sisters with Captain Morrison J. Wilkinson: "Captain Is Given 30 Year Term on Sex Conviction," *Fresno Bee*, June 14, 1944.

Hansen also didn't mention the many chorus girls with no money and no home who had been graciously invited to stay with him: Los Angeles County district attorney grand jury files, "Testimony of Sgt. Finis Brown to D.A. Investigator Frank Jemison," no date given, 25.

Rent was paid in sex, and any refusal would send a girl packing, not only from his house, but also from her much-coveted jobs at the Florentine Gardens: Los Angeles County district attorney grand jury files, "Evidence and Declarations Tending to Connect or Disconnect Mark Hansen with the Murder of Elizabeth Short," 2, 3.

He had even pried sex from a girl who had undergone surgery just days before.: Los Angeles County district attorney grand jury files, "Statement of Ms. Anne Toth," December 13, 1949, 13.

Beth arrived with Mark at the Carlos Avenue house only to discover there was another resident, twenty-four-year-old Anne Toth.: Los Angeles County district attorney grand jury files, "Statement of Ms. Anne Toth," December 13, 1949, 2.

On V-J day in 1945, she was picked up in a hotel by "an extraordinarily wonderful man" who was very well connected in Hollywood: Mary Morris, "Black Dahlia's Life Shows She Was Mixed Up Emotionally," *Des Moines Sunday Register*, March 23, 1947.

She didn't drink, didn't smoke, and was obsessively neat with her wardrobe, never borrowing or lending an article of clothing: Los Angeles County district attorney grand jury files, "Statement of Ms. Anne Toth," December 13, 1949, 7, 15.

Dressmaker Mrs. Ardis and furrier Mr. Barron were frequently called upon by Mark to make bespoke items: Los Angeles County district attorney grand jury files, "Evidence and Declarations Tending to Connect or Disconnect Mark Hansen with the Murder of Elizabeth Short," 3.

Lieutenant Wollock was back in town and picked Beth up for dates at the home on Carlos Avenue.: Los Angeles County district attorney grand jury files, Lt. Frank Jemison, "Summary of the Elizabeth (Beth) Short Murder Investigation," 21.

She had long battled an embarrassing, painful infection that had made sexual activity a challenge.: Los Angeles County district attorney grand jury files, "Lt. Frank Jemison Suspect List and Descriptions," February 20, 1951, 9.

Beth saw him several times throughout the fall of 1946 for the recurring issue.: Los Angeles County district attorney grand jury files, "Grand Jury Testimony of Dr. Melvin Schwartz," February 1, 1950, 1, 4, 5.

To keep Mark Hansen at bay, Beth told him she was a virgin. Los Angeles County district attorney grand jury files, "Statement of Ms. Anne Toth," December 13, 1949, 6.

Beth trusted two brash former servicemen she met on the street named Marvin Margolis and Bill Robinson: Los Angeles County district attorney grand jury files, "Testimony of Sgt. Finis Brown to D.A. Investigator Frank Jemison," no date given, 10.

but he was walking a tightrope over a precarious living arrangement: Los Angeles County district attorney grand jury files, "Testimony of Sgt. Finis Brown to D.A. Investigator Frank Jemison," no date given, 11, 12.

His aunt and uncle, Fanny and Leo Kalish, managed the Guardian Arms and had allowed the boys to stay: Los Angeles County district attorney grand jury files, Lt. Frank Jemison, "Summary of the Elizabeth (Beth) Short Murder Investigation," 11.

When Bacos stopped by one night to pick Lynn up for a date, he found only Beth present. In Lynn's absence, Bacos took Beth out instead.: Los Angeles County district attorney grand jury files, "Statement of George Bacos," February 21, 1950, 3, 4.

An oddly embittered Bacos would later state, "I didn't think I wanted to kiss her because of all the 'goop' she used on her face": Los Angeles County district attorney grand jury files, "Statement of George Bacos," February 21, 1950, 8.

On October 21, Marjorie, Beth, and Marvin popped up at Mark Hansen's house for a visit. Doing all the talking for Beth and Marjorie, Margolis: Los Angeles County district attorney grand jury files, "Statement of Mark Hansen," December 16, 1949, 7, 8.

Fickling for the first time rejected. "Darling, your request impossible at this time, other obligations have me against a wall.": "Elizabeth Short's Letters Reveal Hopes for Service Marriage," *Los Angeles Examiner*, January 21, 1947.

"When you mentioned marriage in your letter, Beth, I got to wondering about that myself. Seems like you have to be in love with a person before it's a safe bet.": James Murray, "'The Black Dahlia' Torture Murder—Even Los Angeles Was Shocked," *St. Louis Globe-Democrat*, February 2, 1947.

Another serviceman named Paul Rosie had written Beth, too. "Your letter took me completely by surprise.": "Elizabeth Short's Letters Reveal Hopes for Service Marriage," *Los Angeles Examiner*, January 21, 1947.

CHAPTER 11: HE'S WAITING FOR ME

Anne described Beth's unbridled rage. "She said in Boston they never did those sort of things, or something.": Los Angeles County district attorney grand jury files, "Statement of Ms. Anne Toth," December 13, 1949, 7.

"Because she insulted another girl, called her a bum. Later we found out she hit the nail on the head.": Mary Morris, "Black Dahlia's Life Shows She Was Mixed Up Emotionally," *Des Moines Sunday Register*, March 23, 1947.

The next morning, Beth desperately called around to various acquaintances and past dates looking for a place to stay.: Los Angeles County district attorney grand jury files, "Evidence and Declarations Tending to Connect or Disconnect Mark Hansen with the Murder of Elizabeth Short," 1.

Roommate Linda Rohr complained, "She was out early every night. She had a lot of telephone calls, mostly from her 'favorite boyfriend' Maurice.": "Death Victim Looked Worried, Says Landlady," *Los Angeles Examiner*, January 18, 1947.

Beth had begun dating a Columbia Studios voice-over artist named Maurice Clement: Los Angeles County district attorney grand jury files, Lt. Frank Jemison, "Summary of the Elizabeth (Beth) Short Murder Investigation," 6.

Jack Egger ushered at CBS Studios and along with the other employees was awestruck by the mysterious lone woman. "She was a striking girl": Los Angeles County district attorney grand jury files, "Statement of John F. Egger," February 7, 1950, 5.

Anne saw Beth every day while she lived at the Chancellor: Los Angeles County district attorney grand jury files, "Evidence and Declarations Tending to Connect or Disconnect Mark Hansen with the Murder of Elizabeth Short," 1.

The second shoot was different. Price demanded that Lynn pose fully in the nude.: "'I Changed My Mind', Killer Writes Police," *Daily News* (Los Angeles, CA), January 29, 1947.

The final nail arrived when police arrested two of her roommates for possession of marijuana: Los Angeles County district attorney grand jury files, "Statement of Anne Toth," February 28, 1950, 13.

Mark arrived home to find Beth crying at his dining room table, "She was sitting there . . . about 5:30 or 6:00 o'clock": Los Angeles County district attorney grand jury files, "Statement of Mark Hansen," December 16, 1949, 10, 11.

First thing in the morning of December 6, Anne called apartment 501 to get the address: Los Angeles County district attorney grand jury files, "Statement of Ms. Anne Toth," December 13, 1949, 18.

Roommate Linda Rohr stated, "The morning she left she was very anxious. She said, 'I've got to hurry he's waiting for me.'": "Death Victim Looked Worried, Says Landlady," *Los Angeles Examiner*, January 18, 1947.

Beth's bus arrived at the Greyhound terminal in downtown San Diego at 6:00 A.M.: Los Angeles County district attorney grand jury files, "Movements of Elizabeth Short," 5.

The movie playing at the Aztec that week was *The Blue Dahlia*: movie showtime listings, *San Diego Union*, December 9, 1946.

"Light, airy and cheerful," all Bayview Terrace government-issued homes came equipped with electric refrigerators, automatic water heaters: John Webster, *Originally Pacific Beach: Looking Back at the Heritage of a Unique Community*" (CreateSpace Independent Publishing Platform, 2013), 207–8.

"I would never be happy in a house alone. I want the kind of happiness everyone else has . . .": Harry Friedenberg, "Betty's Last Letters Tell of Love's Losing Battle," *Boston Traveler*, January 22, 1947.

but was discharged as "mentally unfit for service" on a "psychopathic discharge," though he was found to be mentally "normal.": Los Angeles County district attorney grand jury files, "Summary of various important figures in Short investigation," 2.

He would soon be piloting the airline's new Charlotte-to-Chicago route.: "Firm Pushing Appeal to Cab," *Charlotte Observer*, January 9, 1947. See also: "Letter to Charlottean Believed Last Girl Wrote Before Slaying," *Charlotte News*, January 18, 1947.

CHAPTER 12: SWALLOWED UP BY THE CITY

He recalled her response: "She had met a screwball who had scared her, so she decided to go to San Diego.": Los Angeles County district attorney grand jury files, Lt. Frank Jemison, "Summary of the Elizabeth (Beth) Short Murder Investigation," 14.

Anne Toth detailed what Mark told of her of the January 7 phone call from Beth. "He got a wire from her.": Los Angeles County district attorney grand jury files, "Statement of Ms. Anne Toth," December 13, 1949, 10.

Hansen stated, "She never showed up after she called up and say [sic] she was in San Diego.": Los Angeles County district attorney grand jury files, "Statement of Mark Hansen," December 16, 1949, 13.

"Frankly darling if everyone waited to have everything all smooth before they decided to marry none of them would be together now.": "Elizabeth Short's Letters Reveal Hopes for Service Marriage," *Los Angeles Examiner*, January 21, 1947.

Red obliged, but once on the road she changed her mind and decided against the phone call. She then asked if he would drive her to Los Angeles: "Exonerated Suspect's Story Aids Killer Hunt," *Los Angeles Examiner*, January 21, 1947.

The two drove around the corner to Patrick's Café, at the corner of Balboa and Pacific Avenues, where Beth went to a pay phone to make calls to an unidentified person in Los Angeles.: "Dahlia Phone Call Tracked," *Los Angeles Examiner*, February 5, 1947.

"We didn't make love in the room. I washed and shaved. She combed her hair.":
"Exonerated Suspect's Story Aids Killer Hunt," *Los Angeles Examiner*, January 21,
1947.

"She asked me to get her suitcase out of the car. It was the one with her makeup
and stuff in it. She didn't really seem to be sick.": "Exonerated Suspect's Story Aids
Killer Hunt," *Los Angeles Examiner*, January 21, 1947.

but on the drive back to Los Angeles she instead asked to be dropped off at the
Greyhound bus terminal: Los Angeles County district attorney grand jury files,
"Statement of Robert M. Manley to Investigator Frank Jemison," February 1, 1950,
2, 3.

Manley's recollections of Beth's plans were contradictory and baffling. "She
wanted me to drive her to Los Angeles because she was going North to see her
sister": "Former Air Force Musician Tells of Trip From San Diego," *Los Angeles
Examiner*, January 20, 1947.

Now, at the bus terminal, she had two choices of routes that night, both of which
would depart in four to five hours: Greyhound Bus Timetables pamphlet, 1947.

Red looked to make his exit. "I was anxious to get out of there. . . . I was just glad to
get rid of her.": Los Angeles County district attorney grand jury files, "Statement of
Robert M. Manley to Investigator Frank Jemison," February 1, 1950, 7.

Guests in the lobby claimed they saw her walk to a bank of payphones: Los Angeles County district attorney grand jury files, Lt. Frank Jemison, "Summary of the
Elizabeth (Beth) Short Murder Investigation," 13.

In her unsent letter to Gordon Fickling, Elizabeth Short had written, "I'll never be
settled unless I find my own happiness.": Harry Friedenberg, "Betty's Last Letters
Tell of Love's Losing Battle," *Boston Traveler*, January 22, 1947.

Anne Toth was very unhappy when she stepped off the San Joaquin Daylight train
at Los Angeles's Union Station: Los Angeles County district attorney grand jury
files, "Statement of Leo Sol Hymes," March 1, 1950, 7, 8.

Anne was flabbergasted that Beth had turned up in such a strange location. "I said,
'well, that is like Wrong Way Corrigan'": Los Angeles County district attorney grand
jury files, "Statement of Ms. Anne Toth," December 13, 1949, 10.

She was also surprised by Mark's agitated state. "It was the first thing on his mind
when I came back.": Los Angeles County district attorney grand jury files, "Statement of Ms. Anne Toth," December 13, 1949, 17.

For the next five days, Anne and Mark carried on as usual, with Mark home by
10:00 P.M. each evening.: Los Angeles County district attorney grand jury files,
"Evidence and Declarations Tending to Connect or Disconnect Mark Hansen
with the Murder of Elizabeth Short," 2.

It was 11:19 A.M. on January 15 when Captain Jack Donohoe radioed the call car, a maroon unmarked Chevrolet sedan.: Los Angeles County district attorney grand jury files, Lt. Frank Jemison, "Summary of the Elizabeth (Beth) Short Murder Investigation," 1.

Donohoe signed off with a stark warning, "It sounds bad, Red. Damn bad, It's going to be a rough one.": "Harry Hansen Can't Forget 'Black Dahlia,'" *Los Angeles Times–Washington Post* Service, April 17, 1971.

Detective Lieutenant Paul Freestone had seen the worst of them and yet still claimed, "This is the most brutal example of a sex crime I have ever seen.": "Hunt Torture Den In L.A. Murder," *Los Angeles Herald-Express*, January 16, 1947.

Reporters noted, "Tire tracks indicated the car came from the south and swung hastily to the curb.": "What Has Happened to Justice?" *Press and Sun Bulletin* (Binghamton, NY), February 12, 1950.

An anonymous caller phoned police and reported, "The car, splattered with mud, turned into an alley near the scene": "Hunt Torture Den In L.A. Murder", *Los Angeles Herald-Express*, January 16, 1947.

Smith grabbed the page from the typewriter and ran to the desk of the city editor: Jack Smith, "A Dahlia By Any Other Name," *Los Angeles Times*, January 23, 1975.

CHAPTER 13: FADE TO ZERO

Also present were lead detective Harry Hansen and Ray Pinker: Los Angeles County district attorney grand jury files, "Testimony of Officer Harry Hansen," no date given, 15.

Newbarr pointed out a series of ridges and depressions across the body: Los Angeles County district attorney grand jury files, Lt. Frank Jemison, "Summary of the Elizabeth (Beth) Short Murder Investigation," 3, 4, 5.

The official cause of death was "shock and loss of blood from hemorrhage.": Los Angeles County district attorney grand jury files, "Jemison Memo to H. L. Stanley," October 28, 1949, 7.

Newbarr's autopsy report stated, "There was a marked postmortem lividity on the top side of both parts indicating": Los Angeles County district attorney grand jury files, Lt. Frank Jemison, "Summary of the Elizabeth (Beth) Short Murder Investigation," 1.

Chief of Homicide Jack Donohoe stated, "We believe that a very sharp knife of the long bladed butcher or carving type": "Bossy Blond Friend of 'Black Dahlia' Sought," *Los Angeles Herald-Express*, January 26, 1947.

the well-funded *Daily News, Herald,* and *Examiner* newspapers released armies of reporters called "legmen" to seek witnesses: Jack Smith, "Everyone's Gone To Nowhere City," *Los Angeles Times,* August 2, 1972.

Many legmen would soon get caught up in the world of Elizabeth Short's female acquaintances and "disappear": Jack Smith, "Everyone's Gone To Nowhere City," *Los Angeles Times,* August 2, 1972.

Hundreds of "ecstatically competitive" reporters: Jack Smith, "Everyone's Gone To Nowhere City," *Los Angeles Times,* August 2, 1972.

Smith recalled the jolt of electricity running through his body. "The Black Dahlia. It was a rewrite man's dream.": Jack Smith, "A Dahlia By Any Other Name," *Los Angeles Times,* January 23, 1975.

In the first seventy-two hours, lead detectives Finis Brown and Harry Hansen did not sleep, go home, or change clothes.: Jack Webb, *The Badge* (DaCapo Press, reprint edition, 2005), 26.

While Captain Donohoe marshaled more and more bodies to the case, Chief Horrall issued an all-points bulletin: "Find 'Dahlia' Trail In Night Spots," *Los Angeles Herald-Express,* January 21, 1947.

Having lost sleep from worry, she begged the hotel manager to let her crash in one of the rooms for a few hours: "Vivid Women," *Daily News* (Los Angeles, CA), January 21, 1947.

The next day, she strode into the fabulously appointed Darrin of Paris luxury-car design offices on the Sunset Strip: "Vivid Women," *Daily News* (Los Angeles, CA), January 21, 1947.

"Elizabeth Short's picture was splashed across the front page. Before I read much of the story, I turned sick inside.": "Manley Tells Meeting Girl," *Los Angeles Examiner,* January 20, 1947.

Phoebe pleaded with officers, "I just can't do it. It would be too much for me to do.": "Redhead Grilled In Girl Horror Death," *Daily News* (Los Angeles, CA), January 20, 1947.

Detectives accompanied the Shorts to the coroner's office, but when they arrived, press photographers crowded around: Los Angeles County district attorney grand jury files, Lt. Frank Jemison, "Summary of the Elizabeth (Beth) Short Murder Investigation," 8.

But when asked when she had "first noticed her daughter died": "Seize Man Suspect at Dahlia Inquest," *Hollywood Citizen-News,* January 22, 1947.

neither Phoebe nor her daughter Virginia nor her husband Adrian, who had never even met Elizabeth, could provide any known acquaintances of Beth's in

Los Angeles.: "Slain Girl's One Love Told," *Daily News* (Los Angeles, CA), January 18, 1947. See also: "Police Free Red Haired Salesman As Suspect in 'Black Dahlia' Murder," *Los Angeles Times*, January 21, 1947.

She soon arrived at Room 42 in City Hall's Homicide Division offices with Mark Hansen in tow.: Los Angeles County district attorney grand jury files, "Testimony of Officer Harry Hansen," no date given, 2.

Anne came to her defense. "We used to think the world of that kid. She was always well behaved: "Find Dahlia Trail In Night Spots," *Los Angeles Herald-Express*, January 21, 1947.

He had successfully kept his name out of the newspapers, especially important while he courted Las Vegas impresario Barney Vandersteen: Los Angeles County district attorney grand jury files, "Statement of Bernardus H. Vandersteen," March 29, 1950, 2, 5, 6.

While she was walking on Hollywood Boulevard, a stunned friend handed her a newspaper and muttered, "They're looking for you.": "Seek Aid In Dahlia Case," *Daily News* (Los Angeles, CA), January 22, 1947.

A six-hour interrogation yielded little information from Lynn, until she suddenly cried out, "I didn't think I could get away with it": "Seek Aid In Dahlia Case," *Daily News* (Los Angeles, CA), January 22, 1947.

Detectives announced at least ten men could be prosecuted for sexual relations with the minor, including some "prominent Hollywood personalities": "Film Colony Quiz Slated," *Los Angeles Examiner*, January 26, 1947. See also: Chuck Cheatham, "Society Blamed For Girl's Tragic Life," *Long Beach Independent*, February 3, 1947.

By January 22, the entire homicide squad was assigned solely to the Elizabeth Short case, along with seven hundred police officers, sheriff's deputies: "700 Officers Hunt Clues In Slaying of Black Dahlia," *Bakersfield Californian*, January 21, 1947.

Homicide Captain Donohoe felt the squeeze, and his frustrations bubbled up to the press, "It is unbelievable how a person could be swallowed up by the city: "Hunt Mystery Phone Caller in 'Dahlia' Murder," *Los Angeles Herald-Express*, January 23, 1947.

"The fact that the murdered girl failed to claim her clothes, which were checked for five days prior to her death at the Greyhound bus depot package room, pointed out the captive theory.": "Two Women Sought in 'Dahlia' Slaying, Clews Sought," *Los Angeles Examiner*, January 23, 1947.

"We're right back where we started. We've got nothing," publicly bemoaned lead detective Harry Hansen.: "Dahlia Clues Fail," *Los Angeles Times*, January 23, 1947.

"Some of the evidence points to a woman killer—a brittle, masculine type": "Police Sift Evidence To Learn Sex of Sadistic Killer of Beth Short," *Daily News* (Los Angeles, CA), January 25, 1947.

Evidence of a female killer was listed: The victim's eyebrows were bleached white, which only a woman would know how to do: "What Has Happened to Justice?" *Daily News Sunday Edition* (Los Angeles, CA), February 12, 1950.

CHAPTER 14: THE CITY DOESN'T PAY FOR GENIUSES. IT PAYS FOR DETECTIVES.

By the time he got back to the trashcan, it was being emptied into an LA By-Products trash truck.: "Items Tally With Those Victim Wore," *Daily News* (Los Angeles, CA), January 24, 1947.

Hyman pleaded to save the suspicious items, but the trash collector only brushed him off—"We find lots of things like this": "Bossy Blond Friend of 'Black Dahlia' Sought," *Los Angeles Herald-Express*, January 17, 1947.

At 5:30 P.M., Chief Postal Inspector Judge Wood called the police and then called the five major LA newspapers with news that an alarmingly important package: Los Angeles County district attorney grand jury files, Lt. Frank Jemison, "Summary of the Elizabeth (Beth) Short Murder Investigation," 10.

In some places, 2 pages were missing, in others, 125 pages were missing.: Los Angeles County district attorney grand jury files, Lt. Frank Jemison, "Summary of the Elizabeth (Beth) Short Murder Investigation," 15.

The gasoline had only been applied to the outside of the envelope. All contents found inside were searched for fingerprints, though only smudges were found.: Los Angeles County district attorney grand jury files, "Testimony of Officer Harry Hansen," no date given, 14.

However, the back of the cut-out letters as well as the sticky underside of the Scotch tape used to affix them to the envelope would have picked up: "Slayer Taunts Police, Sends Clues In Mail," *Los Angeles Herald-Express*, January 25, 1947.

On February 6, J. Edgar Hoover responded to LA Police Chief Clemence Horrall: FBI/United States Department of Justice, letter from Director J. Edgar Hoover to Los Angeles Police Department, February 6, 1947.

"This is the big push," Captain Donohoe announced. "Our men are fanning out now to bring in the killer.": "LA Police Find Dahlia Killer's Prowling Area," *Daily News* (Los Angeles, CA), January 24, 1947.

"Several girls rented rooms here at the house. But I never went out with them. She had lots of dates. There was a language teacher that I know of, and with other persons, mostly hoodlums": "Police Checking Names Listed in Address Book," *Los Angeles Examiner*, January 26, 1947.

Risking her relationship with Mark and his home, Anne corrected him on the spot, denying Beth dated hoodlums. "She was a nice girl. She was quiet, she didn't drink": "Dates of Dahlia," *Los Angeles Herald-Express*, January 25, 1947.

Scrambling to avoid suspicion, Hansen twisted his story to the police and the press, directly contradicting earlier statements.: Los Angeles County district attorney grand jury files, "Lt. Frank Jemison Suspect List and Descriptions," February 20, 1951, 10.

This directly contradicted what he anxiously told Anne when she returned to his home on January 10—that Beth had asked him for money, not to stay with him.: Los Angeles County district attorney grand jury files, "Statement of Ms. Anne Toth," December 13, 1949, 10.

One of the names discovered in the killer's packet wasn't written in the address book and didn't appear on a business card. It was written on a loose piece of notebook paper.: "Police Checking Names Listed in Address Book," *Los Angeles Examiner*, January 26, 1947.

He claimed to have also been a salesman for the Marwyn Dairy Products: Los Angeles County district attorney grand jury files, "Summary of Various Important Figures in Short Investigation," 1.

Brown was next handed a report in which "it was established this suspect had on two occasions given different women vicious beatings": Los Angeles County district attorney grand jury files, "Lt. Frank Jemison Suspect List and Descriptions," February 20, 1951, 2.

"A young twenty-two-year-old woman by the name of Dorothy Welsh with whom he had attended a school in Kansas City": Los Angeles County district attorney grand jury files, "Lt. Frank Jemison Suspect List and Descriptions," February 20, 1951, 2.

in 1944 Kansas City Police Lieutenant Charles Welch had contacted LAPD about the murder of Elizabeth Georgia Castaneda in a downtown Los Angeles hotel room: "K.C. Police Reopen Welsh Murder Case," *St. Joseph News Press*, September 10, 1944. See also: "Scour L.B. For Vicious Killer," *Long Beach Independent*, January 25, 1944.

New Police Chief Henry Johnson had been elevated from his position as superintendent of the Traffic and Safety Division.: "As Donnelly Act," *Kansas City Times*, February 19, 1947.

Finis Brown was told KCPD would send on what they had. But the documents never arrived.: Los Angeles County district attorney grand jury files, "Lt. Frank Jemison Suspect List and Descriptions," February 20, 1951, 3.

He and then–Police Chief Lear Reed had both sat on the Kansas City Chamber of Commerce Fire and Police Committee with Carl's father, Herman Balsiger, in 1940 and 1941: "Into Active Year," *Kansas City Star*, December 20, 1940, 20.

With three thousand hours of overtime clocked by twenty-five homicide detectives alone, Donohoe stated, "Sleep is an unknown luxury in this department.": Ralph Dighton, "Los Angeles Police Work Long Hours But Fail to Solve Series of Brutal Crimes on Women," *San Bernardino County Sun*, March 23, 1947.

Jack Kofoed of the *Miami Herald* wrote, "Sometimes it seems girls deliberately stick out their chins": Jack Kofoed, "Unsolved 'Black Dahlia' Murder Case Just a Link In Sordid Delinquency Chain," *Miami Herald*, January 7, 1948.

Jack Webb of *Dragnet* fame implied she was trading sex for money, "Two or three times, friends later remembered, she had hitched rides to the Sixth Street area": Jack Webb, *The Badge* (DaCapo Press, reprint edition, 2005), 28.

Mark Hansen vocalized his own insults. "She's a little tramp. I didn't want her there, and I told her to leave.": Los Angeles County district attorney grand jury files, "Testimony of Officer Harry Hansen," no date given, 5.

"A black dahlia is what expert gardeners call 'an impossibility' of nature. Perhaps that is why lovely, tragic Elizabeth Short": Craig Rice, "Death of the Black Dahlia," *San Francisco Examiner*, November 9, 1952.

she spent most nights alone, attending radio shows at CBS and NBC or movies at the Pantages Theatre.: Los Angeles County district attorney grand jury files, "Statement of John F. Egger," February 7, 1950, 2.

After Bill Robinson hit on Beth, slapped her, and threw her out of his car, Anne stated, "I don't think anyone else tried anything.": Los Angeles County district attorney grand jury files, "Statement of Ms. Anne Toth," December 13, 1949, 7, 8.

Anne proclaimed, "Betty was a nice girl. It was just a coincidence she met up with some lousy man who got nasty.": Mary Morris, "Black Dahlia's Life Shows She Was Mixed Up Emotionally," *Des Moines Sunday Register*, March 23, 1947.

Anne, in turn, blamed the press for the disturbing new narrative, "making us all out [to be] a bunch of bums looking for trouble.": Mary Morris, "Black Dahlia's Life Shows She Was Mixed Up Emotionally," *Des Moines Sunday Register*, March 23, 1947.

"The LAPD records and reports indicate some stupidity and carelessness on the part": Los Angeles County district attorney grand jury files, Frank Jemison, "Elizabeth Short Murder—Los Angeles Police Department Records, Reports, Statements, Correspondence, Evidence and Information." 14.

CHAPTER 15: HOLLYWOOD BABYLON

On February 1, 1950, Robert "Red" Manley was questioned by investigators one more time: Los Angeles County district attorney grand jury files, "Statement of Robert M. Manley," February 1, 1950, 10.

The DA's grand jury report stated, "It was further suspected that this suspect Balsiger had known Short at Camp Cooke and had been court-martialed and sent overseas": Los Angeles County district attorney grand jury files, "Lt. Frank Jemison Suspect List and Descriptions," February 20, 1951, 2.

The LA district attorney's suspect description read, "Claude Welsh, in 1941 was acquitted by Supreme Court jury of the murder of his sister, Dorothy": Los Angeles County district attorney grand jury files, "Lt. Frank Jemison Suspect List and Descriptions," February 20, 1951, 3.

"You're always lonely in Hollywood, even when you're out with people. They don't belong to you—those people.": Caroline Walker, "Tells Hollywood Pitfalls," *Los Angeles Herald-Express*, January 29, 1947.

She was singularly focused on finding her biological siblings.: "Dahlia Trail, Road Easy For Hollywood Girls," *Los Angeles Herald-Express*, January 30, 1947.

Weeks before her death in 1991, a young writer from Hollywood found her and interviewed her for the last time.: *True Crime Garage* podcast, episodes 45 and 46, August 10 and 11, 2016.

Avoiding any interviews with the press, Mark Hansen would slowly sell off his theaters and real estate properties.: "New Theater Opens," *Hollywood Citizen-News*, July 18, 1963.

master of ceremonies Nils Thor Granlund would depart for upstart Las Vegas, where he introduced the glittering, high-kicking showgirl revue to casinos and resorts: Larry Hoefling, *Nils Thor Granlund: Show Business Entrepreneur and America's First Radio Star* (McFarland & Co., Inc., 2010), 195–201.

In 1954, detective Harry Hansen was contacted by doctors at the Veterans Administration in Los Angeles, who relayed that Manley had been confessing to the murder of Elizabeth Short.: "Black Dahlia Suspect Gets Truth Tests," *Los Angeles Times*, August 16, 1954. See also: "Searching Among Dusty Files For 'Black Dahlia' Murderer—Still," *Tyler Courier-Times* (Tyler, TX), January 24, 1982.

In 1982, Hansen shared his thoughts on "the one case that got away": "Searching Among Dusty Files For 'Black Dahlia' Murderer—Still," *Tyler Courier-Times* (Tyler, TX), January 24, 1982.

CHAPTER 16: BLUE BABY

By July 7, she was an accomplished swimmer: "Rites for Betty Balsiger," *Kansas City Star*, July 7, 1927.

After an hour and a half of scouring the bottom of the lake: "Girl, 7, Rides Bicycle Into Lake; Drowns," *Kansas City Kansan*, July 7, 1927.

A spillway at the southwestern corner of the lake provided a slight current in the lake: Author interview with Karen Tennant, Lake of the Forest historian, 2024.

Newspaper reports as far away as Omaha and Texas hinted: "Drowns In Kansas Lake," *Omaha World-Herald*, July 9, 1927.

The death would be kept within the family: Author interview with Karen Tennant, Lake of the Forest historian, 2024. See also: Minutes of "Meeting of the Board of Directors of the Lake of the Forest Club, July 12, 1927."

On June 16, 1915, Herman Carl and twin sister Mary Helen were delivered: Van Brunt Boulevard Presbyterian Church, Register of Baptisms, 1902–1925.

With the outbreak of the Civil War, he joined the 43rd Illinois Infantry: Author interview with Ralph Ells, Balsiger family member, 2022.

But like all grocery markets in Kansas City, real success lay in its butcher shop: *Kansas City Star*, January 17, 1913.

His emotional appeal reached a fever pitch with dire warnings of predatory immigrants: "Higher Standard of Business Urged by Convention Speaker," *Intelligencer* (Mexico, MO), August 18, 1925.

The entire Balsiger family joined him for the business trip: *Illustrated Daily News* (Los Angeles, CA), June 19, 1924.

Local teen Roy Nafziger inherited his father's ailing bakery: Dick Fowler, *Leaders in Our Town* (Burd & Fletcher Co., Kansas City, MO, 1952), 317–21.

Nafziger's private airplane transported Balsiger: *Cincinnati Post*, October 2, 1928.

When a city manager was killed in a drive-by shooting down the street: Author interview with Karl Kanehl, Balsiger family member, 2024.

Thanksgiving and Christmas were not for celebration: Author interview with Ralph Ells, Balsiger family member, 2022.

Nonetheless, Herman would make a statement to the Welshes and other society families: "H.C. Balsiger Buys on Wornall," *Kansas City Star*, June 2, 1929.

Ada had a three-foot-tall statue made of the little girl: Author interview with Karl Kanehl, Balsiger family member, 2024.

a deviated septum that produced a whistling sound: National Archives and Record Administration, military records of Carl Balsiger.

Named after a thirteenth-century grand master of the Knights Templar: *Book of Secret Work of the Order of DeMolay Issued by the Grand Council of the Order of DeMolay* (Grand Scribe's Office, Kansas City, MO, fifth edition, 1930).

Richard wasn't much of a hunter.: Author interview with Amber Hayes, Funk family member, 2024.

He was much more suited to the Saturday night dances at the clubhouse, which every teenager at the lake attended.: *Lake Forest Breeze* (Lake of the Forest community newsletter), 1941.

with probationary pledges who toiled for the brotherhood—washing cars, raking lawns: "Pledge Life at U. of K.C.," *Kansas City Times*, November 5, 1934.

With hundreds of students watching, Balsiger pulled freshman: "Dean Tempers the Hazing," *Kansas City Star*, September 23, 1935.

The paddling continued into Kegon's Hell Week: *UKC UNews*, April 9, 1937.

Despite his domineering presence on campus: "An Honorary Frat," *UKC UNews*, March 18, 1936.

The only news he made were the questions surrounding the dirty, antiquated hat: *UKC UNews*, December 11, 1936.

The *UNews* poked fun at his failed attempt at growing a moustache.: *UKC UNews*, November 15, 1935.

Even his haircut was mocked in the paper: "We Nominate For Oblivion," *UKC UNews*, January 12, 1934.

The paper summed up Carl's reputation in one word: "clown.": *UKC UNews*, May 20, 1936.

CHAPTER 17: MY OWN LITTLE HATCHET

Unsophisticated yet elegant, naïve yet strong-willed, socially adept yet academic: Lear Reed, "Chief Reed's Own Story of the Welsh Case," *Kansas City Star*, December 28, 1942.

Sleeping on blankets by the side of the road: "Back Home With Advice," *Kansas City Star*, September 12, 1936.

Kegon responded with intimidation tactics.: "Poindexter Speaks Out," *KCU UNews*, April 30, 1937.

In her form-fitting blue gown, Leila was the striking picture: "1,000 Attend KCU Ball," *Kansas City Star*, February 12, 1938.

as Richard Funk ascended to the top position and succeeded in helping bring Walt Disney: DeMolay International, https://demolay.org/the-most-famous-demolay -of-all-walt-disney/.

and was upped even further to commander of the DeMolay Group: "Mother Chapter Elects," *Kansas City Times*, October 17, 1938.

In early 1939, Carl made a sudden and surprising move to study: National Archives and Record Administration, military records of Carl Balsiger.

"Last June my folks had a home at Lake of the Forest located in Wyandotte County, Kansas.": Testimony of Richard Funk at Welsh preliminary hearing, May 18, 1942. See also: "His Love Untold," *Kansas City Star*, May 18, 1942.

"Dick's parents had a place at Lake of the Forest in Wyandotte County Kansas.": Lear Reed, "Chief Reed Continues His Story of the Welsh Case," *Kansas City Star*, January 11, 1942.

They whirled on the clubhouse dance floor, feasted on frozen watermelon and crawdads at the lake's community dinners: Wyandotte County Historical Society, documents and newspaper clippings, 1921–1945.

But Carl—or his father—had lied, having actually enlisted on October 19: National Archives and Record Administration, military records of Carl Balsiger.

On November 10, 1940, Carl Balsiger stepped off a bus filled with draftees for intake at Fort Leavenworth: National Archives and Record Administration, military records of Carl Balsiger.

The Quartermaster Corps is one of the three major logistic branches of the U.S. Army: Alvin P. Stauffer, *The Quartermaster Corps: Operations in the War Against Japan* (Center of Military History, United States Army, Washington, DC, 1990), 220–32.

had barely advanced from the primitive days of World War I, when dough was sluggishly kneaded by hand: "Manual for Army Bakers" (United States Government Printing Office, Washington, DC, 1916), 85–97.

With war on the horizon, bread would be a critical secret weapon: Alvin P. Stauffer, *The Quartermaster Corps: Operations in the War Against Japan* (Center of Military History, United States Army, Washington, DC, 1990), 220–32.

By mid-1942, Carl served in a bakery platoon stationed in Pasadena, California: "Doughboys Declare Bread Made By 'Dough Boys' Best," *Pasadena Star News*, October 23, 1942.

In mid-1943, the entire South Pacific Theater of the war had not a single field bakery in operation.: Alvin P. Stauffer, *The Quartermaster Corps: Operations in the War Against Japan* (Center of Military History, United States Army, Washington, DC, 1990), 228.

The Sixth Army's field bakery teams would assemble their ovens under canvas tents in the searing heat of dense jungles.: Alvin P. Stauffer, *The Quartermaster Corps: Operations in the War Against Japan* (Center of Military History, United States Army, Washington, DC, 1990), 226–32.

Balsiger personally devised an ingenious use of jeep motors: Carroll K. Michener, "Stuffed Straights," *Northwestern Miller*, Volume 223, Issue 11, September 12, 1945.

the U.S. Sixth Army landed and established a beachhead on the island of Leyte: National Archives and Record Administration, military records of Carl Balsiger.

Much of the baking equipment from New Guinea was shipped to the wrong islands: Alvin P. Stauffer, *The Quartermaster Corps: Operations in the War Against Japan* (Center of Military History, United States Army, Washington, DC, 1990), 149–50.

Carl returned to form as a salesman for a wholesale baking company: "Aids in Food Conference," *Kansas City Star*, March 31, 1946.

He rented a room on the second floor of a storefront building at Sunset Boulevard and Gardner Street.: Los Angeles County district attorney grand jury files, 1949/1950.

J. W. Costello was to Los Angeles baking history: "Celebrates His 30th Year – J.W. Costello Veteran Weber Head," *San Fernando Valley Times*, October 22, 1940. See also: Author interview with Jamie Costello, 2022.

Carl Balsiger had been introduced to the Costellos years earlier: Author interview with Jamie Costello, 2022.

CHAPTER 18: DESTINY IN THE DIRT

The 1,900 square-foot Spanish Revival structure: Los Angeles Department of Building and Safety records.

Though Carl was busy with wholesale bakery sales runs in the black 1940 Oldsmobile: Los Angeles County district attorney grand jury files, "Movements of Elizabeth Short," 5.

Fate and financial opportunity brought him back in 1940 with his wife: Author interview with Dorothy Parris, daughter of Walter and Jean Thacher, 2023.

Walt had just the place in mind.: "New Bakery to Open Soon in Camarillo," *Camarillo News*, November 8, 1946.

A master baker who had apprenticed in his native Zechin, Germany, from the age of eleven: Author interview with Kurt Sobanja, grandson of Bernhard Sobanja, 2023.

Balsiger and Thacher opened Homecraft Bakery on November 30 to a public: "Homecraft Bakery Opens Tomorrow Here," *Camarillo News*, November 29, 1946.

Carl turned up in Camarillo with a girl: Los Angeles County district attorney grand jury files, "Movements of Elizabeth Short," 1949/1950, 5.

Thacher was subsequently questioned by LAPD: Los Angeles County district attorney grand jury files, Lt. Frank Jemison, "Summary of the Elizabeth (Beth) Short Murder Investigation," 13.

Walt and his wife, Jean Thacher, dined with Carl Balsiger: Author interview with Dorothy Parris, daughter of Walter and Jean Thacher, 2023.

When the bisected body of Elizabeth Short was autopsied, cocoa fibers from a stiff brush were found clinging to her skin: Los Angeles County district attorney grand jury files, Lt. Frank Jemison, "Summary of the Elizabeth (Beth) Short Murder Investigation," 1.

The cocoa fiber bristles, they believed, came from a pastry kitchen scrub brush used to clean surfaces of dough.: Author interview with Dorothy Parris, daughter of Walter and Jean Thacher, 2023.

Homecraft had become every bit the success Sobanja had hoped for: "Local Stores Make Plans to Expand," *Camarillo News*, February 21, 1947.

Without notice, Sobanja showed up to work on February 24: "Local Bakery Closes When Baker Leaves," *Camarillo News*, February 28, 1947.

As part of his court-ordered sentence: "Windshield and Sticker Removal Brings Sentence," *Hollywood Citizen News*, July 19, 1947.

She had attended the University of Nebraska, received her law degree from the University of Iowa: "Jane Balsiger, Madison, Killed in Car Crash," *Lincoln Journal Star* (Lincoln, NE), January 21, 1952.

On June 2, 1949, Los Angeles Police Chief Clemence Horrall: National Archives and Record Administration, military records of Carl Balsiger.

Brown demanded further questioning of Balsiger under administration of a lie detector test.: Los Angeles County district attorney grand jury files, "Lt. Frank Jemison Suspect List and Descriptions," February 20, 1951, 2.

While driving home in Carl's car on Highway 30: Author interview with Karl Kanehl, Balsiger family member, 2024.

The car hit the stock rack of a truck: *The Daily Telegram* (Columbus, NE), January 21, 1952.

work control clerk for TWA airlines: *TWA Skyliner* magazine, December 24, 1953.

Money became increasingly tight; the home on Main Street fell into disrepair.: Author interview with Tabitha "Tibbie" Teall Pearson Ford, daughter of Tabitha Teall, 2022.

CHAPTER 19: UNUSUAL MANNERS AT UNUSUAL HOURS

Tabitha became the center of every room she entered.: Author interview with Laura Smith, daughter of Tabitha Teall, 2022.

As for Tabitha's attraction, she would claim she didn't marry Carl for money or sex. She married for nostalgia.: Author interview with Tabitha "Tibbie" Teall Pearson Ford, daughter of Tabitha Teall, 2022.

On December 8, 1956, Tabitha Teall wed: Marriage License of Teall and Balsiger, Recorder of Deeds, Jackson County.

The filthy, dark home was filled with closed-off rooms: Author interview with Tabitha "Tibbie" Teall Pearson Ford, daughter of Tabitha Teall, 2022.

Tabitha spent lavishly of her own money, fixing the home up: Circuit Court of Kansas City, Missouri, at Kansas City, petition for divorce and other relief, Tabitha Balsiger vs. Carl Balsiger, 1958.

Tabitha filed for divorce, her petition stating: Circuit Court of Kansas City, Missouri, at Kansas City, petition for divorce and other relief, Tabitha Balsiger vs. Carl Balsiger, 1958.

Tabitha Teall put the sordid Balsiger chapter behind her: Author interview with Laura Smith, daughter of Tabitha Teall, 2022.

A restraining order was filed by Fifth & Main Corporation: In the Circuit Court of Jackson County at Kansas City, request for trial by jury, Fifth & Main Corporation vs. Carl Balsiger, 1961.

the company was founded and managed by Kansas City insurance executive Smith F. Brandom: "Mail Fraud Trial Date Set," *Austin American Statesman*, July 2, 1969. See also: "Six Insurance Men Indicted in Milwaukee," *Green Bay Press Gazette*, January 13, 1966.

Balsiger removed $750,000 from the company's Minnesota-based bank accounts: "A Hold Over On Risk From Records," *Kansas City Star*, May 24, 1966.

Finally, in 1971, the charges against him were dismissed.: "Insurance Executive Convicted," *St. Louis Post Dispatch*, March 4, 1971.

But by 1967, Carl had slipped out of the United States for the Bahamas: Author interview with Karl Kanehl, Balsiger family member, 2024.

Back in Kansas City, Balsiger took his white Rambler station wagon out of storage: Author interview with Kathy Allen, Balsiger family member, 2024.

One night, he searched for a rest area, found a well-lit parking lot: Author interview with Karl Kanehl, Balsiger family member, 2024.

Sixty-one-year-old Carl Balsiger's official cause of death was heart attack.: Kansas Department of Health and Environment, Office of Vital Statistics, certificate of death.

CHAPTER 20: ARID SOIL

they could find no evidence of any animosities, any rivalries, any secret boyfriends: Lear Reed, "Chief Reed Continues His Story of the Welsh Case," *Kansas City Star*, January 4, 1942.

"It may be someone who saw the young lady and who was jealous of her achievements in school": "Analysis of Murder Given by Psychiatrists," *Kansas City Journal*, March 10, 1941.

Chief Lear Reed could find no other places where the killer could have hidden.: Lear Reed, "Chief Reed's Own Story of the Welsh Case," *Kansas City Star*, December 28, 1941.

the killer's inexperience was reflected in the mismatched tools he chose for the task: Lear Reed, "Chief Reed Continues His Story of the Welsh Case," *Kansas City Star*, January 4, 1942.

The killer recklessly stood and waited for at least two hours in the open yard next to a chicken-wire fence: "Many To Murder Scene," *Kansas City Star*, March 12, 1941.

The police counted thirty-six windows in neighbors' homes overlooking the Welsh yard: "Many To Murder Scene," *Kansas City Star*, March 12, 1941.

The *Kansas City Star* gathered, "It was a planned crime, carefully and deliberately executed": "Clue in Death Gloves," *Kansas City Star*, March 15, 1941.

"Straight, sharp smears in the folds of the bloody shirt revealed clearly": Lear Reed, "Chief Reed's Own Story of the Welsh Case," *Kansas City Star*, December 28, 1941.

"He had prepared himself as if about to butcher a steer: Lear Reed, "Chief Reed's Own Story of the Welsh Case," *Kansas City Star*, December 28, 1941.

The *Kansas City Star* reported, "Reed stressed the killer showed a knowledge of anatomy": "Kills By Plan," *Kansas City Star*, March 15, 1941.

The psychologists who built the killer's profile for KCPD concluded: "That side of the slayer's personality": "Analysis of Murder Given by Psychiatrists," *Kansas City Journal*, March 10, 1941.

"When I opened the door of the victim's bedroom there were many more reasons to stand still and look": Lear Reed, "Chief Reed's Own Story of the Welsh Case," *Kansas City Star*, December 28, 1941.

CHAPTER 21: CRESTVIEW 1-4666

She had spent three weeks at the Chancellor, the first of which was paid for by Anne Toth, the second week paid for by frequent date Michael Otero: Los Angeles County district attorney grand jury files, Lt. Frank Jemison, "Summary of the Elizabeth (Beth) Short Murder Investigation," 6.

When questioned during the district attorney's investigation, Hymes offered an unusually blunt and illuminating insight: Los Angeles County district attorney grand jury files, "Statement of Leo Sol Hymes to Investigator Frank Jemison," March 1, 1950, 5.

"She seemed to have confidence in a lot of people," Anne recalled with disapproval.: Los Angeles County district attorney grand jury files, "Statement of Ms. Anne Toth," December 13, 1949, 23.

"[Beth] was skeptical of people but despite this she often stumbled into trash.": "Hunt For Woman As New Suspect," *Los Angeles Herald-Express*, January 18, 1947.

She did not wear others' clothing or share her own. Her makeup bag was sacred to her and always at the ready.: Mary Morris, "Black Dahlia's Life Shows She Was Mixed Up Emotionally," *Des Moines Sunday Register*, March 23, 1947.

"These cuts were made by some expert who must have had an education in surgery.": Los Angeles County district attorney grand jury files, Frank Jemison update memo, April 16, 1953.

The *Herald-Express* reported, "Minute examination of the victim's body revealed the tools used in the murder were a sharp butcher knife and a straight razor:

"Bossy Blond Friend of 'Black Dahlia' Sought," *Los Angeles Herald-Express*, January 17, 1947.

Donohoe stated, "We believe that a very sharp knife of the long bladed butcher or carving type was used to sever the body.": "Bossy Blond Friend of 'Black Dahlia' Sought," *Los Angeles Herald-Express*, January 17, 1947.

The LA *Daily News* shrewdly observed, "The cutting indicated a meticulous desire to avoid damaging any vital organs.": "Police Sift Evidence to Learn Sex of Sadistic Killer of Beth Short," *Daily News* (Los Angeles, CA), January 25, 1947.

Elizabeth Short's body was perfectly bisected through the duodenum, a difficult operation: Author interview with Dr. Daniel Winters, 2023.

So successful was the severing of the duodenum that fecal matter within Elizabeth Short's intestines: Los Angeles County district attorney grand jury files, "Evidence and Declarations Tending To Connect or Disconnect Leslie Dillon to the Murders of Elizabeth Short, Jeanne French and Gladys Kern," 9.

Some were only two or three pages, torn out by hand, likely by Short herself.: Los Angeles County district attorney grand jury files, "Testimony of Sgt. Finis Brown to D.A. Investigator Frank Jemison," no date given, 8.

But Carl Balsiger's name was not written in the address book. It was written on a loose piece of paper: Los Angeles County district attorney grand jury files, Lt. Frank Jemison, "Summary of the Elizabeth (Beth) Short Murder Investigation," 9.

Responsible for forty-nine murders, the infamous "Green River Killer," Gary Ridgway, passed a lie detector: Sean Robinson, "Sheriff Not Celebrating As Nemesis Finally Admits Guilt," *News Tribune* (Tacoma, WA), November 6, 2003.

Responsible for as many as forty victims, "Angel of Death" Charles Cullen passed a polygraph: "Killer Passes Polygraph, Innocent Man Fails, Killer Goes On To Kill Again," NITV Federal Services, May 3, 2010.

Lee Anthony Evans killed five New Jersey teenagers in 1978: Gioia Diliberto, "The Night That 5 Boys Vanished," *Record* (Hackensack, NJ), July 5, 1979.

CHAPTER 22: HOW THEY WERE BOUND

Lear Reed offered the public a prediction . . . and a warning. "If the slayer of Leila Welsh": Lear Reed, "Chief Reed Continues His Story of the Welsh Case," *Kansas City Star*, January 4, 1942.

"A young twenty-two-year-old woman by the name of Dorothy [*sic*] Welsh with whom": Los Angeles County district attorney grand jury files, "Lt. Frank Jemison Suspect List and Descriptions," February 20, 1951, 2.

Chief Reed noted, "Her throat had been gashed to the vertebrae. It gaped wide open as though a V had been cut out.": Lear Reed, "Chief Reed's Own Story of the Welsh Case," *Kansas City Star*, December 28, 1941.

Harry Hansen stated, "She had two V-shaped cuts on either side of her mouth": John Bussar, "Hansen Is Technical Advisor on Production About Himself," *Desert Sun* (Palm Springs, CA), January 31, 1975.

While Welsh died from "an acute hemorrhage due to an incised wound to the neck," causing massive loss: "Two Causes of Death," *Kansas City Star*, March 11, 1941.

From Elizabeth Short's left thigh, a four-inch-diameter, one-inch-thick chunk of skin and subcutaneous soft tissue and muscle was sliced: Los Angeles County district attorney grand jury files, Lt. Frank Jemison, "Summary of the Elizabeth (Beth) Short Murder Investigation," 4.

The Short autopsy report stated, "There is an irregular opening in the skin": Los Angeles County district attorney grand jury files, Lt. Frank Jemison, "Summary of the Elizabeth (Beth) Short Murder Investigation," 4.

Coroner Leitch noted of Leila Welsh's missing flesh, "I will say it was a very purposeful act with definitely dexterous handling of the knife.": "Coroner Is Asked Details On Knife in Welsh Trial," *St. Louis Post-Dispatch*, April 9, 1943.

Reed observed of the Leila Welsh murder, "A circular or horseshoe shaped incision": Lear Reed, "Chief Reed's Own Story of the Welsh Case," *Kansas City Star*, December 28, 1941.

When it was discovered in the autopsy, Dr. Newbarr observed a series of "criss-crossing lacerations": Los Angeles County district attorney grand jury files, Lt. Frank Jemison, "Summary of the Elizabeth (Beth) Short Murder Investigation," 4.

"The knife and the [flesh] pattern did not agree. The line of the incision was smooth": "Chief Reed Continues His Story of the Welsh Case," *Kansas City Star*, January 4, 1942.

The letters *E* and *D* were detected in the knife blade marks, though never verified.: Los Angeles County district attorney grand jury files, "Statement of Fred Witman," September 23, 1949, 11.

erotophonophilia, or lust murder, in which an offender achieves sexual climax through the death of another person, not through sexual intercourse.: Jennifer R. Phillips, "Male Serial Killers and the Criminal Profiling Process: A Literature Review" (master's thesis, Eastern Illinois University, 1996), https://thekeep.eiu.edu/theses/1274, 64–68.

"Lust murders are homicides in which the offender stabs, cuts, pierces, or mutilates the sexual regions": Vernon J. Geberth, "Practical Homicide Investigation, Anatomy of a Lust Murder," *Law and Order*, vol. 46, no. 5, May 1998.

Stab wounds and cuts to erogenous zones, genitalia, the face, or neck all replace sexual intercourse: Wade C. Myers, *Juvenile Sexual Homicide* (Academic Press, 2002), 145–47.

Contrary to every account made that morning or since, the body was not posed for public view on the sidewalk: Author interview with Betty and Anne Bersinger, 2022.

The house was just four houses up from the Welsh home, and the officer asked to look into Murphy's backyard.: "Wanted To Tell It All," *Kansas City Star*, May 21, 1942.

Every inch of the yard was scanned and nothing was seen.: "A Link To Welsh," *Kansas City Star*, April 12, 1943.

At George Welsh's trial, defense attorney Roy Rucker grilled Officer Ober about his failure to find the gloves: "Tense Jury Scene," *Kansas City Star*, April 11, 1943.

CHAPTER 23: WEREWOLF

Things were no better in Los Angeles, where the district attorney investigation detailed "extensive trafficking networks of dope peddlers: "Grand Jury Blasts Law Enforcement," *Los Angeles Times*, January 13, 1950.

On March 15, 1947, in just one twenty-four-hour period, the city suffered: *Los Angeles Herald-Express*, March 15, 1947.

INDEX